P9-CLF-858

LEGAL ASPECTS OF LIFE INSURANCE

THE IRWIN SERIES IN INSURANCE

EDITORS

BOILEAU, STALNAKER, & LUCK *Life Insurance Agency Financial Management*

DICKERSON *Health Insurance*

GREGG *Life and Health Insurance Handbook*

MAGEE *General Insurance* Fifth Edition

MAGEE *Life Insurance* Third Edition

MAGEE *Property Insurance* Third Edition

MEHR & CAMMACK *Principles of Insurance* Revised Edition

MCGILL *Legal Aspects of Life Insurance*

MCGILL *Life Insurance*

SNIDER *Readings in Property and Casualty Insurance*

LEGAL ASPECTS OF LIFE INSURANCE

by

DAN M. McGILL, Ph.D., C.L.U.
Frederick H. Ecker Professor of Life Insurance
and
Executive Director, S. S. Huebner Foundation
for Insurance Education
University of Pennsylvania

1959
RICHARD D. IRWIN, INC.
HOMEWOOD, ILLINOIS

First Printing, July, 1959

Library of Congress Catalogue Card No. 59–14265

PRINTED IN THE UNITED STATES OF AMERICA

Willy +

TO HARRY J. LOMAN

For Four Decades of Distinguished Service to Insurance Education and the Wharton School of Finance and Commerce at the University of Pennsylvania

Arthur Miller

Preface

THIS volume is a reprint, with minor modifications, of the legal section of the author's comprehensive text *Life Insurance*. While not originally intended for separate publication, the material contained herein comprises an integral unit of subject matter which may logically be accorded independent status. Separate publication was undertaken at the urging of the American College of Life Underwriters which desired to prescribe the material for use in Part III of the C.L.U. study program. It is hoped that the volume will prove useful to others who have a special interest in the legal phases of life insurance.

The material in this volume is intensely practical. It is not concerned with legal abstractions and esoteric concepts. Rather, it deals with those concrete legal principles and situations encountered in the ordinary course of business by the field and home office representatives of a life insurance company. Knowledge of these principles by those engaged in the life insurance business should reduce the volume of litigation and lead to more effective and economical service to the insuring public.

In the selection and treatment of topics, this material reflects its textbook origin and orientation. In order to keep the parent volume from reaching encyclopedic dimensions, the author had to treat some topics with more brevity than their importance justifies and had to omit other topics altogether. The need to exercise restraint in the choice and development of topics was particularly acute in the area with which this volume is concerned.

Through the gracious assistance of a number of legal experts, this material has been endowed with a high degree of authoritativeness. Berkeley Cox, General Counsel of the Aetna Life Insurance Company; Willis H. Satterthwaite, Vice President and Counsel of the Penn Mutual Life Insurance Company; and Frank W. Hatfield, Attorney for the Penn Mutual Life Insurance Company, reviewed all of the material and rooted out many inaccuracies of fact and law. Edwin W. Patterson, Cardozo Professor Emeritus of Jurisprudence, Columbia University Law School, provided a painstaking and immensely helpful review of Chapters II, III, and IV. Bernard F. Cataldo, Professor of Business Law, University of Pennsylvania, read Chapters II, III, and IV and made many constructive suggestions. Stuart Schwarzschild, Assistant Professor of Insurance, Georgia State College of Business Administration, offered useful comments on the chapter dealing with Protection Against Creditors, the subject of his Ph.D. dissertation at the University of Pennsylvania.

To all of the above and others who responded to requests for specific information, the author expresses his profound gratitude. For any errors or shortcomings that the volume may still possess, he assumes exclusive responsibility.

DAN M. MCGILL

PHILADELPHIA, PENNSYLVANIA
June, 1959

Table of Contents

CHAPTER I

Fundamental Legal Concepts

IT IS not sufficient that a student or practitioner of life insurance understand only the economic and mathematical bases of the subject; he must also have a firm grasp of the basic legal relationships that have largely shaped its formal structure and influenced its content. The law of life insurance is derived predominantly from the general law of contracts; yet, the general law has been profoundly modified by the needs of the insurance business. On the one hand, the insurance companies have sought to condition and limit the risks which they assume; on the other hand, the insuring public has required and obtained protection against excessively legalistic interpretations of policy provisions by the companies. The resulting law is a compromise between these conflicting demands.

This text is not concerned with legal abstractions and with esoteric concepts. It deals with those concrete legal principles and situations that are certain to be encountered by the field and home office representatives in the ordinary course of business. Most of the principles are encountered on a recurring—if not daily—basis. Recognition of situations and actions which have legal significance will enable representatives of life insurance companies to provide better service to the insuring public and more protection to their company against involuntary assumption of risk and unfavorable litigation.

Comprehension of the basic legal principles underlying life insurance should be enhanced by a brief summary of the forms of law, the American judicial system, the general principles of contract interpretation, and the unique legal characteristics of a life insurance contract.

FORMS OF LAW

American law, despite its varied and complex nature, can be classified into two broad, all-inclusive forms: legislation and case law. Legislation consists of those general rules of conduct promulgated by a legally constituted body vested with the authority and power to issue such rules for all or a given portion of the population. Case law consists of those narrow rules of conduct promulgated by the courts and administrative tribunals in the adjudication of particular controversies. Legislation is found chiefly in statute books and is generally identified as a "law" or an "act," while case law is located in the published and unpublished reports of judicial and administrative decisions. The rule of law represented by legislation is stated in an official, exclusive textual form; whereas a proposition of case law must be inferred from the facts, official determinations, and accompanying official opinions of a judicial or an administrative decision. Thus, case law is flexible in form, while legislation is rigid.

Legislation[1]

The term "legislation" is usually used as if it were synonymous with "statute." In this section, "legislation" is used in a broader sense. It is assumed to include all forms of law which have the characteristic of *textual rigidity*. This is a significant characteristic, since the fixed wording of a statute or some other form of legislative law makes the problems of its interpretation and application substantially different from those of the interpretation and application of case law.

The following forms of legislative law are presented in descending order of political authoritativeness.

The Federal Constitution. The primary functions of a constitution are to establish the framework of the government and to set forth the more fundamental principles that should be operative in any democratic society. Thus, the Constitution of the United States provides for a national government of three co-ordinate branches—the legislative,

---

[1] The materials in this section were drawn largely from Noel T. Dowling, Edwin W. Patterson, and Richard R. Powell, *Materials for Legal Method* (University Casebook Series) (Chicago: Foundation Press, Inc., 1946), pp. 14–29. The classification of laws set forth in this section of the chapter was taken from that source.

executive, and judicial—and sets down in some detail the powers and functions of each. At the same time, it provides safeguards against infringement by the government on the basic human rights, such as freedom of speech, freedom of religious worship, and freedom of peaceful assemblage. In short, the federal Constitution prescribes the powers of the various branches of the federal government and sets forth limitations on those powers as they affect private individuals. With a few exceptions, it does not lay down rules of law which create rights in or impose duties on private individuals.

Treaties. The treaties entered into between the government of the United States and foreign governments often contain provisions as to the rights of aliens which are paramount to state constitutions or statutes. For example, a treaty provision which confers on aliens the right to own or inherit land is given effect despite a statute to the contrary in the state in which the land is located. Thus, a treaty of 1850 between the United States and Switzerland, which provided that the heirs of a Swiss citizen who had died owning land in the United States should be entitled to inherit the land, was upheld by the Supreme Court of the United States in the face of a contrary legal doctrine of the state of Virginia, in which the land was located. In so holding, the court said: "It must always be borne in mind that the Constitution, laws and treaties of the United States are as much a part of the law of every state as its own local laws and Constitution. This is a fundamental principle in our system of complex national polity.[2]

It is pertinent to note that the Versailles Treaty, concluded after World War I, contained a provision dealing with life insurance policies lapsed through the exigencies of war. The treaty provided that: "Where the contract of life insurance has lapsed owing to nonpayment of premiums, the payment of which has been prevented by the enforcement of measures of war, the assured or his representatives or the person entitled shall have the right to restore the contract on payment of premiums with interest at 5% per annum within three months from coming into force of the present Treaty." This provision, while binding on European insurers, never became applicable to American life insurance companies, since the United States failed to ratify the treaty.

Federal Statutes. The federal Constitution was, of necessity, couched in general terms. It was intended that the legislative body,

---

[2] *Havenstein* v. *Lynham,* 100 U.S. 483, 25 L. Ed. 628 (1880).

Congress, would address itself to matters requiring specialized rules and regulations. The statutes enacted by Congress within the scope of the powers given by the Constitution to the federal government are of higher authority than any state constitution or statute. As a matter of fact, the Constitution itself states that the Constitution, the laws of Congress made pursuant thereto, and federal treaties shall be "the supreme Law of the Land."

Not all acts of Congress, however, create "law" in the sense in which the term is generally used. Some acts are directed at one individual by name or a specifically identified group of individuals and are known as "private laws." They do not purport to lay down general rules of human conduct. Statutes of general application are labeled "public laws."

Federal Executive Orders and Administrative Regulations. The President of the United States has a power of rather indefinite scope to issue executive orders which, if they prescribe general rules of conduct, are laws, legislative in form. Within their proper scope, executive orders are paramount to state law. In addition, many federal administrative bodies have power to make general rules, ordinarily identified as regulations. These are legislative in character and, when issued pursuant to a constitutional federal statute, are superior to all forms of state laws.

State Constitutions. A state constitution is, within the proper sphere of its operation, the "supreme law" of the state—subject, of course, to the priority of federal legislative law in its proper sphere. In addition to outlining the framework of government and limiting the authority of state officials, state constitutions often prescribe general rules of conduct of the kind normally associated with acts of the state legislature. The purpose of such a provision is to place the rules contained therein beyond the power of alteration by the legislature.

State Statutes. This is a voluminous body of legislative law, since state legislatures have residuary powers to prescribe general rules of conduct. In other words, they have all powers not specifically denied them by the federal Constitution, federal treaties, federal statutes, and the appropriate state constitution. The operations of life insurance companies and the contents of their policies are greatly affected by state statutes. In fact, most states have enacted so-called "standard" provisions which must be included, in substance, in all life insurance policies issued in the states.

Administrative Regulations. Administrative bodies or officials, as a group, are endowed with some of the characteristics of all three branches of government—judicial, executive, and legislative. They sometimes have authority, granted by statute, to adjudicate particular controversies and claims and, in so doing, perform judicial or quasi-judicial functions. Their decisions, with their accompanying explanations, become precedents of administrative case law. They serve as prosecuting and law enforcement officials, in which capacity they exercise executive powers. Finally, they are frequently empowered by statute to make general rules of conduct in their particular areas of responsibility; and these general rules, as "regulations," have the force and effect of law. In many states, no provision is made for the filing and publication of these regulations, and their legal status is uncertain. In New York, a constitutional amendment specifies that no regulation of an administrative agency of that state, unless it relates to the organization or internal management of the agency, shall become effective until the regulation is filed in the office of the Department of State.

Regulations issued by the various state insurance departments constitute one of the most important sources of law for insurance companies.

Municipal Ordinances. The right to govern certain subordinate units of the state—e.g., cities, towns, and villages—is delegated by the state to municipal corporations which have limited legislative powers with respect to matters of purely local concern. The general rules enacted by these municipalities are usually called "municipal ordinances." They exert little influence on the operations of insurance companies.

Rules of Court. Rules of court are the rules adopted by a court, or by a body of judges, which regulate pleading and other procedural matters, or which regulate the internal organization of the court. They are of interest only to lawyers or persons involved in or anticipating litigation.

Case Law

Case law is a by-product of the settling of disputes. From time immemorial, this has been the special province of the courts, and the great body of case law is composed of judicial decisions. Within the last few decades, however, administrative agencies have become an important source of case law. The decisions of administrative tribunals are referred to as *administrative case law,* to distinguish them from the decisions handed down by the judiciary.

Judicial Decisions. When a court is called upon to decide a case involving a point on which there is no legislation, it will look for precedents among cases previously adjudicated. If it finds an applicable precedent, it will ordinarily settle the current dispute on the basis of the principles enunciated in the earlier case. If the court finds no precedent squarely in point or applicable by analogy, it must originate a rule to resolve the dispute. Presumably, the rule will reflect proper consideration of history, custom, morals, and sound social policy.

In creating new rules, the courts are making case law. The more situtations coming before the courts for which there are no existing rules, the more case law there will be. Moreover, each new rule becomes an integral part of the whole body of rules which the courts may use in the future.

American case law of the judicial variety is deeply rooted in the law of England as it existed at the time of the colonization of America. This is natural, since the early settlers brought with them the only law they knew. This law was composed of the rules being followed by the English courts in the settlement of disputes and the statutory enactments of Parliament still in effect. Since the decisions of the English courts were assumed to reflect those principles, maxims, usages, and rules of action which had regulated the affairs of men from time immemorial, they were designated as the "common law" of England. Since that body of principles and rules became the fountainhead of American decisional law, the latter likewise came to be known as "common law." In this sense, the term "common law" distinguishes case law from statutory or constitutional law.[3]

---

[3] It should be noted that in American usage, common law is always the law of some jurisdiction and not a "body of rules universally and automatically applicable like the law of gravitation" (Edmund M. Morgan and Francis X. Dwyer, *The Study of Law* [2d ed.; Chicago: Callaghan & Co., 1948], pp. 41–42). As Mr. Justice Holmes put it: "The common law is not a brooding omnipresence in the sky, but the articulate voice of some sovereign or quasi-sovereign that can be identified. . . . It is always the law of some state" (*Southern Pacific Co.* v. *Jensen,* 244 *U.S.* 205 [1917]). This view is not universally accepted. Some believe that the common law knows no jurisdictional boundaries. This view is exemplified by the reaction of the court to the assertion of the defendant in *St. Nicholas Bank* v. *State National Bank,* 128 N.Y. 26, 27 N.E. 849 (1891), that the contract in dispute was governed by the common law of Tennessee. The New York court stated: "There is no common law peculiar to Tennessee. But the common law there is the same as that which prevails here and elsewhere, and the judicial expositions of the common law there do not bind the courts

1. *Common Law Contrasted with Civil Law.* A broader use of the term "common law" distinguishes the entire system of English law from the legal systems developed in other parts of the world. It has acquired special significance in distinguishing between the English legal system—and the systems based upon it—and the code of law which developed in the Old Roman Empire and today serves as the foundation of the legal systems in continental Europe and in a few American states.

The Roman civil law originated as the law of the historic city of Rome but was gradually extended to the entire Roman Empire. After the fall of the Roman Empire in the fifth century, this law was compiled into a code called "Corpus Juris Civilis." Since the compilation was carried out during the reign of Justinian, it is often referred to as the "Justinian Code."

The Justinian Code attempted to evolve a rule to cover every possible type of legal conflict. An example is the rule which was developed to settle the question of survivorship when two persons perished under circumstances which rendered it impossible to determine which died first.[4] While there are many substantive differences between the Roman civil law and the Anglo-American common law, the most significant difference lies in the impact on the entire legal system of the adjudication of a particular case. Under the civil law code, a case is brought within one of the general provisions and is settled by application of the rule contained therein to the facts of the case. The decision in a particular case is little influenced by previous litigation on the point involved and, in turn, will exert little—if any—influence on similar disputes arising in the future. Under the Anglo-American system of common law, however, a controversy not covered by legislation is decided only after a guiding rule has been sought in previously litigated cases; and—more important—once a decision is made, it forms the basis for the settlement of future disputes. The more frequently a decision is used as a guide to action, the stronger it becomes as a precedent.

2. *Law versus Equity.* The term "common law" is also used to designate the rules applied by the courts of common law as con-

here." Again, in *Slaton* v. *Hall,* 168 Ga. 710 (1929), the court said: "Though courts in the different States may place a different construction upon a principle of common law, that does not change the law. There is still only one right construction. If all the American States were to construe the same principle of common law incorrectly, the common law would be unchanged."

[4] See p. 141 for the rule.

trasted with the rules applied by courts of equity. This is a third meaning of the expression.

The term "equity" is peculiar to Anglo-American law. It arose because of the failure of the common law to give adequate and proper remedy. In the early courts of England, the procedure for pursuing a legal remedy was very rigid. There were a fixed number of "forms of action," and every remedial right had to be enforced through one of these forms. The first step in any action was to apply to the king for a writ, which was a document addressed to the person responsible for the alleged wrong. This writ gave a brief summary of the facts upon which the right of action was based, and contained certain technical formulas indicating the "form of action" being brought and the amount of money damages being sought. The nature of these writs was fixed and could not be substantially altered. A writ had been developed not only for each form of action but also for the facts, circumstances, and events which would constitute the subject matter of the particular action. If no writ could be found in the collection which corresponded substantially to the facts constituting the basis for complaint, the injured party could obtain no relief in the courts. The only course of action available to him was a direct appeal to the conscience of the king.

Over a period of time, the number of direct petitions became so great that the king had to delegate responsibility for dealing with them. Since the appeal was to the king's conscience, he began to refer such matters to his spiritual adviser, the chancellor, who, being an official of the Church, usually favored the ecclesiastical law or the civil law. The practice of delegating cases to the chancellor for his sole decision, once begun, rapidly became the established method of dealing with such controversies. Eventually, a separate court, functioning under the chancellor and called the Chancery Court, was created.

Following the English precedent, the American colonies—and later, the states—established two sets of courts, one applying the rules of common law and called "courts of law," and the other applying rules of equity and good conscience and called "courts of equity." England still maintains separate courts of law and equity; but in this country, the two systems have been merged to the extent that the same court can hear both types of cases. Whether the case is heard in law or equity depends upon the remedy sought. If there is a legal remedy, the action must be brought in law; if there is no legal remedy or the legal remedy is inadequate, the suit can be brought in equity.

The distinction between law and equity is extremely important to life insurance companies. Not only does equity give them access to remedies which would otherwise be unavailable and which are essential to their operations; but suits in equity are, for the most part, tried without a jury, which—in view of the traditionally hostile attitude of juries toward insurance companies—is considered to be a major procedural advantage. Among the equitable remedies frequently invoked by life insurance companies are suits for rescission[5] and restitution, and suits for reformation of contracts.

3. *Restatements of the Law.* The development of rules of law through the adjudication of a series of controversies extending over hundreds of years, whatever the virtues of the system, places an increasing burden on the legal profession. Its members must be familiar with an ever-expanding body of law dealing with subjects becoming ever more diverse and complex. Feeling that the accelerating volume of decisional law posed a real threat to the continuance of the common law system, a group of distinguished legal scholars, in the early 1920's, sought the collaboration of leaders in the three branches of the legal profession—judges, practitioners, and teachers—in a project to simplify the system. The purpose of the project was to determine the basic rules of law, as of the date of the inquiry, in certain important areas of jurisprudence and to restate them without reference to the supporting decisions. The determination was to be arrived at after review, analysis, and synthesis of all reported decisions in the areas covered by the inquiry. The restatements were then to serve as new points of departure for the further evolution of the law. It was anticipated that thereafter, persons pursuing a particular point of law would not find it necessary to consult cases decided prior to the restatement of the law.

The co-operation of many legal scholars—particularly, law school professors—was obtained; and with the financial support of the Carnegie Foundation, the project was launched. Over the next twenty-five years, decisions in such important areas as contracts, trusts, torts, agency, and property were studied and restatements produced.

---

[5] When rescission is sought after the death of the insured, it is usually not possible to avoid trial of the issue by a jury.

Thirty thousand cases were analyzed in the property field alone, the restatement embracing four volumes.[6]

These restatements do not cite cases. Their authority is derived from the insight, skill, wisdom, and care of the legal experts who combed the decided cases in their field. They unquestionably represent an accurate formulation of the law at the date of their respective publications. In many courts, the rule given in the restatement on any question of law is accepted as *the law,* unless a conflicting local decision can be produced.

In order that the lawyers and judges of a particular state can be adequately informed as to the extent to which the decisions of that state conform to—or deviate from—the text of the restatement, local annotations have been prepared in many states for one or more of the restatements.

Administrative Decisions. Reference has earlier been made to the growth of administrative agencies. These agencies, normally created by legislative enactment, are charged with the administration of laws which are general in character and which affect the rights and privileges of private citizens. When they apply a law to a particular set of facts, they are making case law. Their decisions, when officially or unofficially reported and published, have the status of precedents. Precedents in this area, however, are regarded with less sanctity than are judicial decisions and are less likely to be applied to a different set of facts.

An administrative tribunal, unlike the usual court of law, has jurisdiction over a limited class of cases.

RELATIONSHIP OF THE JUDICIARY TO LEGISLATIVE LAW

Attitude of the Judiciary toward Legislation

The courts have always been jealous of their right to create law through the dispute-settling process and, in general, have regarded legislation as an encroachment on their prerogatives. They have long recognized the supremacy of legislative enactments over decision law but have looked upon a statute as something to be contained within the narrowest possible limits. Moreover, they have been unwilling to treat a statute as an exemplification of a general principle or precept worthy of serving as a precedent for the adjudication of a controversy not falling within its precise boundaries. This attitude is criticized in

[6] Dowling, Patterson, and Powell, *op. cit.*, p. 257.

the following excerpt from the writings of an able legal philosopher and Supreme Court Justice:

It is the fashion in our profession to lament both the quantity and quality of our statute-making, not, it is true, without some justification. But our role has been almost exclusively that of destructive critics, usually after the event, of the inadequacies of legislatures. There has been little disposition to look to our own shortcomings in failing, through adaptations of old skills and the development of new ones, to realize more nearly than we have the ideal of a unified system of judge-made and statute law woven into a seamless whole by the processes of adjudication.

The reception which the courts have accorded to statutes presents a curiously illogical chapter in the history of the common law. Notwithstanding their genius for the generation of new law from that already established, the common-law courts have given little recognition to statutes as starting points for judicial lawmaking comparable to judicial decisions. They have long recognized the supremacy of statutes over judge-made law, but it has been the supremacy of a command to be obeyed according to its letter, to be treated as otherwise of little consequence. The fact that the command involves recognition of a policy by the supreme lawmaking body has seldom been regarded by courts as significant, either as a social datum or as a point of departure for the process of judicial reasoning by which the common law has expanded. . . .

. . . I can find in the history and principles of common law no adequate reason for our failure to treat a statute much more as we treat a judicial precedent, as both a declaration and a source of law, and as a premise for legal reasoning. We have done practically that with our ancient statutes, such as the statutes of limitations, frauds and wills, readily molding them to fit new conditions within their spirit, though not their letter, possibly because their antiquity tends to make us forget or minimize their legislative origin. . . . Apart from its command, the social policy and judgment, expressed in legislation by the lawmaking agency which is supreme, would seem to merit that judicial recognition which is freely accorded to the like expression in judicial precedent. But only to a limited extent do modern courts feel free, by resort to standards of conduct set up by legislation, to impose liability or attach consequences for the failure to maintain those or similar standards in similar but not identical situations, or to make the statutory recognition of a new type of right the basis for the judicial creation of rights in circumstances not dissimilar. . . .

That such has been the course of the common law in the United States seems to be attributable to the fact that, long before its important legislative expansion, the theories of Coke and Blackstone of the self-sufficiency and ideal perfection of the common law, and the notion of the separation of powers and of judicial independence, had come to dominate our juristic thinking. The statute was looked upon as in the law but not of it, a formal rule to be obeyed, it is true, since it is the command of the sovereign, but to be obeyed grudgingly, by construing it narrowly and treating it as though it did not exist for any purpose other than that embraced within the strict construction of its words. It is difficult to appraise the consequences of the perpetuation of incongruities and injustices in the law by this habit of narrow construction of statutes and by the failure to recognize that, as recognition of social policy, they are as significant and rightly as much a part of the law, as the rules declared by judges. . . .[7]

Justice Stone ended on a more optimistic note, pointing out that the courts, influenced by the emphasis in law schools on the fusion of judge-made and statutory law, are beginning to recognize that "a statute is not an alien intruder in the house of the common law, but a guest to be welcomed and made at home there as a new and powerful aid in the accomplishment of its appointed task of accommodating the law to social needs."[8]

Interpretation of Legislative Law

While the courts have had to recognize the right of legislatures to make new law through statutory enactments, they have retained the right to interpret or construe the law which is made in that manner. They determine the meaning of the words used in the statute and decide whether a particular set of facts comes within the scope of the law. The same function is exercised with respect to the federal and state constitutions. As a part of this function, the courts determine whether or not a particular statute is in conflict with a constitutional provision.

In the process of determining the scope and meaning of statutory and constitutional provisions, the courts have developed a number of rules. These are known as rules of *statutory construction.* The fundamental purpose of all these rules is to ascertain and give effect to the intention of the legislature. One of the most basic rules is that if the language of the statute is plain and unambiguous, and its meaning clear and definite, there is no room for construction. The statute is said to have a "plain meaning," which the courts must enforce irrespective of their opinion of the wisdom or efficacy of the statute. Normally, the meaning of a statute is sought from the words used by the legislature to express its intent; but if the language of the statute is ambiguous and susceptible of more than one meaning, matters extraneous to the statute—such as its title, legislative history, conditions

---

[7] Harlan F. Stone, "The Common Law in the United States," *Harvard Law Review,* Vol. L, No. 1 (1936), pp. 12 ff.

[8] *Op. cit.,* p. 15.

leading to its enactment, and so forth—can be taken into account in an attempt to arrive at its true meaning.

It stands to reason that all parts of a statute must be considered in any attempt to ascertain its meaning. Furthermore, the interpretation adopted by a court must be one which will give effect to the whole statute. Reflecting the traditional conflict between common and statutory law, the courts have decreed that statutes in derogation of the common law shall be strictly construed. Finally, as between two statutes dealing with the same subject matter, the later one in time is to be given effect as the last expression of legislative intent.

Judicial decisions rendered in connection with the construction of statutes are considered to be case law but do not add to the body of common law. On the other hand, by providing a narrow construction of statutes in conflict with common law, the courts minimize the encroachment of statutory law on common law.

AMERICAN JUDICIAL SYSTEM

Classification of Courts

Federal Courts. The federal Constitution provides for one supreme court and such inferior courts as Congress may, from time to time, establish. At the head of the hierarchy stands the Supreme Court of the United States. The Supreme Court has original jurisdiction over all cases involving ambassadors, ministers, and consuls, and those in which a state is a party. In all other cases which can properly be brought before the Supreme Court, the court has appellate jurisdiction. Hence, the principal jurisdiction of the court is appellate. It is the court of last resort for all cases involving *federal* law and for all cases coming to it from the inferior or lower federal courts involving questions of state law.

In 1891, Congress made provision for intermediary courts of appeal, in order to lessen the burden on the Supreme Court. These tribunals are known as the Courts of Appeals, of which there are now ten.[9] Each of these courts has a minimum of three judges, who preside as a group, there being a total of forty-eight circuit judges at present. The jurisdiction of the Courts of Appeals is exclusively appellate. In most cases, the decision of a Court of Appeals is final, subject only to being reviewed by the Supreme Court at its discretion.

---

[9] These tribunals were originally called Circuit Courts of Appeals.

The general courts of original jurisdiction are the District Courts. The country is presently divided into eighty-four judicial districts, with each state having at least one district and no district embracing territory in more than one state. There is one District Court for each judicial district, but some courts have more than one judge. In total, there are roughly two judges for each District Court. The District Courts have jurisdiction over all cases arising under the federal Constitution or laws of Congress and those cases involving litigants with diversity of citizenship where the amount in dispute exceeds $10,000. The amount in controversy need exceed only $500, however, when the action is in the form of a bill of interpleader or a bill in the nature of a bill of interpleader.[10] For purposes of federal jurisdiction, diversity of citizenship is considered to exist whenever the litigating parties are citizens of different states in the United States or one is a citizen of the United States and the other is a citizen of a foreign country. For this purpose, a corporation is considered to be a citizen of the state in which it is chartered. If the jurisdiction of the federal courts is based on diversity of citizenship, the subject matter of the dispute may be state law.

In addition to these courts of general jurisdiction, there are a number of federal courts which have jurisdiction—not always exclusive—over certain types of disputes. Among such courts are the Court of Claims, the Tax Court, and the Customs Court.

State Courts. In each state, there exists—by constitutional provision and legislative enactment—a system of judicial tribunals, which embraces various courts of original jurisdiction and one or more of appellate jurisdiction. Usually, there is one court of unlimited original jurisdiction which has the power to entertain any action, regardless of the amount involved or the nature of the relief requested, although it does not ordinarily have authority over the probate of wills or administration of estates of deceased persons. This type of court usually hears cases at the county seat of the various counties in the state and is known variously as the District, Circuit, Superior, or Common Pleas Court. There are usually several inferior courts, with jurisdiction limited as to subject matter, amount in controversy, or relief sought. These are commonly designated by some such name as Municipal Court, Police Court, Magistrate's Court, or Justice of the Peace Court. There may be a separate court or a special division

---

[10] See p. 169.

of a court to deal with problems of domestic relations or juvenile delinquency. In many states, there is but one appellate tribunal, a court of last resort. In some, however, there is an intermediate tribunal with powers somewhat similar to those of the Courts of Appeals of the United States. The name of the court is not necessarily indicative of its place in the judicial hierarchy. In New York, for example, the court of original jurisdiction (the trial court) is known as the "Supreme Court," while the court of last resort is known as the "Court of Appeals." In most states, however, the court of last resort is called the "Supreme Court."

Jurisdiction of Courts

The jurisdiction of a court refers not only to its power to hear a case but also to its power to render an enforceable judgment. The constitutional or statutory provision creating a particular court defines its jurisdiction as to subject matter, parties, geographical area, and amounts involved. Jurisdiction over the person of the defendant is of especial importance. This jurisdiction is given effect by a summons from the court in which the case is to be tried, which is delivered to the sheriff, to be served upon the individual or organization made defendant to the suit. The summons must be served within the geographical area subject to the jurisdiction of the court issuing the summons. If a person comes into the state or county, as the case may be, and is served with a summons by the sheriff while there, such person is then under the authority and jurisdiction of the court.

If the defendant is a nonresident of the place where the suit is brought, service of process may be accomplished by publication. This, however, does not normally give the court authority to render a personal judgment for damages. Accompanied by proper attachment proceedings, however, service by publication brings under the court's jurisdiction all attached property of a nonresident which lies within the territorial limits of the court, so that such attached property is liable for the judgment debt and may be used to satisfy the judgment. Moreover, under the Unauthorized Insurers Service-of-Process Act, which is discussed in the following chapter, a policyholder residing in one state may obtain and enforce a judgment against an out-of-state insurance company by serving the summons on the insurance commissioner or other designated official of the state of the insured's domicile.

If a particular controversy falls within the jurisdiction of the federal courts, the plaintiff may bring his action in a federal court. If he brings the action in a state court and the defendant acquiesces in the choice of jurisdiction, the case will be tried in the state court. If, however, the defendant does not wish the case to be heard in the state court, he can have it removed to the appropriate federal court.[11] If a case involving a federal question is adjudicated in a state court, the decision of the state court on that question is subject to review by the Supreme Court of the United States, subject to the conditions and limitations imposed by Congress.

Insurance companies may prefer to have their cases tried in the federal courts because of the caliber of the federal judges, as a class, and the less hostile environment. If the sum in question exceeds $10,000, the case usually goes before a federal court, since diversity of citizenship is likely to be involved. In view of the fact that the insurance business is regulated by the states, insurance cases seldom get into the federal courts through the involvement of a federal statute.

Conflict of Laws

The jurisdiction of a court has reference to its power to hear a controversy and to enforce its decision; it is not determinative of the law which will be applied. A court of one state may have to apply the law, either statutory or common, of another state. The manner in which this could come about involves the whole topic of *conflict of laws,* which is one of the most complex and unsettled branches of the law.

The question of which law will govern the validity and interpretation of a life insurance contract is extremely important, since the states have different attitudes toward various company practices and policy provisions. Broadly speaking, the matter is resolved on the basis of the *contacts* which a life insurance contract has with various territorial sovereigns which might be deemed to have an interest in determining the rights and duties of the parties to—and beneficiaries of—the contract. These contacts might arise out of the relationship of the state to the home office, a branch office, the insured, or the beneficiary, to mention only the major possibilities. Theoretically, if a state has *any* relationship to—or contact with—an insurance contract, it has some—though perhaps only slight—claim to a voice in the determination of the rights and duties thereunder. Since, in the typical case, there will be at least two states concerned with the policy

[11] See Morgan, and Dwyer, *op. cit.*, pp. 27–31, for a more detailed statement of the conditions under which a case can be removed to the federal courts.

—the state in which the home office is located and the state in which the insured is domiciled—and there can easily be five or more, rules must be developed to determine which state has the paramount interest in interpreting and enforcing the contract.

The rule followed by the majority of jurisdictions is that questions concerning both the validity and the interpretation of a life insurance contract will be resolved by the law of the state in which the contract was made,[12] which will be the state in which the last act necessary to bring the contract into existence took place. This is the so-called "place-of-making rule." Since, under the usual circumstances, the contract becomes effective at the moment it is delivered by the agent to the insured and the first premium is collected,[13] the place of making is typically the state in which the insured resides. On the other hand, if the first premium is paid with the application and a conditional receipt is issued contingent on approval at the company's home office, the act which brings the contract into existence occurs at the home office of the company, producing a different result.

Disturbed by the fortuitous nature of the place-of-making rule and convinced that all policyholders should be protected by the laws of their states, several courts have adopted the rule that all policies shall be governed by the laws of the state in which the insured is domiciled, irrespective of where the contract came into existence.[14] Other courts —feeling that the control of a state over a company incorporated under its laws assures equality of treatment of all policyholders, wherever they live—follow the rule that the laws of the insurer's state of incorporation shall be applied in determining the validity and interpretation of a life insurance contract.[15] In all these cases, the choice of the governing law is determined by the conflict-of-law rule of the state in which the case is being adjudicated.

The policy may contain a provision that its validity and interpretation shall be governed by the law of a designated state, which may be neither the state of domicile of the insured nor the state in which

[12] *Mutual Life Insurance Company* v. *Johnson,* 293 U.S. 335, 55 Sup. Ct. 154, 79 L. Ed. 398 (1934).

[13] See pp. 33–43 for an explanation of the methods by which life insurance contracts come into existence.

[14] *Great Southern Life Insurance Company* v. *Burwell,* 12 F. (2d) 244 (C.C.A. Miss., 1926); *Dolan* v. *Mutual Reserve Fund Life Assn.,* 173 Mass. 197 (1899); *Keatley* v. *The Travelers Insurance Company,* 187 Pa. 197 (1898).

[15] *Equitable Life Assurance Society* v. *Nixon,* 81 Fed. 796 (C.C.A. Wash., 1897); *Fidelity Mutual Life Assn.* v. *Ficklin,* 74 Md. 172 (1892); *Jones* v. *Metropolitan Life Insurance Co.,* 158 Misc. (N.Y. Sup. Ct.) 466 (1936).

the home office is located. It appears that the insured or beneficiary can enforce this provision if the laws of the designated state are more favorable to him than the laws which would apply under the conflict-of-law rule, but the insurance company is not permitted to invoke the provision.[16] This has led one insurance law authority to conclude that "the general principle that, *in case* of ambiguity in an insurance contract, it will be construed most strictly against the insurer (*contra proferentem*) and most favorably to the insured or beneficiary has been stretched to a principle that *even an unambiguous* provision as to the choice of law will be enforced only if favorable to the insured or beneficiary."[17]

It should be noted that when the courts of one state apply the laws of another state, they apply *their* interpretation of what the law is in the other state. This may differ from the interpretation adopted by the courts of the other state.

It was provided in the act creating the federal judiciary[18] that in trying cases based on diversity of citizenship, federal courts would be bound by the applicable laws of the state in which they were sitting (assuming no conflict of laws). In the famous case of *Swift* v. *Tyson*,[19] decided by the United States Supreme Court in 1842, it was held that the word "laws" used in the act referred to statutory law and not case law. Thus, the federal courts were free to apply their own version of the common law in settling disputes not involving a federal or state statute. This ruling turned out to be highly significant for insurance companies, inasmuch as federal precedents were more favorable to the companies in many respects than the common law of the various states. This happy state of affairs was ended in 1938, when the United States Supreme Court, in the case of *Erie Railroad Company* v. *Tompkins,*[20] overruled its earlier doctrine and held that the federal courts were obliged to apply the common law, as well as the statutory law, of the state in which the case is being heard. Three years later, the Supreme Court held that the federal courts would also have to follow the conflict-of-law rules of the state in which they sit.[21] Thus,

[16] See Edwin W. Patterson, *Essentials of Insurance Law* (2d ed.; New York: McGraw-Hill Book Co., Inc., 1957), pp. 54 and 55, nn. 114 and 116, for citations.

[17] *Ibid.*, p. 55.

[18] Judiciary Act of 1789, 1 Stat. 92, 28 U.S.C., Sec. 725.

[19] 16 Pet. 1 (1842).

[20] 304 U.S. 64 (1938).

[21] *Griffin* v. *McCooch,* 313 U.S. 549 (1941); *Klaxon* v. *Stentor Electric Manufacturing Co.,* 313 U.S. 487 (1941).

"for purposes of diversity jurisdiction, a federal court is in effect, only another court of the state."[22]

GENERAL NATURE OF A LIFE INSURANCE CONTRACT

A valid agreement between a life insurance company and the applicant for insurance, represented by an instrument called the *policy* (from the Italian word *polizza,* meaning a rolled document), is a contract and, as such, is subject to the general rules of contract law. However, in adapting these rules, which are familiar to all students of business law, to the life insurance contract, the courts have introduced substantial modifications because of certain peculiar characteristics of the life insurance contract. These characteristics—which, with one exception, are common to all types of insurance contracts—are briefly described herewith.

Aleatory Contract

The agreement contained in a life insurance policy is *aleatory* in nature, rather than *commutative.* In a commutative agreement, each party expects to receive from the other party, in one way or the other, the approximate equivalent of what he himself undertakes to give. Thus, in an agreement to purchase real estate, the buyer agrees to pay a sum of money which represents the approximate value of the property to him, while the seller agrees to sell the property for a price which represents its approximate value to him. In other words, both parties contemplate a fairly even exchange of values.

In an aleatory agreement, on the other hand, both parties realize that, depending upon chance, one may receive a value out of all proportion to the value which he gives. The essence of an aleatory agreement is the element of chance or uncertainty. The prime example of such a contract is the wagering agreement. The term may also be applied to an industry where the potential gain or loss is governed largely by chance. Thus, the exploration and drilling functions of the oil industry may be described as aleatory in nature. So is prospecting for gold, silver, or uranium.

In a life insurance transaction, the present value of the potential premium payments at the inception of the agreement is precisely equal, on the basis of the company's actuarial assumptions, to the

---

[22] *Angel* v. *Bullington,* 91 L. Ed. 557 (U.S., 1947).

present value of the anticipated benefits payable under the contract. In this sense, the life insurance transaction is not aleatory. Moreover, the sum total of insurance transactions for a company, or the whole life insurance industry, is not aleatory because of the predictability and stability provided by the theories of probability and the law of large numbers. It remains true, however, that a particular policy-holder may pay in to the insurance company a sum of money considerably smaller than the sum promised under the contract. Indeed, the face of the policy may become payable after the insured has paid only one installment of the first premium. This *chance* of obtaining a disproportionate return from an "investment" in a life insurance policy has motivated—and continues to motivate—many unscrupulous persons to seek life insurance through fraudulent means and for illegal purposes. The remedies for breach of warranty, misrepresentation, and concealment are invoked by the companies to protect themselves and society against fraudulent attempts to procure insurance. The requirement of an insurable interest is also designed to deal with the problems created by the fact that the life insurance policy is an aleatory contract.

The aleatory nature of the insurance contract accounts in large measure for the modifications of contract law in the field of insurance.

Unilateral Contract

Most contracts in the business world are *bilateral* in nature. This means that each party to the contract makes an enforceable promise to the other party. The consideration for such a contract is the exchange of mutual promises. Thus, an order from a wholesaler to a manufacturer for a specified quantity of a particular item at a specified price, if accepted, is a bilateral contract. The manufacturer agrees to deliver the desired merchandise at an agreed-upon price, while the wholesaler agrees to accept and pay for the merchandise when it is delivered.

Under a *unilateral* contract, on the other hand, only one party makes an enforceable promise. This arises out of the fact that the other party to the contract carries out his part of the bargain *before* the contract comes into existence. For instance, if the wholesaler in the foregoing example had remitted cash with his order, the transaction would have become unilateral in nature, inasmuch as only the manufacturer had anything to perform. In general, unilateral contracts are confined to situations in which one party is unwilling to extend credit to the other or to take his word for future performance.

As a general rule, a life insurance policy is a unilateral contract, in that only the insurance company makes an enforceable promise thereunder. The consideration demanded by the company—namely, the application and the first premium, or the first installment thereof—is given by the insured before the contract goes into effect. The insured is under no legal obligation to pay premiums subsequent to the first, although, if he does not do so, the company will be released from its original promise to pay the face of the policy. Nevertheless, he incurs no legal penalties through failure to continue premium payments. On the other hand, the company is obligated to accept the periodic premiums from the insured and to keep the contract in force in accordance with its original terms.

If a life insurance policy is delivered in exchange for the applicant's promissory note or oral promise of the insured to pay by an agent having the authority to waive cash payment of the first premium, a *bilateral* contract is created. The insurer's promise is exchanged for the insured's promise.

Conditional Contract

Closely related to the foregoing is the fact that the life insurance policy is a *conditional* contract. This means that the company's obligation under the contract is contingent on the performance of certain acts by the insured or the beneficiary. This does *not,* however, make the contract bilateral.

A condition is always inserted in a contract for the benefit of the promisor and hence is disadvantageous to the promisee. Conditions are not confined to unilateral contracts; a party to a bilateral contract can condition his promise in any manner acceptable to the other party. Conditions are classified as either precedent or subsequent. A condition *precedent* must be satisfied before legal rights and duties are created or continued, whereas a condition *subsequent* must be fulfilled in order to prevent the extinguishment of rights and duties already created in the contract. Whether a condition is precedent or subsequent depends upon the intention of the parties to the contract. When the intention is not clear, the tendency of the courts is to classify a condition as precedent, in order to avoid a forfeiture.

The legal significance of a condition is quite different from that of a promise. Failure to perform a promise subjects the promisor to liability for damages to the promisee. Failure to perform or fulfill a condition does not subject the person involved (the promisee) to liability for damages, but merely deprives him of a right or privilege which he otherwise would have had. It releases the promisor from his obligation to perform. As Professor Patterson puts it, "A condition is a shield, not a sword."[23]

The promise of a life insurance company is conditioned on the timely payment of premiums subsequent to the first. Payment of these premiums is considered to be a condition *precedent* to the continuance of the contract under its original terms. If this condition is not fulfilled, the company is relieved of its basic promise but remains obligated to honor various subsidiary promises contained in the surrender provisions and the reinstatement clause.

The company's promise to pay the face of the policy is always conditioned on the insured's forbearance from committing suicide during a specified period (usually, one or two years) after issue of the policy and may be conditioned on his death from causes not associated with war or aviation. Finally, the company has no liability until satisfactory proof of death has been submitted by the beneficiary or the insured's personal representative.

Contract of Adhesion

A life insurance policy is also a contract of *adhesion*. This means that the terms of the contract are not arrived at by mutual negotiation between the parties, as would be the case with a *bargaining* contract. The policy, a complex and technical instrument, is prepared by the company and, with minor exceptions, must be accepted by the applicant in the form offered to him. The prospective insured may or may not contract with the company, but in no sense is he in a position to bargain about the terms of the contract if he does decide to seek insurance. He must reject the contract entirely or "adhere" to it. Any bargaining which precedes the issuance of a life insurance contract has to do only with whether or not the contract is to be issued, the plan and amount of insurance, and—to some degree—the terms of the settlement agreement, although the agreement is actually drafted by the company.

The adhesive nature of the life insurance contract is highly significant from a legal standpoint. This importance derives from the basic rule of contract construction that a contract is to be construed or inter-

---

[23] Patterson, *op. cit.*, p. 69.

preted most strongly against the party who drafted the agreement. The avowed purpose of this rule is to neutralize any advantage that might have been gained by the party which prepared the contract. This means that if there is an ambiguity in the life insurance policy, the provision in question will be given the interpretation most favorable to the insured or his beneficiary. The view is rather prevalent in insurance circles that in their zeal to protect the insured, the courts find ambiguities in contracts where none exists.

Some who readily admit the soundness of this rule in general and of its application to life insurance policies prior to the turn of the century question its continued application to policies currently being issued, in view of the large number of provisions which are required by state statutes to be incorporated in such policies. Although these statutes do not prescribe the exact language to be used, many states require that the language of all policy provisions, including those voluntarily included, be approved by the state insurance department before sale of the policy form to the public. Such a requirement has the purpose, among others, of preventing the use of any deceptive or misleading language, or any provisions that would be unfair to policyholders. These factors have produced a relaxation of the strict rule of construction in some courts; but in general, all ambiguous provisions of the policy continue to be construed against the insurer.

Contract to Pay Stated Sum

Contracts issued by property and casualty insurance companies are contracts of *indemnity*. This means that the insured can collect only the amount of his loss, irrespective of the face of the policy—except, of course, that the recovery cannot exceed the face of the policy. Moreover, upon payment by an insurer of a loss caused by the negligence of a third party, as in the case of an automobile accident, the insurer acquires the insured's right of action against the negligent third party, up to the amount of its loss payment and any expenses incurred in enforcing its rights. This is known as the doctrine of *subrogation;* and while a provision giving effect to this doctrine is virtually always included in property and casualty insurance policies, it applies even in the absence of a policy provision.

The foregoing is background to saying that a life insurance policy is not a contract of indemnity, but one to pay a *stated sum*. This is presumably based on the assumption that the value of a man's life to himself is without limit; and thus, no sum payable upon his death will be in excess of the loss suffered. Thus, even though the insured has reached an age or a circumstance where he no longer has an economic value, upon his death the company will still have to pay the sum agreed upon. The practical significance of this principle is that the insurance company, after paying the face of the policy, is not subrogated to the right of action of the decedent's estate when his death was caused by the negligence of a third party.

CHAPTER II

Formation of a Life Insurance Contract

TO BE enforceable, the agreement between a life insurance company and the person seeking insurance, represented by a written instrument called the policy, must meet all the requirements prescribed by law for the formation of a valid contract. In this and the following chapter, it will be explained in specific terms how each of these requirements is satisfied in the formation of a life insurance contract.

LEGAL CAPACITY OF THE PARTIES

Parties to the Contract

There are two parties to the life insurance contract—the insurance company and the applicant. The applicant is normally, but not necessarily, the person whose life is the subject matter of the contract. The person on whose life a policy is issued is technically known as the *insured.* A person who takes out insurance on the life of another is sometimes referred to as the assured, to distinguish him from the *insured.* Such person may also be referred to as the *owner-applicant.* The person whose life is insured is not a party to the contract unless he is also the applicant. Occasionally, two or more persons may jointly apply for insurance on the life of another person, as in the case of business continuation agreements. In that event, the joint applicants would constitute parties of the second part.

The designation of a third party to receive the proceeds upon maturity of the policy does not make such a person a party to the contract in the technical sense. The third-party beneficiary need not know of the contract at its inception, may disclaim any benefits thereunder, and incurs no duties by virtue of his designation. The beneficiary does acquire certain rights which are enforceable against the company, but he acquires them only through the agreement between the company and the applicant. Furthermore, the beneficiary's rights can be negated by any defenses available against the applicant.

An assignee, while possessing rights quite distinct from those of a beneficiary, occupies a position similar to that of the beneficiary, in that he is an *interested* party but is not a party to the contract in a strict sense.

It is worthy of noting that the voluntary payment of premiums by a person having no other relationship with the policy bestows no contractual rights or privileges on the premium payer.

The relationship between the insurance company and the other contracting party, be he the insured or the assured, is that of conditional debtor and creditor. The insurance company incurs obligations only if certain conditions are fulfilled, and then its duty is only to carry out the terms of the contract. The insurance company is not a trustee in any sense of the word and is under no legal obligation to render an accounting of the premiums received or, in the absence of a showing of bad faith, of the apportionment of dividends.

Competency of the Insurer

In the absence of specific legislation to the contrary, there is no reason why any person who has the legal capacity to enter into a contract cannot become the insurer under a life insurance contract. Freedom of contract is a constitutional and common-law privilege which must not be abridged unless the nature of the subject matter of the contract is such as to make it a proper subject for the exercise of the police power of the state. Insurance—because of its magnitude, nature, and intimate bearing on the welfare of society—has been adjudged a proper subject for the exercise of such power. The United States Supreme Court has ruled that a state may prohibit the making of insurance contracts by persons, either natural or artificial, who have not complied with the requirements of the law of the state. In many states, the statutes specifically prohibit natural persons from acting as life insurers; and even in those states that have not so legislated, the nature of the business—with its need for continuity and permanence of the insurer—has brought about the same result. Hence, while individual insurers were common in the early days of life insurance, today the business is conducted exclusively by corporate insurers.[1]

If a corporation seeking to write life insurance in a particular state is legally organized, the only question that can arise with respect to its capacity to contract is whether it has complied with all the requirements for doing business in that state. The most important requirement is that the corporation obtain a license to do business in the state. In certain lines of insurance, notably accident and sickness insurance, the transacting of business, frequently by mail, by companies which have not obtained a license in the state where the policyholders reside is a major problem and creates difficulties for policyholders attempting to enforce claims against such unauthorized insurers. In life insurance, however, the problem of the unlicensed or unauthorized insurer is of less serious proportions. A more likely form of noncompliance on the part of a life insurance company would be failure (perhaps through inadvertence) to file policy forms and other blanks as required by law.

A contract issued by an unlicensed insurer is usually enforceable by the policyholder. This rule of law recognizes that a person who is solicited to buy insurance cannot be expected to inquire into the affairs of the insurance company to determine whether or not it has complied with all the statutory and regulatory requirements governing its operations and is fully qualified to enter into the proposed contract. On the contrary, the prospective insured is permitted to assume that the insurer is legally competent to enter into the proposed contract and will not be permitted to erect as a defense against claims its own violation of statutory requirements. In order to assist the insured in enforcing his claims against an unauthorized out-of-state insurer, several states (fourteen, at the present writing) have enacted the so-called Unauthorized Insurers Service-of-Process Act, which designates the insurance commissioner or some other state official as agent of the unauthorized insurer for the purpose of accepting service of process. Designed to deal with companies which do business by mail, these statutes permit the insured to secure a judgment against the insurer in the courts of his own state, which judgment must be given "full faith and credit" by the courts of all other states in which

[1] Including fraternal associations.

the insurer has assets. Agents of unauthorized insurers are subject to both criminal and civil penalties and, in some states, are personally liable for claims under contracts which they sold. It hardly seems necessary to add that an unlicensed insurer cannot maintain an action to enforce any claim arising out of an insurance contract made in violation of the laws of the state in which the suit is brought.[2]

If the insurer is duly authorized to do business in a particular state but has failed to comply with some other requirement of the state law, the validity of its contracts will usually not be affected by the noncompliance. The contracts will be binding upon both parties; but the insurer will be subject to whatever penalties are imposed for the violation of the law; and if the statute requires certain provisions in such a contract, the contract will be deemed to contain such provisions.

Competency of the Applicant

All individuals are presumed to have legal capacity except those comprising the clearly defined groups that are held by law to have no capacity or only limited capacity to contract. For life insurance purposes, the two most important classes of persons with impaired capacity are minors and alien enemies.

Minors—or infants, as they are known to the law—do not lack capacity in the absolute sense and may enter into contracts which are binding on the other party. However, subject to certain restrictions, a minor can disaffirm his contract at any time and demand a return of the monetary consideration that passed to the other party. Limitations on the right of a minor to void his contract are found in the general rules that an infant is bound to pay the reasonable value of necessaries actually furnished to him and that if he can make restitution of that which he received for it, he must do so. Up to this point, no American court has held a life insurance policy to be a necessity for a minor, in the legal sense of the word. Hence, a minor can disaffirm a life insurance contract at any time and recover all premiums paid. A majority of the courts permit full recovery of premiums, with no deduction for the cost of protection,[3] while a few courts authorize the company to retain that portion of the aggregate premiums applied

[2] *Farmers etc. Insurance Co.* v. *Harrah,* 47 Ind. 236 (1874); *Isaac Fass, Inc.* v. *Pink,* 178 Va. 357 (1941).

[3] *Simpson* v. *Prudential Insurance Co.,* 184 Mass. 348, 68 N.E. 673 (1903).

toward the cost of protection.[4] In the latter case, the recovery is limited to the cash value or reserve. It is clear that only by permitting the insurer to deduct the cost of protection does the court compel the minor to make restitution to the other party.

In recognition of the importance of life insurance and of the unfavorable position of a life insurance company in dealing with minors, several states have enacted statutes conferring on minors, of a specified age and over, the legal capacity to enter into valid and enforceable life insurance contracts on their own lives. The age limit varies from fifteen to eighteen, with fifteen predominating. A minor who satisfies the age requirement is permitted not only to purchase a life insurance policy but also to exercise all ownership rights in the contract. The statutes usually require that the beneficiary be a close relative, the eligible relationships being set forth in the laws. Since the statutes bestow legal capacity on a minor only for the purpose of negotiating insurance on his own life, he is still under legal disability in dealing as owner or beneficiary with a policy on the life of another person.

A life insurance contract entered into between an American company and a resident of a foreign country is just as valid as one made with an American citizen, unless a state of war exists between the two countries, in which event the contract would be a nullity. In the first instance, the resident of the foreign country would be described as an alien friend; and in the second, as an alien enemy. A contract made with an alien friend is valid in all respects, while one with an alien enemy is void. No difficulties are likely to arise unless an alien friend with whom a contract has been made becomes an alien enemy through the outbreak of hostilities. In that event, it will generally be impossible, as well as contrary to public policy, for the parties to carry out the terms of the contract. In the case of life insurance, premium payments could not be made (unless the company had a branch office in the foreign country), and a question arises as to the status of the policy.[5]

The rulings of the courts in cases involving this problem have been diverse. In Connecticut, Georgia, and a few other states, it is held that

[4] *Johnson* v. *Northwestern Mutual Life Insurance Co.*, 56 Minn. 365, 57 N.W. 934, 59 N.W. 992 (1894).

[5] This problem has frequently originated through the sale of life insurance to an alien residing in the United States who returned to his native country before the outbreak of hostilities.

all rights in such contracts are terminated and all equities forfeited. This is a harsh rule and permits the enrichment of the insurance company at the expense of one whose nonperformance was beyond his individual control. A number of states, including New York and New Jersey, hold that the contract is merely suspended during hostilities and can be revived by payment of all past-due premiums. Under this rule, the policy of a deceased policyholder can be revived and the company forced to pay the face amount. This rule obviously exposes the company to a high degree of adverse selection. A third group of courts, including the United States Supreme Court, hold that the contract is terminated with the outbreak of hostilities, but the policyholder is entitled to the reserve computed as of the date of the first premium in default. The reserve would be paid over to the governmental agency charged with the responsibility of assembling and holding property belonging to alien enemies. Under this rule, no action can be brought to recover the face of the policy, nor is the company under any obligation to revive the policy. None of the solutions to the problem is perfectly satisfactory, but the basis of settlement prescribed by the Supreme Court would seem to be the most equitable.

MUTUAL ASSENT

As in the case of other simple contracts, there must be an expression of mutual assent before a life insurance contract can be created. One party must make an offer to enter into an insurance transaction, and the other must accept the offer. One would naturally assume that the company, through one of its soliciting agents, makes the offer, which the prospective insured is free to accept or decline. That is not necessarily the case. In many situations, the prospect is considered to have made the offer. As a general rule, and subject to the exceptions noted later, the prospect is considered to have made the offer whenever the application is accompanied by the first premium, whereas the company is regarded as the offeror whenever the first premium is not paid (or, at least, definitely promised) with the application. In the first situation, the prospect has indicated his unqualified willingness to enter into a contractual relationship with the company, even to the point of putting up the consideration; while in the second situation, the prospect may refuse, without any legal penalties, to accept and pay for the contract issued by the company. The question of who is the offeror and who the offeree is important in determining the exact time at which the contract comes into existence, which may be of crucial significance. This matter is dealt with in a later section.

The Application

The chain of events which culminates in the formation of a life insurance contract is inaugurated by a conversation between a soliciting agent of the company and a prospect for insurance, during the course of which the prospect is invited or—more accurately—urged to extend an offer to the company. Such invitations to deal have no legal consequences in the formation of the contract, although they may contain representations that will have consequences after the contract is made.[6] If the invitation to deal comes from a broker, the representations will have no legal effect either before or after formation of the contract, since a broker is considered to be the agent of the applicant for the purpose of procuring insurance.[7]

The prospective insured's offer to the company, or his invitation to the company to make him an offer, as the case might be, is communicated in the form of an application. As far as the law is concerned, the application can be oral or written; and in many branches of insurance, such as fire insurance, oral applications are the custom. In life insurance, however, written applications are required as a matter of company practice.

The application for a life insurance contract serves the following purposes:

1. It requests the insurer to issue a specific type of policy, providing a designated amount of insurance, in exchange for a specified premium.
2. It gives the name and address of the applicant, the name and relationship of the person or persons to whom the proceeds are to be paid, and the manner in which the company's obligation is to be discharged.
3. It provides a detailed description of the risk which the insurer is asked to underwrite, including statements or representations as to the applicant's occupation, travel plans, family history, personal medical history, present physical condition, and habits.
4. It puts the applicant on notice, and requires an acknowledgment from him of the fact, that the soliciting agent has no authority to modify any terms of the application or of the policy to be issued pursuant thereto (the *nonwaiver clause*).

---

[6] See pp. 95, 96.

[7] On the other hand, a broker is considered to be an agent of the insurer for the purpose of collecting the first (and subsequent) premium and delivering the policy.

The contents of the application relating to the first two functions constitute the offer in the technical sense, since they fix the terms of the policy to be issued by the company as an acceptance of the offer. While the identification of the person whose life is to be insured is a necessary part of the offer, the detailed description of the risk is not actually a part of the offer. From a legal standpoint, the representations of the applicant as to his medical history, present physical condition, and so on, are merely inducements to the insurer; they are not promises or conditions of the contract. Neither does the nonwaiver clause relate to the offer. It is intended merely to prevent the applicant from successfully contending afterwards that he was misled as to the apparent authority of the agent.[8]

In the typical commercial transaction, the offer becomes a part of the contract ultimately consummated. This is not true of the offer leading to a life insurance contract, unless the application is specifically made a part of the contract. It has long been established—first by court decisions and later by statutes—that once a life insurance policy is issued, the entire contract is contained in the policy. This rule, known historically as the *parol evidence rule* but more recently as the rule of *legal integration,* has been stated as follows: "All preliminary negotiations, conversations and oral agreements are merged in and superseded by the subsequent written contract and unless fraud, accident or mistake be averred, the writing constitutes the agreement between the parties, and its terms cannot be added to or subtracted from by parol evidence."[9]

Since the company places great reliance on the information contained in the application and—in the event of a contested claim—would undoubtedly want to introduce evidence therefrom, it customarily incorporates the application into the contract, by reference as well as by physical attachment of a copy (usually a photostat) of the application to the policy. The application can be incorporated by reference only through a statement in the policy that the application is made a part of the policy. It cannot be accomplished by a statement to that effect in the application itself. When a copy of the application is also physically attached to the policy, there can be no doubt of the sufficiency of the incorporation. This practice has been sanctioned in

[8] The effect of such notice is discussed on pp. 94, 95.

[9] H. M. Horne and D. B. Mansfield, *The Life Insurance Contract* (2d ed.; New York: Life Office Management Association, 1948), p. 46.

many states by statutes, usually identified as *entire-contract statutes,*[10] which require that a copy of the application be attached to the policy before it is delivered to the insured.

Effective Date of Coverage

The coverage under a life insurance policy becomes effective the instant the contract comes into existence. The latter event, however, takes place only after certain conditions have been fulfilled, and those conditions can be fulfilled in more than one manner. The procedure by which a contract is brought into existence after submission of the application depends upon whether the latter is regarded as an offer or only an invitation to the company to make an offer. That, in turn, depends upon the time at which and the circumstances under which the first premium is paid. In that regard, it is necessary to distinguish among three different sets of circumstances. The first set of circumstances to be considered is that under which the application is submitted without payment of the first premium.

Application without First Premium. It will be recalled that when the applicant does not tender the first premium with the application, the latter is regarded as only an invitation to deal,[11] and the approval of the application and issue of the policy constitute an offer from the company to the prospective insured which is normally communicated by delivery of the policy. The applicant manifests his acceptance of the company's offer by accepting delivery of the policy and paying the first premium. Most companies specify in the application that the prospective insured must be in good health at the time of delivery of the policy, and some condition the contract on the absence of any medical treatment during the interim between submission of the application and delivery of the policy. All these requirements—delivery of the policy, payment of the first premium, good health of the applicant, and absence of any interim medical treatment—are treated as conditions precedent which must be fulfilled before the contract comes into existence and the coverage becomes effective. Each of these requirements will be discussed.

---

[10] See p. 72.

[11] This is true only when the soliciting agent does not have authority to extend credit. If the agent has authority to take a promissory note or even an oral promise of the insured, in lieu of cash, an application accompanied by such a promise is an offer from the applicant to make a *bilateral* contract—an exchange of the applicant's promise for the insurer's promise.

1. *Delivery of the Policy.* Delivery of the policy is a legal prerequisite to the validity of the life insurance contract only because the companies specifically make it so. Neither by statute nor by common law is the delivery of a formal policy requisite to the completion, validity, or enforceability of a contract of insurance. This is contrary to real estate law, for example, which holds that legal title to real estate is not transferred until the deed is delivered. The company could conceivably communicate its offer to the applicant in some other manner, and the applicant could manifest his acceptance by notification to the company or to the soliciting agent. The controlling reason why the companies make delivery of the policy a condition precedent to the formation of the contract is that it provides a means of establishing definitely the moment at which coverage under the contract becomes effective. Several other actions of the company—such as approval of the application by the underwriting department, issue of the policy, or mailing of the policy to the soliciting agent for delivery—might be construed as the inception of coverage, leading to much confusion and litigation, unless the parties agree in advance that a definitely determinable event, such as delivery of the policy, shall mark the beginning of coverage.

Despite this attempt to achieve certainty, litigation has developed over the meaning of the word "delivery." The issue is whether the condition can be satisfied only by a manual delivery or whether constructive delivery will be sufficient. If it is clearly evident from the terms of the application and the policy that actual, manual delivery is contemplated, the requirement will be strictly enforced.[12] If, however, the requirement is couched in terms of a simple "delivery," the general rule is that the condition can be fulfilled by constructive delivery.[13] Constructive delivery has been held to take place whenever a policy, properly stamped and addressed to the company's agent, is deposited in the mails, provided no limitations are imposed upon the manual delivery of the policy to the insured by the agent.[14] There are a number of decisions, however, which hold that the requirement of "delivery"—and especially "actual delivery"—is itself a condition

---

[12] *Pruit* v. *Great Southern Life Insurance Co.,* 202 La. 527, 12 So. (2d) 261 (1942).

[13] *Massachusetts Mutual Life Insurance Co.* v. *National Bank of Commerce,* 95 F. (2d) 797 (1938).

[14] *Life and Casualty Insurance Co.* v. *McCrae,* 193 Ark. 890, 103 S.W. (2d) 929 (1937); *Republic National Life Insurance Co.* v. *Merkley,* 59 Ariz. 125, 124 P. (2d) 313 (1942); *Jefferson Standard Life Insurance Co.* v. *Munthe,* 78 F. (2d) 53 (1935); *Jackson* v. *New York Life Insurance Co.,* 7 F. (2d) 31 (1925).

precedent which cannot be met by a constructive delivery. It should be remarked that the issue of constructive delivery is not material if the other conditions—notably, payment of the first premium and the applicant's good health—are not met.

To a large extent, delivery is a matter of the intention of the parties. It is a question of who has the *right* to possession of the policy, rather than who has actual possession. That being true, possession of the policy by the insured is, at most, only prima-facie evidence of its delivery.[15] The presumption of proper delivery can be rebutted by evidence that the insured obtained possession of the policy by fraud, for the purpose of inspecting it, or in any other manner manifesting a lack of intention on the company's part to effectuate a legal delivery of the policy. On the other hand, it has been held that if the first premium has been paid, the applicant is in good health, and the company has implicitly expressed its intention of being legally bound under the contract by delivering the policy to the agent to be unconditionally passed on to the applicant, the contract is in force; and, although the insured may die without actual possession of the policy, the company is liable for payment of the insured amount.[16]

In view of the foregoing presumption, an agent must observe proper safeguards in relinquishing physical possession of a policy to an applicant before all conditions precedent have been fulfilled. The need for caution is greatly magnified if the policy, on its face, acknowledges receipt of the first premium, which is sometimes the case. The most common circumstance under which the agent may find it necessary to relinquish control over a policy without making a legal delivery is when the applicant expresses a desire to study the policy. In that event, the applicant is asked to sign a receipt in which he acknowledges that the policy is in his hands only for examination and approval, and that he has not paid the first premium. This acknowledgment is called an *inspection receipt*.

2. *Payment of First Premium.* It is customary for the application —and sometimes, the policy itself—to stipulate that the first premium must be paid before the coverage can become effective. Payment of the full amount in cash is usually specified; and unless the company agrees to extend credit, any payment smaller than the full premium will fail to satisfy the requirement. The agent is usually not authorized to extend credit on behalf of the company, but he may pay

[15] *Eaton* v. *New York Life Insurance Co.,* 315 Pa. 68, 172 Atl. 121 (1934).

[16] *New York Life Insurance Co.* v. *Baker,* 33 F. (2d) 434 (1929).

the premium for the insured and seek reimbursement on a personal basis. If an agent is authorized to accept the promissory note of an applicant in payment of the first premium, the tendering of such a note by the applicant will satisfy the condition precedent, but failure of the insured to pay the note at maturity may cause the policy to lapse.[17]

Payment by check may be taken as absolute or conditional payment, depending upon the intention of the parties. If the check is accepted in absolute payment of the first premium, failure of the bank to honor the check would not affect the validity of the policy, merely giving the company the right to sue the applicant for the amount of the check. On the other hand, if the check is accepted only as conditional payment, nonpayment of the check would cause the contract to fail. Most companies stipulate that checks are accepted subject to being honored by the bank, which is the common-law rule in the absence of evidence that the check was accepted as absolute payment.

3. *Good Health of Applicant.* The *delivery-in-good-health clause* is a by-product of the process by which risks are underwritten in life insurance. In most lines of property and casualty insurance, the local agent is clothed with the authority to underwrite the risk and bind the coverage. There need be no lag of any consequence between the inspection of the risk and the binding of the coverage. In life insurance, on the contrary, all underwriting information is forwarded to the home office, and the right to bind the risk rests solely with the executive officers of the company. Under such a system, which seems to be the only feasible one, there is an inevitable time lag between the submission of the application and the assumption of the risk by the insurer. In a large case, where the investigation of the applicant must be very comprehensive and the collection of medical data may involve correspondence with attending physicians and requests for supplemental diagnostic procedures, the lag might be as long as a month. The company naturally would like to be protected against a deterioration of the applicant's health during the time it is considering the application. The means which the companies have chosen to accomplish this objective is the delivery-in-good-health clause.

The exact wording of the good-health clause varies from company to company; but the gist of the clause is that the policy shall not take effect unless, upon the date of delivery, the applicant shall be alive and

---

[17] See pp. 48–50.

in good health. Some clauses provide that unless the first premium is paid with the application, the applicant must be alive and in good health upon payment of the first premium. Such a clause has the effect of making the good health of the applicant a condition precedent to the effectiveness of the contract.[18]

The fact that the good-health requirement is a condition precedent, and has been enforced by the courts as such, has great significance in protecting the companies against fraud. In attempting to rescind a contract on the grounds of misrepresentation or concealment,[19] the companies are frequently required to prove that the applicant deliberately misrepresented the facts of the case. In fact, most states have enacted legislation which stipulates that no misrepresentation shall void the policy unless such misrepresentation was made with actual intent to deceive, or unless it would increase the risk. To prove intent to defraud is always difficult and is frequently impossible. The difficulty is avoided with the good-health clause, since intent is not involved. The clause is concerned with the existence of a condition and not with what may or may not have been known to the applicant. If the company can prove to the satisfaction of a court that the applicant was not, in fact, in good health at the date of delivery of the policy, it can avoid liability under the contract. In practice, however, companies generally raise the issue only when they suspect that the applicant did not act in good faith, or when there has been a material deterioration in the applicant's health in the interval between the date of the medical examination and the date of delivery of the policy.

As might be expected, the courts have frequently been called upon to define the meaning of the terms "good health" and "sound health." A Georgia court[20] has ruled that "good health," as used in the context of the clause under discussion, is a relative term, meaning not absolute freedom from physical infirmity but only such a condition of body and mind that one may discharge the ordinary duties of life without serious strain upon the vital powers. A Texas court[21] has stated that "good health" does not mean perfect health, but a state of health

---

[18] Under the laws of some states, including Pennsylvania, if the applicant underwent a medical examination, the good-health requirement can be invoked only with respect to changes in the applicant's health occurring after the medical examination.

[19] Such action must be taken during the period of contestability. See pp. 119, 120.

[20] *National Life and Accident Insurance Co.* v. *Bonner,* 58 Ga. App. 876, 200 S.E. 319 (1938).

[21] *Texas Independence Life Insurance Co.* v. *Pickens,* 153 S.W. (2d) 884 (Tex. Civ. App., 1941).

free from any disease or ailment that seriously affects the general soundness of the system. A Nebraska court[22] distinguished between a mere temporary indisposition, which does not tend to weaken or undermine the constitution, and an ailment which must be regarded as serious. One of the most comprehensive definitions was supplied by a Kansas court:

> [Good health] is not apparent good health, nor yet a belief of the applicant that he is in good health, but it is that he is in actual good health. Of course, slight troubles or temporary indisposition which will not usually result in serious consequences, and which do not seriously impair or weaken his constitution, do not establish the absence of good health, but, if the illness is of a serious nature, such as to weaken and impair the constitution and shorten life, the applicant cannot be held to be in good health.[23]

There has been a tendency on the part of some courts to narrow the application of the clause to those cases where a change in the applicant's health occurs between the time of the medical examination and delivery of the policy to the applicant. This line of decisions is exemplified by a fairly recent Pennsylvania case,[24] in which the court stated that the good-health clause has no application to a disease the applicant may have had at the time of the medical examination, unless fraud or misrepresentation can be proved, since presumably his physical condition was satisfactory to the company; otherwise, the policy would not have been issued. "The legal scope of that provision is restricted to mean only that the applicant did not contract any new disease impairing his health, nor suffer any material change in his physical condition between the time of such examination and the date of the policy. . . ."[25]

This interpretation of the clause is certainly at variance with the common understanding of the term "good health" and with the legal definition cited earlier, but it is consistent with the apparent purpose of the clause. As a matter of fact, the companies have usually invoked the clause as a defense against a claim only where there has been a change in the applicant's health, or where there has been fraud or misrepresentation in the application.

---

[22] *Gugelman* v. *Kansas City Life Insurance Co.,* 137 Neb. 411, 289 N.W. 842 (1940).

[23] *Klein* v. *Farmers and Bankers Life Insurance Co.,* 132 Kan. 748, 297 Pac. 730 (1931).

[24] *Davidson et al.* v. *John Hancock Mutual Life Insurance Co.,* 159 Pa. Super. 532, 49 A. (2d) 185 (1946).

[25] *Ibid.,* 535 and 49 A. (2d) 186.

The burden of proving that the applicant was not in good health at the time of delivery of the policy is usually on the company. A minority of the courts have held that the insured or his beneficiary must prove compliance with the clause.

4. *Medical Treatment after Submission of Application.* Some policies issued today contain a clause which provides that the policy shall not take effect if the applicant has received medical or hospital treatment between the time that the application was signed and the date of delivery of the policy.[26] Like the good-health clause, this clause is designed to deal with a change in the physical condition of the applicant during the time the application is being processed. It is intended to be a condition precedent, and the courts generally treat it as such. In other words, if during the contestable period, the company can prove that the applicant received medical or hospital treatment between the date of the application and delivery of the policy, and failed to disclose the fact to the company, the latter can avoid liability under the contract. If the fact of medical treatment is disclosed at the time the policy is delivered, the company, after consideration of the ailment, may conclude that the applicant's insurability is not impaired and waive the clause. The courts are very zealous in seeking a waiver of the clause in the conduct of the company or its agents.

5. *Justification of Conditions Precedent.* When the premium is not paid with the application, all conditions precedent must be fulfilled before the contract becomes effective. In general, this means that the policy must be delivered by the agent while the applicant is alive and in good health, and the full amount of the first premium must be paid in cash or by a valid check at the moment of delivery. Delivery of the policy and payment of the first premium are supposed to be simultaneous transactions.

Some may feel that this procedure is unduly legalistic and should be replaced by a system under which the company would approve retroactively all applications from persons who were insurable at the time of application, paying the face of the policy to the beneficiaries of those who die before the policy can be delivered and placing into full effect the policies requested by those whose health deteriorates in the interim. The impracticality of this scheme is apparent when it

---

[26] Industrial life insurance policies usually contain a provision which permits the company to void the contract (within the contestable period) if within two years prior to application for the policy, the insured received hospital or medical treatment which he failed to disclose or to prove immaterial to the risk.

is realized that in issuing a policy which has not been paid for, the company is making an offer to the applicant which the latter is free to reject without any liability on his part. In other words, the applicant can refuse to take a policy which he requested, even after the company has incurred considerable expense in having him examined by a physician, securing an inspection report, and processing the application through various channels. The company would be exposed to serious antiselection if it should honor all insurance applications from persons who die or suffer an impairment of health before the policy can be delivered, and yet not be able to force those applicants who are still alive and in good health to accept delivery of their policies. Recognizing the advantages to both the applicant and the company of having the coverage attach at the date of application, the companies have devised a procedure to accomplish the objective. This procedure, involving the use of a so-called *conditional receipt,* is described in the following section.

Prepayment of First Premium. The applicant can avoid the legal consequences of the aforementioned conditions precedent by the simple expedient of remitting the first premium with his application for insurance. In that event, the companies generally acknowledge receipt of the premium with a document called a *conditional* or *binding receipt,* which binds the coverage without reference to delivery of the policy.

There are several forms of conditional receipt in general use today; but perhaps the most typical one makes the coverage effective at the time of the application, provided the applicant is found to be insurable in accordance with the general underwriting rules of the company. Some receipts make the coverage effective on the date of the application or the medical examination, whichever is later.

The coverage under such a clause is not automatic. The applicant is considered to have made an offer to the insurer, which, by the issuance of the binding receipt, accepts the offer, subject to a condition —the condition being that the applicant be found to be insurable. If the home office finds the applicant to have been insurable in accordance with its general underwriting rules on the date of the application or medical examination, the coverage attaches retroactively to the date cited. If the company finds that the applicant was not insurable at the time he submitted the application, the coverage never attaches under the policy applied for, and the premium is refunded. For the coverage to be binding as of the date of application, the risk must be acceptable to the company under its underwriting rules on the plan and for the amount applied for, and at the premium rate envisioned in the application. If the risk is acceptable, but only on a plan or at a premium rate different from that contemplated in the application, the company is construed to have made a counteroffer which must be accepted by the applicant before the coverage can become effective. A few companies have adopted a form of receipt which provides retroactive coverage under the counterproposal if the applicant, within a specified period, accepts the counteroffer and pays any additional premium that might be involved. If the applicant should die before he has had a reasonable opportunity to accept the counteroffer, he is deemed to have accepted it, and the company is obligated to pay the amount of insurance that would have been purchased on the altered terms by the premium actually paid.

If the applicant is found to have been insurable at the date of application, the coverage attaches retroactively even though, in the meantime, the applicant may have died or suffered a serious impairment of his health. Companies are frequently called upon to consider the application of a person known to have died since applying for insurance, and they are careful not to permit that circumstance to influence their underwriting decision. The same code of ethics is followed in reviewing the applications of persons who have suffered heart attacks or other physical impairments. If the applicant is to receive the fullest benefit of the conditional receipt, it is absolutely essential that the company apply general underwriting standards rather than standards tailored to fit the individual case.

In that connection, the older forms of conditional receipt, which are still used by some companies, made the coverage effective from the date of application, provided the company *approved the application.* The approval was not made contingent on the applicant's meeting the general requirements for insurability; and presumably, the company could apply arbitrary standards in deciding whether to approve the application. Moreover, the company was not on the risk if the applicant died before his application was acted upon. The reaction of one federal court to this aspect of the receipt form under discussion is revealed in the following excerpt from its decision: "[The] ordinary applicant who has paid his first premium and has successfully passed his physical examination, would not by the remotest chance understand the clause as leaving him uncovered until the insurer at its leisure approved the risk; he would assume that he was getting immediate coverage for his money."[27] One insurance authority[28] has expressed the view that companies using this type of binding receipt today would, as a rule, honor the claim when death occurs before the application has been acted upon if the facts of the case indicate that the application would normally have been accepted under the company's rules and that no misrepresentation or fraud was involved.

A few companies use a form of conditional receipt that places the company unconditionally on the risk from the date of application, usually for a limited period of time, such as sixty days, the insurance remaining in full effect unless and until the application is declined. Under this form, the applicant enjoys coverage for a brief period even when he is definitely an uninsurable risk.

The conventional binding receipt arrangement offers real benefits to both the insured and the insurer, and is widely used. It protects the applicant against loss of insurability during the period his application is being processed, and it protects the company against a declination of the policy by the applicant after it has been issued—at considerable expense. The arrangement is feasible, since all applicants using the plan pay their premiums in advance, and the company is not exposed to adverse selection. Moreover, the arrangement does not involve any relaxation of underwriting standards. Unfortunately, only a relatively small percentage of applicants take advantage of the opportunity of obtaining immediate coverage.

Advance Payment of First Premium without Conditional Receipt. The first premium may be remitted with the application without a conditional receipt being issued to the applicant. This situation could arise out of the practice of issuing conditional receipts only when the applicant specifically requests immediate coverage or through inadvertence, as where an inexperienced agent failed to issue the receipt. Under such circumstances, the coverage does not attach until the application has been approved and the policy has been "delivered."[29] The applicant is considered to have made an offer which he can with-

---

[27] *Gaunt* v. *John Hancock Mutual Life Insurance Co.,* 160 F. (2d) 599 (1947); certiorari denied, 331 U.S. 849 (1947).

[28] J. B. Maclean, *Life Insurance* (7th ed.; New York: McGraw-Hill Book Co., Inc., 1951), p. 522.

[29] A few courts have held to the contrary. Moreover, California has a statute which binds the insurer as of the moment of premium payment if the risk meets the underwriting requirements of the company.

draw at any time before acceptance by the company. Acceptance is manifested by "delivery" of the policy.

In this case, as with policies whose premiums are not paid in advance, delivery can take the form of an actual physical transfer of the policy from the agent to the applicant, or transmission through the mails in such manner as to constitute constructive delivery. However, if the application requires that the policy be delivered to the applicant while the latter is in good health, mailing of the policy to the agent for delivery to the applicant is not likely to be regarded as constructive delivery, since a condition has been imposed on its release. Direct mailing of the policy to the applicant would be regarded as a waiver of the delivery requirement, but would be treated as a waiver of the good-health requirement only if the insurer had knowledge of a breach of the condition. The contract would become effective the instant the policy is placed in the mails, even though the insured never receives it.

Delay in Consideration of the Application

A life insurance company owes a moral duty and—in a minority of the states—a legal duty to the insuring public to consider all applications within a reasonable period and to render prompt decisions on the insurability of those seeking insurance. Two questions may arise in case of an unreasonable delay on the part of a company in determining the insurability of an applicant: (1) Does the unreasonable delay constitute an acceptance of the applicant's offer? (2) Is the insurer liable for the damages caused by its delay in case the applicant dies before the application is either accepted or rejected?

It seems clear that no presumption of acceptance should be allowed when the application is not accompanied by the first premium. In that event, no offer has been made to the company, and the silence of the latter could hardly be construed as acceptance of a nonexistent offer. A different situation obtains, however, when the applicant remits the first premium with his application and thus makes a valid offer to the company.

As a general rule, silence is not construed as acceptance of an offer. To the contrary, after a reasonable time, the offeror can assume that the offer has been rejected and he is free to deal with another party. If this were not the rule, people with goods to sell could flood the country with offers which the recipients would be obliged to reject if they were not to become obligated to buy the goods. The writing of rejections could become an intolerable burden. A majority of courts have applied this general rule to the insurer's silence and have held that no matter how long the company delays, its silence will not bind it to a contract of insurance.[30]

A few courts have made a distinction between *unsolicited* offers, the usual kind, and those which are made in response to the activities of agents who are paid to solicit offers, as is the case in life insurance. These courts have held that the insurer's unreasonable delay in rejecting an application constitutes an acceptance which completes the contract.[31]

While in most states, delay in consideration of an application does not make an insurer liable under *contract,* some courts have recognized a liability of the company in *tort*—i.e., a civil liability arising other than from a contract.[32] These courts hold that since the company is operating under a franchise from the state, it is under duty to act promptly and with due care upon all applications received by it. They argue that the state issues a charter or license in order that the public may have access to an important form of protection which, in the public interest, should be made available to all who can qualify for it. The company solicits the application and, having obtained it along with the applicant's consideration, is bound to furnish the insurance which the state has authorized or to decline to do so within a reasonable time. "Otherwise the applicant is unduly delayed in obtaining insurance he desires and for which the law has afforded the opportunity, and which the insurer impliedly has promised if conditions are satisfactory."[33] Failure to live up to this obligation makes the insurer liable to the applicant for damages. If an applicant who was insurable at the time of application dies before the company—in disregard of its duty to act promptly—has approved the risk, many courts would hold that the applicant's estate could recover the amount of insurance applied for. It would seem that if the insurer is adjudged guilty of a tort, the beneficiary would be the logical person to receive damages; but with a few

[30] *Steinle* v. *New York Life Insurance Co.,* 81 Fed. 489 (1897).

[31] *American Life Insurance Co.* v. *Hutchinson,* 109 F. (2d) 424 (1940); *Columbia Law Review,* Vol. XL (1940), p. 1072.

[32] See Edwin W. Patterson, *Essentials of Insurance Law* (2d ed.; New York: McGraw-Hill Book Co., Inc., 1957), p. 78, n. 28, for case citations and a list of the states in which such doctrine has been approved and rejected. Pennsylvania courts have rejected the doctrine.

[33] *Duffie* v. *Bankers Life Assn.,* 160 Iowa 19, 139 N.W. 1087 (1913).

exceptions, the courts hold that she cannot recover, since she is not a party at interest until the coverage becomes effective.

The question of tort liability is not likely to arise under a conditional receipt situation, since the forms in general use provide for retroactive coverage.

Operative Date of Policy

The foregoing discussion was concerned with the determination of the date on which coverage under a life insurance contract becomes effective. Such date is usually referred to as the *effective date* of the policy. It may or may not be the same date as that on the face of the policy, which is significant for other reasons. The latter governs the status of various policy provisions after the contract has gone into effect and is sometimes referred to as the *operative date* of the policy.

The policy may bear the date on which it was issued, the date on which the coverage becomes effective, or the date on which it was applied for. The most common practice is to date the policy as of the date of issue, unless there is a conditional receipt, in which event the policy will bear the date of the application or the medical examination, whichever is later. Occasionally, the policy will bear a date earlier than the date of application. This is known as *antedating* the policy and is done only at the request of or with the consent of the applicant, usually for the purpose of producing a lower insurance age and hence a lower premium.[34] The practice is not generally regarded to be in conflict with anti-rebating laws, but several states prohibit it when an age change is involved. Other states have attempted to control the practice by forbidding the issue of a policy which bears a date more than six months earlier than the date of the application, a limitation which many—if not most—companies have voluntarily adopted.

The practice of antedating policies—which, from a legal standpoint, refers to the use of any date earlier than the effective date of the policy—raises three important questions: (1) When does the next premium fall due? (2) From what date does extended term insurance run? (3) From what date do the incontestable and suicide clauses begin to run? When the antedating was done at the request of

---

[34] A person's insurance age for ordinary insurance is his age at the nearest birthday. For insurance purposes, he becomes one year older six months and one day after his last birthday. It is possible to obtain a lower insurance age by dating a policy back only one day, but most cases involve a much longer period.

the applicant and resulted in a lower contract age for the applicant, the overwhelming majority of both state and federal courts hold that the due date of the next premium is established by the date of the policy. Even when the antedating does not benefit the applicant—i.e., no age change is involved—the majority of the courts support the view that the policy date establishes the due date, on the grounds that certainty is preferable to uncertainty. In some jurisdictions, however, it is held that the payment of an "annual" premium entitles the insured to a full year of protection and that the due date of the next premium is determined by reference to the effective date of coverage. For this reason, many companies do not refer to the first premium as an "annual" or "quarterly" premium but indicate, rather, the exact period covered by the first premium and the due date of the second premium.

Closely related to the problem of determining the due date of the second and subsequent premiums is the fixing of the period of extended term insurance in the event that there is a default in premium payments. Clearly, it would bc to thc advantage of the insured and his beneficiaries to have the date of default from which the period of extended term insurance runs calculated by reference to the effective date of the contract, rather than from an earlier date of issue. The timing of the insured's death could be such that the choice of beginning date for the term insurance could make the difference between payment of the face of the policy and total avoidance of liability by the company. It is generally held, however, that the anniversary date fixed for premium payment purposes also controls the inception date for extended term insurance.

With respect to the incontestable and suicide clauses, the general view is that the date of issue establishes the point of departure. A few courts, arguing that the suicide clause is completely independent of the provisions dealing with premium payment, hold that the effective date of the policy controls. Some policies specify a certain date as being the "date of issue" for the purpose of these clauses, which date is usually recognized by the courts.

In summary, then, it may be said that antedating, if done without fraud or mistake and not in violation of a state statute, is given effect whether it benefits the insured or the insurer.

CHAPTER III

Formation of a Life Insurance Contract (Continued)

CONSIDERATION

Nature

The life insurance contract, like other contracts, must be supported by a valid consideration. A consideration is always given in exchange for a promise and, in the case of a bilateral contract, is itself a promise. The life insurance contract, however, is a unilateral contract, since only the company makes an enforceable promise. The consideration for the insurer's promise is the first premium or, if premiums are to be paid more frequently than annually, the first installment of the first premium. The policies of some companies state that the promise of the company is given in consideration of the *application* and the first premium. This is apparently intended to give greater legal effect to the application, on which the company places such great reliance.

Premiums subsequent to the first are not part of the legal consideration, since otherwise the contract could not come into existence until they are all paid. Rather, they are conditions precedent to the continuance of the contract. The promise of the insurer is conditioned on the continued payment of periodic premiums. If the insured defaults in the payment of a subsequent premium, the company is released from its original promise to pay the face of the policy but remains obligated to honor various subsidiary promises contained in the surrender provisions and the reinstatement clause.

Form

The insurance company is entitled to receive the first premium, or the first installment thereof, in cash; it may, however, agree to accept any valuable property. The premium may be paid in cash, by check, by promissory note, or—in the absence of a prohibitive statute—by services, such as printing work or advertising. Some states forbid an insurance company to accept payment of any premium in services, presumably because the practice lends itself too readily to rebating. By placing an excessive value on the services rendered, a company or its agent could, in effect, refund a portion of the contractual premium charge.

Checks are readily accepted by insurance companies, but they are generally treated as conditional payments. That is, crediting of the premium is usually conditioned upon the honoring of the instrument by the bank upon which it is drawn. Hence, if the check is not honored when presented, the company holds that the premium has not been paid, and its promise is no longer operative. This is true even though the check was tendered to the insurer in good faith by the insured. However, where the insured had sufficient funds in the bank to cover the check and the bank's failure to honor the check was based on a technical defect in the instrument, such as an improper signature or an incorrect date, or a clerical error on the part of the bank, the companies are inclined to recognize a contractual obligation, provided the premium is subsequently paid in cash or by valid check by the insured or his beneficiary.

A company or its properly authorized agent may agree that the check constitutes an absolute payment of the premium. That is, the company accepts the liability of the parties to the instrument in satisfaction of the premium. This occurs when the agent gives the applicant an unconditional premium receipt in exchange for his check. In this case, if the check is not paid when presented, the company may enforce its rights on the instrument but cannot validly claim that the premium has not been paid.

A company may authorize some or all of its agents to accept a promissory note of the insured in payment of the first premium (and subsequent premiums, for that matter). If the note is honored at maturity, no complications are involved; but a real question arises as to the status of the policy in the event that the note is not paid when due. In anticipation of such an eventuality, a company may include on the note, premium receipt, or policy, or all three, a stipulation to the effect that if the note is not paid at maturity, the policy shall be discontinued. If such a provision is included in all three instruments, it will be enforced according to its terms. Hence, as soon as the maturity date of the note arrives and the note remains unpaid, the company is entitled to repudiate the contract. If the aforementioned stipulation is included in the note or in the premium receipt, *but not in the policy,* there is a conflict of opinion as to the rights of the company. Some courts hold that the provision is nugatory, on the grounds that it violates the statute, found in most states, which provides that the policy and the application shall constitute the entire contract between the parties. Other courts uphold the provision, on the grounds that the statute means simply that the policy shall contain the entire contract as of the time it was issued. The courts which entertain this view feel that the statute does not prevent the execution of subsequent agreements. They point out that if the policy is construed to contain all possible agreements relating to the contract, it would be contrary to the statute for the company to agree to an extension of time for the payment of a premium, whereas such agreements are generally recognized. The latter view would seem to be in accord with the evident intention of the parties.

If the forfeiture provision is contained in the policy but not in the note or the premium receipt, there is also a conflict of opinion. In those states in which the entire-contract statute is strictly followed, the provision contained in the policy will be enforced according to its terms. In other states, the decision turns on the interpretation of the note and the receipt. If the note and the receipt evidence an intention on the part of the insurer to accept the note as an unconditional payment, this subsequent agreement will override the provision contained in the policy. On the other hand, if there is no indication of an intention to accept the note as an unconditional payment, the provision in the policy will prevail.

If there is no forfeiture provision in the policy, or the note, or the premium receipt, the note is considered to be an absolute payment of the premium, and the insurance company is limited to its rights on the note in the event that it is not paid at maturity. This is the usual case.

It should be observed that if the insurer or its authorized agent extends credit to the insured, the contract will be bilateral rather than unilateral. In this case, the consideration for the insurer's promise is the insured's promise to pay the amount of the first premium.

An agent who is not authorized to extend credit on behalf of the company may pay the premium for the applicant. In doing so, he is acting as the applicant's agent, and failure of the applicant to reimburse the agent will not invalidate the policy.

LEGALITY OF PURPOSE

General Considerations

To be enforceable, a contract must be entered into for a legal purpose. All contracts are assumed to have a legal purpose, except those that contemplate a course of action that would contravene a statute or some other rule of law. It is not sufficient, however, that the agreement refrain from an act specifically prohibited by law; it must not tend to encourage illegality, immorality, or other conduct contrary to public policy.

Life insurance clearly does not require either party to perform an illegal act and, in that respect, qualifies as a perfectly valid contract. As a matter of fact, it is universally recognized as having a purpose highly beneficial to society and worthy of favorable legislative treatment. On the other hand, it has been recognized that without adequate safeguards, life insurance could lend itself to behavior that would be socially harmful and contrary to public policy. Specifically, it could provide the motivation for wagering, murder, and suicide.

Inducement to Wagering. With respect to the first of these dangers, life insurance, being aleatory in nature, offers the opportunity of a return out of all proportion to the investment in the contract. This characteristic of the transaction early attracted elements of the populace who were hopeful of enriching themselves through the operation of the laws of chance. In eighteenth-century England, life insurance became the means of satisfying a mania for gambling, which was discouraged but not prohibited. Speculative life insurance was likely to be taken out on anyone who was in the public eye. Persons accused of crimes punishable by death and those in disfavor with the royal court were favorite subjects for life insurance contracts. Prominent persons became the object of speculative insurance as soon as press notices revealed them to be seriously ill, and the premium for new policies on such persons fluctuated from day to day in accordance with the reports or rumors on their condition. Newspapers of the day even carried premium quotations on the lives of persons known to be the object of speculative insurance, with the consequences described by a contemporary writer. "This inhuman sport affected the minds of men depressed by long sickness; for when such persons casting an eye over a newspaper for amusement, saw their lives had been insured in the Alley at 90 p.c., they despaired of all hopes, and thus their desolution [*sic*] was hastened."[1] The situation became so intolerable that in 1774, Parliament enacted a law which provided that a person contracting for insurance had to have an insurable interest in the life of the person to be insured and, moreover, upon the death of the insured, could not recover a sum in excess of the monetary interest.[2]

In this country, an insurable interest has always been required; but with the exceptions noted later, no attempt has been made to apply the indemnity concept. In most states, the requirement of insurable interest is not based upon statute, but results from a judicial application of the public policy against the enforcement of wagering contracts. The states of New York, Pennsylvania, and California, among others, have statutes requiring an insurable interest.

Murder of Insured by Beneficiary. The insurable interest requirement originated as a means of controlling wagering in human lives and still finds its greatest significance in that function, but it was also intended to reduce the threat of murder created by the insuring of one person's life for the benefit of another. The thought was that if the class of persons who can legally insure the life of another is restricted to those who are closely related to him by blood, or possess such a financial relationship with him that they stand to gain more by his continued life than by his death, the temptation to murder the insured would be greatly curtailed. A further safeguard is sometimes provided in the form of a requirement that a person whose life is to be insured by another must give his consent to the transaction. Presumably, he will not permit his life to be insured in favor of a person whose integrity is questionable or whose motives he distrusts. The same reasoning underlies the rule, discussed later, that the beneficiary of a policy taken out by the insured himself need not have an insurable interest in the insured. The law presumes that the insured, whose life is at stake, is capable of choosing beneficiaries who will not be moti-

---

[1] David Scott, *Every Man His Own Broker* (1761), quoted in C. Walford, *Insurance Cyclopaedia* (London: Charles and Edwin Layton, 1876), Vol. IV, p. 187.

[2] Stat. 14 Geo. III, Chap. 48 (1774).

vated to commit murder to hasten the enjoyment of the insurance proceeds.

The foregoing deterrents are supplemented not only by criminal penalties for murder but by statutes and judicial rulings which prohibit the payment of insurance proceeds to a beneficiary who murders the insured. This restriction is based on a general rule of law that a wrongdoer is not permitted to profit by his wrongdoing. The insurance company is not relieved of its obligation to pay, the proceeds going to contingent beneficiaries or the heirs of the insured.

Suicide. A final area in which there exists the possibility of a conflict between life insurance and the public interest is the treatment of the suicide hazard. Suicide is contrary to many religious laws, and attempted suicide is ordinarily a penal offense. Thus, suicide is contrary to public policy. Any contract that would encourage or act as an inducement to suicide would, by the same token, be contrary to public policy. Some of the early court decisions in this country indicated that death by suicide should not be covered by a life insurance policy. In a leading case, the United States Supreme Court expressed the view that "death intentionally caused by the act of the insured when in sound mind—the policy being silent as to suicide—is not to be deemed to have been within the contemplation of the parties. . . . [A] different view would attribute to them a purpose to make a contract that could not be enforced without injury to the public. A contract, the tendency of which is to endanger the public interests or injuriously affect the public good, or which is subversive of sound morality, ought never to receive the sanction of a court of justice or be made the foundation of its judgment."[3]

This view, which has since been rejected by the American courts but is still the law in England, was not universally entertained; and in order to protect themselves against persons who might apply for insurance with the deliberate intent of committing suicide, the companies adopted the precaution of inserting in their policies a clause which limited their liability to a return of premiums in the event that the insured should commit suicide within a specified period—usually, one or two years—after the date of issue. It was felt that such a clause would properly protect the interests of the companies and yet, after a preliminary period during which any abnormal impulse toward self-destruction should have passed away or else been carried out, would

---

[3] *Ritter* v. *Mutual Life Insurance Co.,* 169 U.S. 139 (1898).

provide coverage against a hazard of life to which all are subject. Such a clause was adjudged by the United States Supreme Court to conserve the public interest, and a number of states have gone so far as to impose statutory restrictions on the right of the companies to avoid liability because of suicide. The most common type of restriction is to limit the period during which a company can avoid coverage of the hazard. The Missouri statute precludes the defense of suicide at any time.[4] This statute has been upheld by the United States Supreme Court as not being in conflict with the state constitution or the federal Constitution, but the court intimated that the statute was inconsistent with public policy and sound morality.[5] New York prohibits exclusion of suicide while the insured is insane.

For all practical purposes, the requirement of a legal object or purpose is concerned with the issue of insurable interest, and the remainder of this section will be devoted to that subject.

Insurable Interest

Insurable interest is difficult to define precisely. In its broadest sense, it is a "relation between the insured and the event insured against such that the occurrence of the event will cause substantial loss or harm of some kind to the insured."[6] As applied to life insurance, an insurable interest may be defined as such a relationship between the person applying for insurance and the person whose life is to be insured that there is a reasonable expectation of benefit or advantage to the applicant from continuation of the life of the insured or an expectation of loss or detriment from the cessation of that life. It should be noted that this definition does not require a *pecuniary* interest; it is broad enough to recognize a sentimental interest or one based on love and affection. Legal opinion in this country is divided as to whether a sentimental interest can satisfy the insurable interest requirement; but since a respectable group of courts do support the view that a sentimental interest is sufficient, the definition was made

[4] The Missouri statute reads as follows: "In all suits upon policies of insurance on life, hereafter issued by any company doing business in this state, it shall be no defense that the insured committed suicide, unless it be shown to the satisfaction of the court or jury trying the case, that the insured contemplated suicide at the time he made his application for the policy, and any stipulation in the policy to the contrary shall be void." The difficulty of proving intent is so great that the companies do not even attempt it.

[5] *Whitfield* v. *Aetna Life Insurance Co.*, 27 Sup. Ct. 578, 205 U.S. 489 (1907).

[6] Edwin W. Patterson, *Essentials, of Insurance Law* (2d ed.; New York: McGraw-Hill Book Co., Inc., 1957), p. 154.

broad enough to encompass both points of view. It should be further noted that the pecuniary interest need not be capable of exact measurement. Nor need it be based on a legal right. It is sufficient that there be a *reasonable expectation* of some financial gain or advantage.

Various relationships can give rise to an insurable interest. Before they are discussed, however, it seems preferable to indicate when the interest must be present.

Incidence of Insurable Interest. In property and casualty insurance, an insurable interest need not be present at the inception of the contract, but it must exist at the time of loss if there is to be any recovery under the contract. The requirements are just reversed in the case of life insurance. In life insurance, an insurable interest must exist at the inception of the contract but need not be present at the time of the insured's death. This striking difference in the application of the requirement results from the fact that property insurance is based on the principle of indemnity, while life insurance is not. To use property insurance terminology, a life insurance contract is a *valued* policy; it is a contract to pay a stated sum upon the occurrence of the event insured against. Since the beneficiary has a legal claim to a fixed sum of money upon the insured's death, he need not prove that he sustained loss by reason of the death.

One may concede that the insurable interest of one person in another person's life should not be the *measure* of recovery and still argue that if the former's interest has become *wholly* extinguished, his right to the face amount of the policy should likewise be extinguished. To permit a person whose interest in the life of the insured has been completely terminated to collect the proceeds upon the insured's death gives the appearance of speculation and offends the sense of justice of many persons. However, the rule was adopted by the courts (English) at a time when surrender values were not available and termination of a policy before maturity meant the forfeiture of all accumulated values. For the courts to force a policyholder to lapse his policy and forfeit the entire investment element because of the extinguishment of an interest which was perfectly valid at the time the policy was issued would have been harsh.[7] The courts were faced

[7] As a matter of strict accuracy, the English courts at first held that a policy did become unenforceable as soon as the insurable interest was extinguished (*Godsall* v. *Bolders*, 9 East 72 [1807]). The insurers did not take advantage of the ruling, however, and continued to pay the full amount of the policy even when the insurable interest was lacking at the date of death. When the matter came up again, almost a half

with the alternative of permitting the owner of the policy to collect the full face of the policy or nothing at all. It is probable that if the matter were being adjudicated today, without regard to precedent, the courts would hold that extinguishment of insurable interest terminates a policy and the policy owner would be permitted to recover the cash value as of the date of extinguishment, together with premiums paid thereafter in mistaken reliance on the contract.

As the matter now stands, an incipient interest is all that is necessary to sustain the validity of a life insurance contract. Thus, if a creditor procures insurance upon the life of his debtor and the debt is subsequently extinguished, the creditor may keep the policy in force and collect the full amount of the policy when the insured dies.[8] A policy procured by a partnership on the life of a partner is unaffected by the dissolution of the partnership and the transfer of the policy to a former member of the firm who no longer has an insurable interest.[9] A corporation that procures a policy upon the life of a valuable manager may collect at his death the full amount of insurance, despite the fact that the manager had meanwhile been discharged.[10] A divorce does not deprive a wife-beneficiary of the right to the proceeds of her husband's life insurance, even though she no longer has an insurable interest in his life.[11]

The foregoing rules are not followed in Texas. The Texas courts have traditionally required a countinuing interest. That is, a person who takes out insurance on the life of another person must have an insurable interest in the insured at the maturity of the contract in order to receive the proceeds. The recent statute[12] which eliminated the requirement of an insurable interest for the beneficiary or assignee of a policy procured by the insured left undisturbed the mandate of a continuing interest for the person who procures insurance on another's life.

The discussion in this section has made no reference to policies pro-

---

century later, the court yielded to the custom of the insurers and permitted full recovery under the policy (*Dalby* v. *India & London Life Assurance Co.,* 15 C.B. 365 [1854]). The latter case has served as a precedent for American courts.

[8] *Ferguson* v. *Massachusetts Mutual Life Insurance Co.,* 32 Hun (N.Y.) 306 (1884); affirmed, 102 N.Y. 647 (1886). Under such circumstances, however, the debtor usually takes over the policy and continues premium payments upon repayment of the debt.

[9] *Gerstel* v. *Avens,* 143 Fla. 20 (1940).

[10] *Wurzburg* v. *New York Life Insurance Co.,* 140 Tenn. 59 (1918).

[11] *Connecticut Mutual Life Insurance Co.* v. *Schaefer,* 94 U.S. 457 (1876).

[12] Texas Acts, 1953, 53d Legislature, Chap. 113, p. 400.

cured by the person whose life is to be insured, since in such cases, there is no question of a continuing interest. If the view is accepted that a person has an insurable interest in his own life, then certainly the interest continues throughout life.

Relationships Evidencing Insurable Interest. In considering the relationships which give rise to an insurable interest, it is helpful to distinguish between the cases in which the applicant is applying for insurance on his own life and those where he is seeking insurance on the life of another.

1. *Policy Procured by the Insured.* The question of insurable interest is not involved when a person, on his own initiative, applies for a policy on his own life. It is commonly said that a person has an unlimited insurable interest in his own life; but the expression would appear to be inaccurate, since a person does not suffer a financial loss by his own death or, at least, does not survive to claim indemnity for a loss. Hence, it seems preferable to state that the issue of insurable interest is immaterial when a person applies for insurance on his own life. Regardless of how the status of the insured is characterized, the law considers the insurable interest requirement to have been met—for any amount of insurance.

For underwriting purposes, the companies do not accept the view that the applicant has an unlimited insurable interest or that the question is immaterial. The financial circumstances of an applicant are carefully investigated, and the company limits the amount of insurance to that which can be justified by the applicant's financial status and earning capacity.

The law is well settled that when a person procures a policy on his own life, it is not necessary that the beneficiary have an insurable interest in the insured's life, either at the inception of the contract or at the time of the insured's death. Prior to the enactment of the 1953 statute previously referred to, Texas required that the beneficiary have an insurable interest at all times. The law is now unanimous on that point (except in England), the rationale being that the insured should be permitted to dispose of his human life value with the same freedom that he can exercise in disposing of his other property at death.[13] The temptation to murder is considered minimized by the judgment of the insured in choosing the objects of his bounty.

[13] As a matter of fact, the insured enjoys much greater latitude in disposing of his human life value, since insurance proceeds are not subject to a wife's dower rights (or statutory equivalent), restrictions on bequests to charitable organizations, or claims of creditors (if properly set up).

The courts take a different view of the situation when the policy is applied for at the instigation of the beneficiary. Such a transaction may arise out of a legitimate business relationship and have a useful purpose, or it may serve as a cloak for a wagering contract. When the application does not stem from a business or personal situation which would seem to justify the designation of the particular beneficiary as payee and the beneficiary agrees in advance to pay all premiums under the policy, the courts are inclined to regard the transaction as speculative in nature. For example, where a woman was induced to make application for insurance on her life in favor of the mortgagee of her husband's land,[14] her employer,[15] and her sister-in-law,[16] the beneficiary in each case paying all premiums, the contract was declared to be a wager. Likewise, a policy procured at the instigation of a college upon the life of a wealthy man who was a prospective donor to its endowment fund was declared invalid because the college had no insurable interest in his life.[17] The payment of premiums by the beneficiary is not conclusive proof of wagering, but it gives rise to a strong inference. Since the question of insurable interest is of importance only at the inception of the policy, it is immaterial that later, owing to a change of circumstances, the beneficiary assumes responsibility for premium payments in order to keep the policy in force.

In practice, a company makes no distinction between applications submitted at the initiative of the prospective insured and those submitted at the instigation of the prospective beneficiary. In all cases, it requires that the original beneficiary have an insurable interest of some sort as a precaution against wagering, homicide, or other untoward moral hazard. If the prospective beneficiary does not appear to have a legitimate insurable interest, the company will request an explanation of the relationship; and if the explanation is unsatisfactory, it will almost certainly reject the application. Once the policy is issued, however, the company has no right to withhold approval of a change of beneficiary on the grounds that the proposed beneficiary lacks an insurable interest—or on any other grounds, for that matter, except failure to comply with the prescribed procedure for effecting such a change. Of course, if the circumstances surrounding the request for change of beneficiary are indicative of an attempt to evade the under-

---

[14] *Hinton* v. *Mutual Reserve Fund Life Assn.* 135 N.C. 314 (1904).

[15] *Gerald* v. *Metropolitan Life Insurance Co.,* 167 Miss. 207 (1933).

[16] *Carter* v. *Continental Life Insurance Co.,* 115 F. (2d) 947 (D.C., 1940).

[17] *Trinity College* v. *Travelers Insurance Co.,* 113 N.C. 244 (1893). The college was not even permitted to recover the surrender value under the policy.

writing requirements of the company or the legal requirement of insurable interest, the company may be permitted to rescind the policy, on the grounds of fraud or on the grounds that the entire transaction was a subterfuge for the procurement of insurance by a person lacking an insurable interest in the insured.

The insured may make the policy payable to a third party by means of an assignment; and as a general rule, it is not necessary for the assignee to have an insurable interest. The position of the courts is that it is immaterial whether the insured designates the payee of the policy within the contract itself, as by a conventional beneficiary designation, or by means of a separate instrument—i.e., an assignment. Five states[18] require the assignee to have an insurable interest, at least under certain circumstances. All states require an insurable interest if the insured was induced by the assignee to take out the policy, since that would be tantamount to the assignee's applying for the insurance directly. If there is any indication at the time of application that an assignment is contemplated, the insurance company, as a matter of underwriting practice, will usually require evidence of the insurable interest of the prospective assignee.

Under the doctrine adopted by the majority of American courts, there is nothing to invalidate successive assignments of a life insurance policy once it is validly issued. None of the assignees need have an insurable interest, and the insured need not give his consent to the assignments. This rule is based on the doctrine that a life insurance policy is a form of personal property and should be freely transferable. If a life insurance contract could be sold only to persons having an insurable interest in the life of the insured, the market would be severely limited, and the owner of the policy would be handicapped in disposing of it. Nevertheless, it would probably be held contrary to public policy today for life insurance policies to be sold on the auction block to the highest bidder.

A special set of rules is applicable when a policy is made payable to a creditor of the insured, whether the designation be as beneficiary or as assignee. The creditor situations will be discussed in the next section.

Most policies are issued upon the application and at the initiative of the insured himself. Hence, the foregoing principles may be regarded as those governing the typical situation. The rules applica-

---

[18] Alabama, Kansas, Kentucky, Missouri, and Texas.

ble to the exceptional cases where the applicant and the insured are not one and the same are set forth in the following section.

2. *Policy Procured by Person Other than Insured.* Contrary to popular belief, in most jurisdictions, consent of the person to be insured is not essential to the validity of a life insurance contract taken out by a person other than the prospective insured. Those states which do require such consent[19] usually make an exception of applications submitted by a spouse on the life of the other spouse or by a parent on the life of a child too young to apply for insurance in his own right. As a practical matter, the signature of the prospective insured is needed on the application in affirmation of the accuracy of the information in the application. Hence, the companies always require the signature of the person whose life is to be insured, except when such person is a minor.

In all jurisdictions, a third-party applicant must have an insurable interest in the life of the person to be insured. This statement presupposes that the applicant will be the owner of the policy and the person to receive the proceeds upon maturity of the contract. A more accurate statement of the requirement—as it is prescribed in some states, at least—is that the *person who procures the policy and is to receive the proceeds* must have an insurable interest in the insured. The New York Insurance Law, for example, states the requirement in such terms and provides that if the proceeds should be paid to a person not having an insurable interest in the insured *at the time the contract was made,* the insured or his personal representative,[20] as the case may be, may maintain an action to recover such proceeds from the person so receiving them.

The insurable interest required under such circumstances may arise out of either a family relationship or a business relationship. If it arises out of a family relationship, it may be based on *love and affection* or on a legal or factual expectation of *financial* advantage from continuance of the life of the insured. Interests originating in business relationships are regarded as economic in nature.

a) Family Relationships. The doctrine that an emotional attachment constitutes a sufficient insurable interest, apart from financial considerations, has been expounded in various judicial opinions and

---

[19] At the present time, eleven states—including New York, Pennsylvania, Delaware, and Maryland—require the consent of the person whose life is to be insured, with certain exceptions.

[20] Executor or administrator.

incorporated into the statutes of several states, including New York and Pennsylvania. The courts which subscribe to the doctrine usually justify their action on the grounds that the natural affection engendered by close ties of blood and affinity operate more efficaciously to protect the life of the insured than would any other consideration. Such an argument tacitly assumes that the primary purpose of the insurable interest requirement is to protect the insured against the possibility of being murdered by those who would profit by his death. It will be recalled, however, that the requirement of an insurable interest was introduced to stamp out indiscriminate gambling on the lives of public men and vocational or professional wagering on the lives of persons with whom the applicant-owner had no business or family ties. This has led to the argument[21] that justification for the love-and-affection doctrine can be found in the "restricted class" concept enunciated by Oliver Wendell Holmes in the landmark insurance case, *Grigsby* v. *Russell.*[22] In his opinion, Justice Holmes recognized the aleatory nature of the life insurance transaction and asserted that the chief purpose of the insurable interest requirement is to limit the opportunities for wagering on the life of a particular individual to that relatively small group of persons having close ties of blood or affinity with the individual or possessing a substantial economic interest in his life. He pointed out that "the whole world of the unscrupulous" should not be "free to bet on what life they choose." It is apparent that the love-and-affection doctrine is quite consistent with that view. Thus, it would appear that the doctrine serves both of the major objectives of the insurable interest requirement: the minimization of wagering and the prevention of murder.

In applying the doctrine, the closeness of relationship needed to satisfy the requirement is of critical importance. The relationship of husband and wife is universally conceded to be close enough, although it is virtually always accompanied by an economic interest arising out of the wife's legal right to support from her husband and the husband's expectation of domestic services from the wife. A growing minority of courts have recognized the relationship of parent and child, brother and sister or brother and brother or sister and sister, and grandparent and grandchild as sufficient.[23] Blood relationships more remote than the foregoing, such as uncle and niece, uncle and

[21] Patterson, *op. cit.*, p. 179.

[22] 222 U.S. 149 (1911).

[23] Patterson, *op. cit.*, p. 181.

nephew, and cousin of any degree, have generally been rejected as insufficient. Aside from that of husband and wife, no tie growing out of affinity alone—such as an interest of an individual in his father-in-law, mother-in-law, brother-in-law, stepfather, or stepchild—has been recognized as a sufficient insurable interest.

The courts that do not subscribe to the belief that a sentimental value alone will satisfy the insurable interest requirement still find a valid insurable interest in close family relationships, apparently on the assumption that a legal or factual expectation of pecuniary value exists in such cases. Thus, the legal obligation of a man to support his wife gives her an insurable interest in his life, and the legal duty of a woman to render household services to her husband gives him an insurable interest in her life. The father (and in some instances, the mother) is entitled to the services of a minor child and hence has an insurable interest in the child's life. A woman has an insurable interest in the life of her financé, at least in those states where the agreement to marry is a legal obligation.

An expectation of financial advantage from the continued life of a person which is not based on a legal obligation is referred to as a *factual expectation*. A factual expectation is generally not sufficient to support a contract of indemnity, such as those found in the property and casualty insurance branches, but it has long been regarded as sufficient in life insurance. In the earliest reported American decision involving life insurance, the Supreme Judicial Court of Massachusetts upheld a policy in favor of the insured's sister, on the grounds that he had been voluntarily supporting her and probably would have continued to do so had he lived.[24] A foster child, though not legally adopted and hence without legal claim to support, has been held to have an insurable interest in the life of his foster father.[25] A woman living with a man under the honest but mistaken belief that she was lawfully married to him was held to have had an insurable interest in his life because of her expectation (possibly misplaced) that he would have continued to support her.[26] An illegitimate child is considered to have an insurable interest in the life of its putative (supposed) father, who has contributed to its support.[27]

---

[24] *Lord* v. *Dall,* 12 Mass. 118 (1815).

[25] *Carpenter* v. *United States Life Insurance Co.,* 161 Pa. St. 9 (1894).

[26] *Scott's Administrator* v. *Scott,* 77 S.W. 1122 (Ky., 1904). In this case, the putative husband was legally married to another woman.

[27] *Overton* v. *Colored Knights of Pythias,* 173 S.W. 472 (Tex. Civ. App., 1915).

It is sometimes said that a *moral* obligation gives rise to a legally adequate insurable interest. Such an interest might be found in a moral obligation to provide support or to reimburse a benefactor for support gratuitously provided. Some courts have accepted that view; but the majority reject it, on the grounds that the obligation is too vague and uncertain.

When an insurable interest is based on a family relationship, there is no legal limit to the amount of insurance that may be validated by it. This is based on the concept that a life insurance policy is not a contract of indemnity and hence does not purport to reimburse a beneficiary for a specific pecuniary loss. It would be extremely difficult, if not impossible, to place a precise valuation on an interest based on love and affection. Interests arising out of a legal entitlement to support could perhaps be valued, but those based on a factual expectation could be measured only in the roughest terms. Interests based on business relationships can usually be valued and, in general, can support only an amount of insurance that bears a reasonable relationship to the value of the interest.

b) Business Relationships. A variety of business relationships give rise to an insurable interest. One of the most common is a contractual arrangement calling for personal services of a unique or distinctive character. Innumerable examples of such arrangements can be found in the entertainment world. Thus, a theatrical producer has an insurable interest in the life of an actor who would be extremely difficult to replace in a role which he has contracted to perform over a definite period. Likewise, the producer of a motion-picture film has an insurable interest in the lives of the principal performers, an interest which comes into sharper focus as the film gets into production and the death of a "star" would disrupt operations and require the refilming of all the scenes in which the deceased appeared. Professional baseball clubs have an insurable interest in the lives of their outstanding performers.

The foregoing examples are based on contractual or legal obligations, but factual expectations may also support an insurable interest. The increasing importance of the business manager has led to the recognition that a corporation or other form of business enterprise may have an insurable interest in the life of a manager or some other official whose services and skill are vital to the prosperity of the enterprise, even though the person has not assumed a legal obligation to work for the firm for any specified period of time. The interest of a firm in its key officers and employees has been recognized by statute in many states and judicially sanctioned in most, if not all, of the other states. Insurance taken out to protect such an interest is called *key-man insurance* and is widely sold.

Another business relationship that gives rise to an insurable interest is that existing among partners in a partnership and stockholders in a close corporation. The consequences of the death of a general partner or an active stockholder in a close corporation are such that the parties involved frequently enter into agreements for the disposition of the business interest of any such individuals who might die while still active in the management of the firm. Specifically, the agreement binds the surviving members of the firm to purchase the interest of the deceased member at a price specified in the agreement, and the deceased member's estate to sell his interest. The agreements are usually financed by insurance on the lives of the individuals involved, the insurance on any particular individual being applied for by either the other members of the firm or the firm itself.[28] In such cases, the courts have recognized an insurable interest, based on the factual expectation of a loss in the event that the business should have to be liquidated, capable of supporting the insurance.

Perhaps the most common business or commercial relationship that produces an insurable interest is that created by the lending of money. Despite the fact that the obligation to repay a loan is not discharged by the death of a debtor, the obligation being enforceable against the deceased's estate, a creditor is everywhere conceded to have an insurable interest in the life of the debtor. This rule is based on recognition of the fact that the creditor may not be able to collect the sum of money due him from the debtor's estate because of insufficiency of assets. The creditor may protect his interest by taking out insurance on the life of the debtor or by requiring the debtor to designate him as payee under a policy taken out by the debtor.

If the creditor takes out insurance on the debtor's life *and pays the premiums,* he is permitted to retain the full amount of the proceeds, even though they exceed the amount of the debt, plus accumulated interest. As a matter of fact, he can retain the full amount of the proceeds, even though the debt has been completely extinguished. The only limitation imposed in most jurisdictions is that the amount of in-

[28] See Dan M. McGill, *Life Insurance* (Homewood, Ill.: Richard D. Irwin, Inc., 1959), pp. 22, 23.

surance must not be disproportionate to the amount of the debt as it existed at the time the policy was issued or as it was reasonably expected to be thereafter. The purpose of this requirement is to prevent the use of a debt as a cloak for a wagering transaction. In a leading case, a policy for $3,000 taken out on the basis of a $70 debt was held to be a wager and hence invalid.[29] Yet, policies have been upheld where the amount of insurance was several times the debt. A Maryland court upheld a policy for $6,500 on a debt of $1,000,[30] while a New York court validated a policy for $5,000 taken out to protect a debt of $2,823.[31] These liberal decisions are largely due to the notion that a creditor should be allowed to insure the debtor's life for a sum estimated to be sufficient to reimburse the creditor, at the debtor's death, for premiums paid on the policy, with interest thereon, plus the debt and accumulated interest. This formula was first applied by the Supreme Court of Pennsylvania, which estimated the premiums to be paid on the basis of the insured's life expectancy as projected in the Carlisle Tables.[32] The limitation imposed by this rule is a specious one, since the premiums that would be paid during the insured's life expectancy, plus interest, would exceed the face of the policy. By this test, a creditor could justify any amount of insurance on a debt of $1. This rule, however, is not strictly followed by the courts today; and in general, the amount of insurance must bear a reasonable relationship to the size of the debt.

If a debtor assigns an existing policy to the creditor *as security* for a loan, the creditor is permitted to retain only the amount of his interest and must pay the excess, if any, to the insured's estate. The creditor's interest is construed to comprise the unpaid portion of the loan, accumulated interest on the loan, and expenses connected with the loan, including any premiums paid on the policy. The same rule applies when the creditor is designated beneficiary, if it is clear that the arrangement was intended to serve as security for the debt. In general, the creditor's rights are the same when the debtor procures new insurance and assigns it as collateral, provided the debtor pays the premium. Most courts will permit the creditor to retain the full amount of proceeds under any arrangement which contemplates payment of premiums by the creditor.

---

[29] *Cammack* v. *Lewis,* 82 U.S. 643 (1872).

[30] *Rittler* v. *Smith,* 70 Md. 261 (1889).

[31] *Wright* v. *Mutual Benefit Life* Assn., 118 N.Y. 237 (1890).

[32] *Grant's Administrators* v. *Kline,* 115 Pa. 618 (1887).

Occasionally, a policy is assigned to the creditor *in satisfaction of the debt,* and not as security for it. In those instances, the creditor is allowed to keep all the proceeds, even though they greatly exceed the amount of the debt canceled. The validity of such an arrangement has been upheld even when the creditor has induced the debtor to procure the policy.

Legal Effect of Lack of Insurable Interest. A life insurance contract not supported by an incipient insurable interest is a wagering contract and hence illegal. This does not mean, however, that the contract cannot be carried out according to its terms. The courts will not enforce an illegal contract, but they do not necessarily forbid the parties to observe the promises made under the illegal agreement. If an insurance company feels that the applicant honestly believed that he had an insurable interest in the life of the person to be insured, it may honor its promise, despite later evidence that there was no insurable interest. On the other hand, if the company feels that the applicant knew he had no insurable interest and sought the insurance for speculative purposes, it may deny liability, on the grounds of illegality. If the court sustains the company's contention, there will be no obligation under the contract. Not only will the company be relieved of paying the face of the policy (if the insured has died); but, in some states, it will not be obligated to return the premiums paid under the contract. Several states have relaxed the rule against non-enforcement of illegal contracts to allow the applicant or his personal representative to recover all premiums paid where he applied for insurance in the honest belief that he had an insurable interest. In all jurisdictions, recovery of premiums would be permitted if the insurer's agent induced the applicant to apply for insurance by falsely leading him to believe that he had a legitimate insurable interest.

Moreover, the courts have not strictly applied to wagering policies the doctrine that a partial illegality taints the entire transaction and makes it void for all purposes. The rule is frequently modified when a person applies for insurance on his own life at the instigation of a third party who lacks an insurable interest in the applicant, with the third party paying the premiums and being designated beneficiary. From a strict legal standpoint, such a contract is illegal, but the courts may choose to nullify the interest of the offending beneficiary and direct the insurance company to pay the proceeds to the insured's estate[33]

---

[33] In a recent case which has caused considerable apprehension on the part of the life insurance industry, the father of a murdered child was awarded $75,000 in puni-

Under such circumstances, however, the courts are practically unanimous in permitting the beneficiary to recover out of the proceeds the premiums which he paid on the policy. The same attitude is taken toward the case where a policy is assigned to a third party without insurable interest who induced the insured to apply for the policy.

FORM

Some types of contracts have to be in a particular *form* in order to be legal. From a practical standpoint, this aspect of the formation of a contract refers to whether or not the contract has to be in writing or can be in oral form.

The Statute of Frauds, which was originally enacted in England in the seventeenth century and has become a part of the statutory law of nearly all the states of the United States, requires certain types of contracts to be in writing in order to be enforceable. The only section of the statute that might be construed to apply to a contract of life insurance is that which requires written and signed proof of an agreement which, by its terms, is not to be performed within one year from its effective date. This provision has been interpreted to apply only to agreements which *cannot possibly* be performed within one year. Since the insurer's promise may have to be fulfilled within one year or even one day from issue of the policy, a life insurance contract falls outside the statute. Hence, it may be said that in the absence of specific legislation requiring a life insurance contract to be in writing, such a contract can be oral in nature.

Georgia has long required life insurance contracts to be in writing, while several states have construed statutes prescribing standard provisions to require such contracts to be in writing. While all states have prescribed a set of standard provisions that must be included—in substance—in all contracts of life insurance such standard provisions do not necessarily invalidate oral contracts. The standard provisions are simply assumed to be a part of the oral contract.

tive damages against three insurance companies for issuing insurance on the life of the child to an aunt-in-law who had no insurable interest in the life of the insured. The aunt subsequently poisoned the child to collect the insurance and was executed for the crime. The court held that the failure of the companies to insist on an insurable interest on the part of the applicant was the proximate cause of the insured's death (*Liberty National Life* v. *Weldon*, 100 So. [2d] 696 [1957]). For a complete account of this case and a summary of the insurable interest requirements in every American jurisdiction, see John W. Gillon, "Tort Liability of Life Insurers Resulting from Violation of the Insurable Interest Rule," *Proceedings* of the Legal Section of the American Life Convention, 1958.

Statutes invalidating any terms in a policy which appear in a type face smaller than a designated size and those requiring a policy to be signed have been interpreted as not requiring a written contract. Charter provisions requiring all contracts to be in writing are usually disregarded by the courts if proof is furnished that an agent of the company led the "insured" to believe that he was covered under an oral agreement.

As a practical matter, oral contracts are rare, and usually occur only when an agent oversteps his authority and the company is estopped from denying responsibility for the agent's conduct. Oral contracts are a fruitful source of misunderstanding and litigation, and are completely unsuitable for a transaction involving life insurance.

CHAPTER IV

Avoidance of the Contract by the Insurer

THE DECISION of a life insurance company to enter into a contractual arrangement with an applicant for insurance is based largely on the information furnished to the company by the applicant himself. Consequently, it is vitally important to the company that the information be accurate and complete. Unfortunately, the applicant sometimes defaults in his legal duty to supply factually accurate underwriting information; and if the company feels that it has been misled to its detriment, it may seek to avoid liability under the contract it has entered upon. Its action may take the form of either a suit for rescission of the contract, usually but not necessarily instituted during the insured's lifetime, or, more commonly, a defense to a claim brought by the beneficiary after the death of the insured. These rights must be asserted, if at all, during a specified period following issue of the policy —usually, one or two years in duration—since the incontestable clause, to be discussed in Chapter VI, prohibits the company from denying the validity of the contract after the expiration of such period.

During the contestable period, the company can avoid a contract on any one of three grounds: breach of warranty, misrepresentation, or concealment. Each of these grounds is subject to its own set of rules and restrictions and, consequently, will be discussed separately.[1]

[1] For a comprehensive and authoritative treatment of this subject, see Edwin W. Patterson, *Essentials of Insurance Law* (2d ed.; New York: McGraw-Hill Book Co.,

BREACH OF WARRANTY

A warranty is a technical concept which has acquired peculiar significance in insurance and, in this context, may be defined as a clause in an insurance contract that prescribes, as a condition of the insurer's liability, the existence of a fact affecting the risk assumed under the contract. The doctrine of warranties originated in marine insurance more than two hundred years ago and still plays an important role in that branch of insurance. It was developed for the purpose of controlling the risk associated with a particular insurance venture. If a certain state of affairs was deemed to be a risk-reducing factor and insurance was arranged on the assumption that such a state of affairs would continue throughout the term of the policy, the policy would condition the coverage on the existence of the favorable state of affairs. The policy would *warrant* that the desired conditions would prevail. For example, the frequent wars during the eighteenth century made it highly desirable that British merchant vessels sail under the convoy of British warships, and it was customary for marine insurers to require an insured vessel to sail under convoy or pay a higher premium. If a shipowner warranted that his vessel would sail only under convoy and then permitted it to sail alone, his coverage would be nullified. It was not necessary for the insurer to prove that the breach—i.e., the failure to sail with convoy—materially increased the risk; materiality was assumed. Neither was it necessary to establish bad faith or fraud on the part of the insured. The insurer had only to prove that the warranty was breached. This is still the law in marine insurance.

The use of warranties gradually spread to other branches of insurance where they were less suitable. They were no longer confined to contracts sold to businessmen familiar with trade and insurance practices but were liberally interspersed in contracts sold to the general public, the members of which had no concept of the significance of warranties. Abuses inevitably developed. The situation was particularly bad in fire insurance where there was no incontestable clause to ameliorate the effect of a breach of warranty. The courts strained the law in an effort to protect the insuring public, but most states found it necessary to provide statutory relief for those persons procur-

---

Inc., 1957), pp. 272–473. Patterson's discussion deals with all forms of insurance, but there are specific references to life insurance.

ing life and health insurance and, less commonly, those seeking other types of insurance. The general effect of the statutory modifications is that no breach of warranty will void a contract unless it increased the risk, contributed to the loss, or occurred with fradulent intent.

The special legislation directed at life insurance—and, in many states, at accident and sickness insurance—was brought about by the fact that, for one reason or another, most companies had begun to incorporate the application into the policy, which, according to common-law doctrine, made all statements in the application warranties. To make doubly sure of this result, some companies, by express provision, made the applicant warrant the truth of all statements in the application. This meant that the company was in a position to void the contract if any one statement in the application was not literally true. This caused more than half of the states to enact legislation which, in effect, provides that "in the absence of fraud, all statements in the application shall be deemed representations and not warranties." A few states, including New York, have dropped the words "in the absence of fraud," making the statements in the application representations under all conditions. The significance of this modification of the common law will be apparent after the discussion in the next section.

In those states that have not enacted legislation of the type described in the preceding paragraph, the statements in the application could presumably be treated as warranties, provided the application were made part of the contract. However, the standard provisions for life insurance policies prescribed in all states contain the language quoted above and thus eliminate the requirement of literal accuracy.

The doctrine of warranties is not entirely without significance in the field of life insurance, since in some jurisdictions, conditions precedent dealing with the insurability of the applicant are regarded as warranties. For example, the New York Insurance Law defines a warranty as follows:

> The term "warranty" as used in this section, means any provision of any insurance contract which has the effect of requiring, as a condition precedent of the taking effect of such contract or as a condition precedent of the insurer's liability thereunder, the existence of a fact which tends to diminish, or the non-existence of a fact which tends to increase, the risk of the occurrence of any loss, damage, or injury within the coverage of the contract. . . .

The definition goes on to state that the expression "occurrence of loss, damage, or injury" is deemed to include death. Thus, the delivery-in-good-health clause and the medical treatment clause would be construed as warranties in New York and several other states.

In a sense, the statement of the insured's age in the life insurance policy is a warranty, since a misstatement of age which reduces the periodic premium payable is clearly material. However, as a result of a standard provision required in most states, the life insurance policy is not voidable because of such a misstatement, but the amount payable is reduced or increased according to the insurer's premium table. The only other adjustment of this type is that found in some accident and sickness contracts which provide for a reduction in the amount of weekly benefits in the event that the insured should change to a more hazardous occupation.[2]

MISREPRESENTATIONS

Nature and Legal Effect of Representations

Generally speaking, a representation is an oral or written statement made by a party to a contract prior to or contemporaneously with the formation of the contract. It is not a part of the contract but rather is an inducement to the contract. It may refer to facts or conditions existing at the time the statement is made, in which event it is known as an *affirmative representation;* or it may refer to facts or conditions expected to exist in the future, in which case it is referred to as a *promissory representation*. It may be a fact within the knowledge of the person making the statement, or it may be merely an expression of opinion or belief. A representation does not bind the party making it to anything that may happen after the contract is made; if it did, it would be a promise or condition of the other party's promise and would have to be embodied in the contract. It would be the equivalent of a warranty. Finally, a representation need be only substantially true when made.

In life insurance, representations are made by both the applicant and the soliciting agent; but for all practical purposes, only the applicant's statements have legal significance. Hence, the discussion in

---

[2] There is a statute in New Hampshire (*New Hampshire Revised Laws,* 1942, Chap. 326, Sec. 4) which provides for a reduction *in the amount of insurance*—not necessarily the recovery—when, in connection with a fire insurance policy, there occurs a mistake or misrepresentation which contributed to the loss.

this chapter will be concerned only with representations of the applicant.

Since representations do not purport to change the *terms* of a contract, they are not subject to the parol evidence rule, discussed earlier, and, in the absence of a prohibitory statute or policy provision, can be oral in form. However, most states have enacted statutes, directed at life insurance and referred to as *entire-contract statutes,* which state, in substance, that the policy and the application attached thereto constitute the entire contract between the parties. These statutes have been interpreted by the courts to exclude all representations of the insured other than those contained in the application attached to the policy. In other words, the application, or a copy thereof, must be attached to the policy if the company is to treat the statements in the application as representations. In addition, most states require the inclusion in every policy of a provision that has the effect of excluding from consideration all statements of the applicant other than those contained in the application. A typical provision of that nature reads as follows: "No statement of the insured shall avoid this policy or be used in defense of a claim hereunder, unless it is contained in the application and a copy of such application is attached to the policy when issued."

Technically, when the application is made a part of the contract, either by physical attachment to the policy or by reference to it in the policy, all the statements in the application pertaining to the risk become warranties. In order to avoid this untoward result, more than half of the states have enacted laws, previously referred to, which convert statements in the application from warranties to representations. Other states have removed the sting from warranties by requiring that the matter misrepresented be material or, stricter still, have contributed to the loss, before a company can use the breach of warranty as a basis for voiding the contract. Apart from statute or judicial ruling, the policies of most companies provide that all statements in the application shall be deemed representations and not warranties. As a matter of fact, it is customary for the companies to incorporate into one omnibus clause provisions which state that the policy and the application attached thereto shall constitute the entire contract, that statements in the application shall be deemed representations, and that no statement of the insured shall be used to avoid the policy or to contest a claim unless it is contained in the application attached to the policy.

Legal Consequences of a Misrepresentation

A representation has legal consequences only if a person, acting in reliance thereon, is induced to enter into a contract to which he would not otherwise have become a party. If the representation turns out to be false, the aggrieved party can sue to recover damages from the person who made the misstatement or rescind the contract which he was induced to make. The first remedy is available against anyone who *fraudulently* or *deceitfully* makes a misrepresentation, while the second remedy is available only if the person who makes the misrepresentation is a party to the contract. Thus, if a life insurance company is induced to issue a policy because of the fraudulent misrepresentation of the medical examiner, it can recover damages, if any, from the medical examiner, but it cannot rescind the policy unless it can prove that the applicant conspired with the doctor to have the misrepresentation made or, at least, knew of the fraud before the policy was issued. Cases of this sort are occasionally unearthed, but the typical remedy for a misrepresentation in a life insurance application is rescission of the contract.

A misrepresentation does not of itself make a contract void; it only makes it voidable. The aggrieved party may elect to affirm the contract, in which event he is bound by its terms (but not precluded from suing for damages for any fraud involved); or he may elect to rescind the contract. He is under obligation to exercise his option within a reasonable time after discovering the falsity of the representation. In this respect, a misrepresentation differs from a breach of warranty, in that the latter can be offered in defense of a claim even when the company has delayed beyond a reasonable period in making its election between affirmation and rescission. However, this distinction has lost some of its significance because of a number of court decisions which treat the insurer's retention of premiums after discovery of either a misrepresentation or a breach of warranty as a *waiver* or *estoppel.*[3] In any event, the insurer's delay bars its power to rescind, on the ground of misrepresentation, only if the insured was prejudiced by the delay.

An insurance company's notice of rescission must be accompanied by a tender of all premiums paid under the contract. This is necessary, since the purpose of rescission is to wipe out the contract and restore

---

[3] See pp. 96, 97.

the parties to the position which they occupied before the contract was made.

To make its rescission conclusive, the insurance company must obtain an adjudication of its power to rescind. This it may do by defending a judicial proceeding brought by the beneficiary to recover on the policy or by instituting a suit in equity to obtain a decree of rescission. In the former case, the question of misrepresentation is left to a jury when there is any conflict in the evidence, since the beneficiary's suit to recover the sum payable by the terms of the policy is an *action at law* and his right to a jury trial is protected by the federal Constitution. The Constitution does not guarantee a jury trial for suits in equity, and such cases are ordinarily tried by a judge who determines both the law and the facts. Insurance companies prefer the latter type of proceeding because of the tendency for juries to favor the adversary of an insurance company. In most states, however, the equitable remedy is available only under exceptional circumstances.

To obtain a rescission of a life insurance policy on the grounds of a misrepresentation, the company must prove that one or more statements of *fact* in the application were both *false* and *material* to the company's decision to approve the application. It is not necessary, unless required by statute, to prove that the statement was made with intent to deceive the insurer. While considerable authority can be found for the argument that only a *fraudulent* misrepresentation of a material fact will provide grounds for rescission, a majority of cases hold that an innocent misrepresentation of a material fact suffices to make a policy voidable. The doctrine is well established that the test of a misrepresentation is the *effect* on the insurer, and not the *culpability* of the insured or his agent in making it. By the same token, it is held that a fraudulent misstatement of an *immaterial* fact will not make a policy voidable. The purpose of rescission is to protect the company—and, indirectly, its policyholders—against an increase in risk arising out of a misrepresentation, and not to punish the insured whose dishonesty caused the company no harm.

An important exception to the rule that a misrepresentation need not be fraudulent exists when the misstatement is concerned with a matter of opinion, belief, or expectation. It is not sufficient that the applicant's belief as to the status of a matter material to the risk turned out to be erroneous. If the applicant's statement accurately reflected his state of mind at the time he made the assertion, no misrepresentation occurred. A statement of opinion is false only if the person making it does not have such an opinion at the time the statement is made. Therefore, to void a policy on the ground of a false statement of opinion, the insurer must prove that the insured spoke fraudulently. This leads to the conclusion that a statement of opinion must be *false, material,* and *fraudulent* before it makes a policy voidable.

If the statement in the application is qualified by words denoting mental processes, such as "in my opinion" or "to the best of my knowledge and belief" or "the above is as near correct as I can recall," it is clearly one of opinion or belief. However, even unqualified statements will be construed by the courts to be statements of opinion if the fact to which they relate is deemed to be one not susceptible of accurate and conclusive determination by the insured. In other words, an unqualified assertion as to a situation or an event about which there may obviously be differences of opinion may be construed as a statement of opinion.

A statement by the applicant that he "is in good health" has been held to be a statement of opinion,[4] since it calls for an inference rather than a report on observed facts. Statements as to the future are construed as expressions of intent or expectation and are thus opinions, rather than representations of facts. The following questions taken from the application form of a large life insurance company call for a declaration of intentions:

> Are you contemplating any hazardous undertaking or any trip or residence outside of this country? (State why, when, and each country.)
>
> Do you contemplate making any aircraft flights in any capacity other than as a passenger?
>
> Do you contemplate any change, temporary or permanent, in occupation? (Details.)

Negative answers to such queries are of no avail in litigation unless the insurer can prove that at the time of application, the applicant had a definite intention of doing the thing which was the subject of the inquiry.

A representation need be true only at the time it is made; it is not necessary that it continue to be true until the contract is consum-

---

[4] *Sommer* v. *Guardian Life Insurance Co.,* 281 N.Y. 508 (1939). A *statement* that the applicant is in good health must be distinguished from the requirement that the applicant *be* in good health upon delivery of the policy, which requirement, as a condition precedent, is strictly enforced.

mated. At one time, the federal courts and some state courts accepted the view that a representation had to be true at the moment the contract became effective, a doctrine referred to as the rule of *continuing representation;* but with some exceptions, the view today is that the intervening falsity of a representation will provide grounds for rescission only if notice of the changed circumstances is fraudulently withheld from the insurer. In other words, the applicant must be aware of the change, must realize that the change is material to the company's underwriting decision, and must deliberately withhold notice of the change to the company. Legally, such subterfuge of the applicant is not construed to be a misrepresentation, but a concealment, which is discussed at a later point in this chapter.

Concept of Materiality

A representation of the insured is of significance only if it is communicated to the insurer and in some way influences its decision with respect to a contract. If a statement of the insured induces the insurer to enter into a contract which it would not have made had it known the true statement of the fact, or would have made only on different terms, the statement is said to be *material.* More accurately, the *facts misrepresented* in the statement are material.

Extent of Falsity. A distinction must be made between the materiality of the subject matter of a question in the application and the materiality of the misrepresentation made in the answer to the question. Not all statements made by the insured in response to questions of the insurer about matters of consequence to the risk are material. To avoid a policy on the ground of a material misrepresentation, the company must prove not only that the insured made a misstatement about a matter of concern to the company, but that the *extent* of the falsity was substantial enough to be of significance. In other words, the *difference* between the actual facts relating to a matter material to the risk and the facts as falsely represented must have been sufficient to induce the company's decision. This is simply another way of saying that knowledge of the true facts would have caused the company to reject the risk or to accept it only on different terms.

The distinction between a material matter and the materiality of a false response relative to the matter can be illustrated in terms of any number of questions in the typical application form. For example, the application form of one large company contains the following question: "Have you now or have you ever had or been treated for any disease or disorder of the nose, throat, lungs, or pleura?" Suppose that an applicant should give a negative answer to that question when, in fact, he had suffered an attack of tonsilitis ten years earlier which was severe enough to require medical treatment. Obviously, the condition of the applicant's throat is material to the company's consideration of the risk; but was the undisclosed attack of tonsilitis ten years ago of sufficient consequence to justify rescission of the policy?

Tests of Materiality. In adjudicating cases involving a misrepresentation, the courts may attempt to test the materiality of the misrepresented facts by reference to the underwriting practices of insurers generally or by reference to the practices of the particular company involved in the litigation. The first test has been characterized as the *prudent-insurer* standard, while the second has been designated the *individual-insurer* standard.

The prudent-insurer standard has been adopted in the majority of jurisdictions, presumably because it is thought to provide an objective standard of judgment on an issue as to which judgments are likely to be subjective or emotional. It is argued that the judgment of the officers of the litigating company is likely to be warped by the general assumption that anyone who dies within one or two years after issuance of the policy must have concealed some physical impairment. Under this standard, the judgment of objective experts on underwriting practices, usually officials of other companies, is substituted for the subjective opinions of the officers of the company which accepted the risk. The test is subject to a fundamental weakness, in that it presupposes a uniformity of opinion and practice which does not exist. The medical directors of the various companies disagree as to the significance of many types of impairments. To rely exclusively on the testimony of outside experts may impose liability on an insurer, particularly a conservative one, for a risk which that company would unquestionably have rejected with knowledge of the facts misrepresented. A weakness of another sort is that the claimant (the beneficiary, as a rule) may have difficulty in persuading qualified experts to testify against the insurance company.

The individual-insurer test is applied in many jurisdictions and has been adopted by statute in several important states. The New York Insurance Law, for example, states that: "No representation shall be deemed material unless knowledge by the insurer of the facts misrepresented would have led to a refusal by the insurer to make such contract."[5] This text conforms to the basic principle of rescission for misrepresentation and has considerable support in judicial precedents involving transactions other than insurance contracts.

One would naturally assume that in applying this test, the courts would place great reliance on testimony of officials associated with the company involved in the litigation. At one time, however, testimony as to the underwriting practices of the litigating company was, in most jurisdictions, either inadmissible or severely restricted. In some jurisdictions, for example, the only testimony that the medical director was permitted to give was that he had read the application before signing it. Rejection of testimony as to what the company would have done was defended by the courts on the ground that witnesses from one of the parties to the litigation should not be permitted to "substitute" their judgment for that of the jury on the very issue that the jury had to resolve. This meant that the members of the jury had to surmise, from their general knowledge of the human body and the consequences of various diseases, what the insurer would have done had it been in possession of the true facts. This is still the law in some jurisdictions; but many states, by statute or court ruling, have legalized testimony as to the practices of the insurer involved in the litigation. The New York Insurance Law expressly provides that the underwriting practices of the litigating insurer shall be provable: "In determining the question of materiality, evidence of the practice of the insurer which made such contract with respect to the acceptance or rejection of similar risks shall be admissible."[6]

Under this provision, the insurer's medical director or some other qualified official is permitted to testify in court that it is the practice of the company to reject applications that reveal facts similar to those proved in the case under consideration. In fact, if qualified, the witness will be permitted to testify that the insurer, with knowledge of the facts misrepresented, would have rejected the application in dispute. If the testimony is uncontroverted, the evidence is ordinarily (i.e., if not patently absurd) deemed conclusive, and the question of materiality will not go to the jury. In several other states, the insurer is permitted to prove what it would have done had it known the facts later disclosed, but such evidence is not deemed conclusive.

---

[5] Sec. 149 (2). For purposes of this statute, a contract issued on the basis of a higher premium is considered a different contract.

[6] Sec. 149 (3).

The individual-insurer test enables an insurer to apply its standards of insurability in all cases, including those in which the applicant did not disclose all the facts that the insurer requested. This, of course, assumes that the insurer is permitted to prove its standards of insurability, rather than leaving the matter to the conjecture of the jury or the judge. The maintenance of underwriting standards benefits not only the insurer, but also the host of honest policyholders who made no misrepresentations. Moreover, the test of what a particular insurance company would have done in a specific factual situation can be more accurately formulated and more reliably proved than what insurance companies in general would have done.

The principal disadvantage of the individual-insurer test is that the proof of materiality comes from the files of the insurance company and the testimony of its officials, and the counsel for the beneficiary has but little chance of controverting it. His only hope is to prove that the company has not consistently followed its alleged practices; but in attempting to do so, he is not permitted to subpoena the records of the insurance company. If the company should claim to follow a practice which violates common sense, the beneficiary's lawyer could request the judge to let the question go before the jury. If the request were granted, the outcome would not be very much in doubt.

Some recent decisions have ruled that misrepresented facts are material if knowledge of the facts *might* have caused the insurer to reject the application. This is a much stricter standard from the standpoint of the insured and also one much more difficult to apply in practice. It would treat, as material, facts which would cause the company to seek a further investigation of the applicant, even though in the end, the company would have approved the application. A California statute even holds misrepresented facts to be material if knowledge of them would have led the company to make further inquiries or to delay acceptance of the application.[7]

Statutory Modification of the Common Law

The common-law effect of misstatements by an applicant for life insurance has been modified by statute in many states. The most significant modification is that wrought by the type of statute, enacted in most states and discussed earlier, which converts statements in the application from warranties into representations. The effect of

---

[7] California Insurance Code, Sec. 334.

such a statute is to eliminate the conclusive presumption of materiality of statements in the application, forcing the company to prove their materiality.

A second type of statute, far less prevalent, is that which permits a company to void a contract only if the matter misrepresented increased the risk of loss. Such statutes usually apply to warranties as well as representations. They were apparently intended to provide a more objective test of materiality than that furnished by the common-law definition. However, any fact that would be considered an inducement to contract under the common-law concept of materiality would, if so unfavorable as to be misrepresented by the applicant, tend to increase the risk. Hence, these statutes by judicial construction have been given the same effect as the prudent-insurer test of materiality.

A few states[8] have statutes that require the misrepresented fact to have contributed to the loss. Illustrative of this type of legislation is the Missouri statute, which reads as follows:

> No misrepresentation made in obtaining or securing a policy of insurance on the life or lives of any person or persons, citizens of this state, shall be deemed material or render the policy void, unless the matter misrepresented shall have actually contributed to the contingency or event on which the policy is to become due and payable, and whether it so contributed in any case shall be a question for the jury.[9]

Under this type of statute, an applicant can conceal or misrepresent a condition which—if known to the insurer—would unquestionably have caused it to decline the risk; and yet, the company will be held liable if the insured's death resulted from a cause not related to the misrepresented condition. For example, if an applicant concealed a serious heart impairment and later met death in an automobile accident not caused by his heart condition, the company would have to pay the face of the policy, despite the fact that it would not have been on the risk if the heart condition had been revealed at the time of application. The position of the insurance companies under such statutes has been made even more difficult by the construction placed on the statutes by the courts. One of the most extreme examples is provided by the construction of the Missouri statute by the Supreme Court of that state. The court rules that a false statement as to a medical consultation could never be a defense to a claim, since a

---

[8] Missouri, Kansas, Oklahoma, and Rhode Island.

[9] *Vernon's Annotated Missouri Statutes,* Secs. 376.580 and 377.340 (Supp., 1953).

medical consultation is not capable of contributing to a person's death![10] It would seem that the "matter misrepresented" in such a case would be the ailment disclosed by the consultation, but the federal and state courts in Missouri continue to follow the original ruling of Missouri's highest court.

Source of Litigation

Any statement in the application that is designed to elicit information directly relevant to the risk is a potential source of litigation. Yet, some subject areas of the application seldom serve as the basis for denial of a claim, while others are a fruitful source of dispute. Whether the applicant's answer to a particular question is construed to be a statement of fact or a statement of opinion makes a significant difference.

Answers to questions concerning the amount of insurance carried by the applicant and the disposition of applications submitted to other companies are generally regarded to be statements of fact rather than of opinion. Rarely in recent years, however, has an insurance company successfully invoked an answer to this group of questions as a material misrepresentation. Since the companies that do the bulk of the business are members of the Medical Information Bureau, they will ordinarily have access to information about impairments discovered by other companies. If a company were to be put on notice as to detrimental information in the M.I.B. files, it would be permitted to void the contract only if there were other information of a material nature which the applicant should have disclosed.[11]

Answers to questions about the applicant's past and present occupation, if unequivocal, are regarded as statements of fact. Yet, there are few reported cases where the insurer attempted avoidance of the contract on the basis of a misrepresentation as to occupation. The chief explanation for this is probably found in the fact that the inspection report would be likely to uncover any discrepancy in the applicant's statement as to occupation. Statements as to a change of occupation are considered to be declarations of expectation and could serve as a basis for avoidance only if false and fraudulent.

Answers to questions about family history, in so far as they call for information about events that occurred many years before or hap-

---

[10] *Keller* v. *Home Life Insurance Co.,* 198 Mo. 440 (1906).

[11] *Columbian National Life Insurance Co. of Boston, Mass.* v. *Rodgers,* 116 F. (2d) 705 (C.C.A. Kan., 1941); certiorari denied, 313 U.S. 561 (1941).

pened to relatives long separated from the applicant, are deemed to be opinions. Rarely have answers to such questions been used as a basis for litigation. It would ordinarily be difficult for the insurer to prove the materiality of the facts misrepresented without also proving that the applicant suffered from a serious medical impairment traceable, in part, to family history. In that event, it would be simpler to avoid the contract on the grounds of the physical impairment. Answers to questions about exposure to contagious diseases, while significant for underwriting purposes, are of little value in litigation because of the difficulty of proving the materiality of the exposure.

Statements of the applicant as to his habits are usually treated as opinions. The questions are directed at the use of intoxicating beverages and narcotics, and call for distinctions of degree, such as infrequent, moderate, or excessive use. Moreover, the applicant is asked to rate himself, which he cannot be expected to do objectively. For these reasons, and because of the fact that the inspection report reveals the most serious cases of addiction to alcohol or drugs, the applicant's statements as to habits seldom constitute the basis for litigation.

Answers to questions about specific ailments or diseases are in most—but not all—jurisdictions deemed to be statements of fact, and not merely of opinion. An applicant is expected to know whether or not he has ever had—or been treated for—disorders of important organs of the body. Some courts infer the applicant's knowledge of the falsity and materiality of his answer from the serious consequences to him of the disease and the treatment.[12] On the other hand, if the evidence indicates that the applicant's physician did not inform him as to the nature of his ailment—for instance, when it was an incurable disease—the applicant's statement as to that particular disease is likely to be treated as an opinion and not sufficient to permit avoidance of the contract by the insurer.

Answers to general questions about medical treatment, consultation, or hospitalization have been the ones most frequently invoked as defenses in recent litigation. The questions usually are directed at such treatment as has taken place only during the last five years, and the applicant is expected to have a sufficiently keen awareness of such events as to provide the insurer with accurate information. With some exceptions, the answers are treated as statements of fact and not of

[12] See, for example, *Mutual Life Insurance Co. of New York* v. *Moriarity,* 178 F. (2d) 470 (C.A. Ariz., 1949).

opinion. The fact can, except in those states which have adopted the physician-patient privilege (see below), be proved by the testimony or records of the physician or of the hospital.

Of course, the applicant's failure to disclose, or positive misrepresentation of, an instance of medical treatment is of itself neither material nor immaterial. The thing that is material is what the company would have learned, with the full co-operation of the physician or the hospital, if it had been put on notice as to the medical treatment and had made inquiry as to its nature. In order to avoid any disputes or disagreements about the materiality of an applicant's misrepresentation of his recent medical history, the New York Insurance Law states that:

> A misrepresentation that an applicant for life, accident or health insurance has not had previous medical treatment, consultation or observation, or has not had previous treatment or care in a hospital or other like institution, shall be deemed, for the purpose of determining its materiality, a misrepresentation that the applicant has not had the disease, ailment or other medical impairment for which such treatment or care was given or which was discovered by any licensed medical practitioner as a result of such consultation or observation.[13]

It does not follow that in all cases, the facts misrepresented by the applicant's failure to disclose a medical consultation will be sufficient to avoid the contract. If the consultation was for the purpose of obtaining treatment for a common cold or some other slight ailment of a temporary nature, the facts misrepresented would not, because of their immateriality, constitute grounds for avoidance of the contract.

Many states have enacted statutes which provide that information about a patient's physical condition obtained by a physician through medical treatment or professional consultation shall be regarded as a *privileged communication,* which can be divulged only with the consent of the patient, or—if he is deceased—his personal representative. In those states, a physician is not permitted to give testimony as to his medical treatment of an applicant for insurance unless the latter or his personal representative is willing that the physician's findings be made public. If the physician is not permitted to testify, a suspicion arises that the ailment was one material to the defense of misrepresentation. The suspicion is so strong that, since 1940, the New York Insurance Law has contained a provision that if the insurer proves that an applicant misrepresented the facts relating to a medical con-

[13] Sec. 149 (4).

sultation and the applicant or any other person claiming a right under the insurance contract prevents full disclosure and proof of the nature of the medical impairment, such misrepresentation shall be presumed to have been material.[14] The presumption can be rebutted by evidence from the claimant that the ailment was not material to the risk. This provision, which followed a decision of the highest court of New York to the same effect, has been successfully invoked in New York courts and in federal cases governed by New York law. In other states having the physician-privilege statute, no such presumption of materiality arises.

CONCEALMENT

The doctrine of concealment is the final legal defense of the insurance company in its efforts to avoid liability under a contract which was obtained through the misrepresentation or concealment of material facts. Of the three basic grounds for avoidance, concealment is the narrowest in scope and the most difficult to prove. The three grounds are discussed in this chapter in the order of the success with which they can be invoked by the insurance company.

Nature and Legal Effect of a Concealment

In general law, concealment connotes an affirmative act to hide the existence of a material fact. In insurance law, however, a concealment is essentially a nondisclosure; it is the failure of the applicant for insurance to communicate to the insurer his knowledge of a material fact that the insurer does not possess.

It is general law of long standing that one party to a contract is under no legal obligation during the period of negotiation to disclose to the other party information which the first party knows is not known to the second party and, if known, would be deemed material to the contract. The rationale of this rule is that prices in the market place should be set by the best-informed buyers and sellers; and as a reward for performing this economic function, such persons should be permitted to profit by their special knowledge of affairs. For some years, however, there has been a marked trend in the other direction. Among the numerous exceptions to the general rule are the requirements that one party not actively try to prevent the second party from discovering facts known only to the first party or give deliberately mis-

[14] Sec. 149 (4), last sentence.

leading answers to questions designed to elicit information material to the contract.

In insurance, the law of concealment, like the other two doctrines discussed in this chapter, developed during the eighteenth century out of cases involving marine insurance, and the law still reflects the conditions of that period. The relative inaccessibility of the property to be insured and the poor communication facilities, combined with the aleatory nature of the contract, caused Lord Mansfield, the father of English commercial and insurance law, to hold that the applicant for insurance was required by good faith to disclose to the insurer all facts known to him that would materially affect the insurer's decision as to acceptance of the risk, the amount of the premium, or other essential terms of the contract, whether or not the applicant was aware of the materiality of the facts. Even though conditions affecting marine insurance have changed, the law has not. The person seeking marine insurance today, whether he be the shipowner or shipper, must disclose all material facts in his possession to the insurer; and failure to do so, even though innocent, will permit the insurer to void the contract. Under the British Marine Insurance Act, enacted in 1906, the applicant is even "deemed to know every circumstance which, in the ordinary course of business, ought to be known by him."[15]

In English law, the doctrine of innocent concealment is strictly applied to all branches of insurance. In the United States, it is applied only to marine insurance. The American courts have felt that the circumstances surrounding fire and life insurance are so different from those obtaining in marine insurance—particularly in 1766, when the marine rule originated—that a different rule is justified. Under American law, except for marine insurance, a concealment will permit the insurer to void the contract only if the applicant, in refraining from disclosure, had a fraudulent intent.[16] In other words, *except for marine insurance, a concealment must be both material and fraudulent*. In marine insurance, it need only be material.

Test of Materiality

The doctrine of concealment may be regarded as a special manifestation of the doctrine of misrepresentation. The relationship be-

[15] 6 Edw. VII, Chap. 41, Sec. 18 (1).

[16] This is not true in California. The Insurance Code (Section 330) of that state provides that "concealment, whether intentional or unintentional," entitles the insurer to rescind the contract.

tween a misrepresentation and a concealment has been compared with that existing between the heads and tails of a coin. If a misrepresentation is the heads of a coin, a concealment is the tails. One is affirmative; the other is negative. A concealment is misrepresentation by silence. It has legal consequences for the same reason that a misrepresentation does—namely, that the insurer was misled into making a contract that it would not have made had it known the facts. Hence, the general concept of materiality applied to a concealment is the same as that applicable to a misrepresentation: the effect on the underwriting decision of the insurer. "Fraudulent intent" is a subjective concept difficult to prove; many courts take the attitude that if the fact not disclosed by the applicant was *palpably* material, this is sufficient proof of fraud.[17]

The degree of relevance to a risk required of a fact in order to be "palpably" material has never been judicially defined. An illustration was provided in a famous decision by William Howard Taft,[18] then a judge of the Circuit Court of Appeals, who indicated that an applicant for life insurance who failed to reveal to the insurer that he was on his way to fight a duel would be guilty of concealing a palpably material fact. This illustration was almost contradicted by a fairly recent decision that an applicant's failure to disclose that he was carrying a revolver because of his fear of being killed by his former partner, whom he had accused of committing adultery with his wife, was not a palpably material concealment, even though the applicant was murdered a few months later by a person unknown.[19] Experts are occasionally called upon to testify as to the materiality of a concealed fact; but in those cases settled in favor of the insurer, the judge has usually decided from his own knowledge that the fact concealed was palpably material.

The palpable materiality test is applied to the applicant's knowledge of materiality, while both the prudent-insurer and individual-insurer tests of materiality apply only to the *effect* on the insurer. In concealment cases, which are governed by statutes only in California and states that have adopted its laws, the prudent-insurer test seems to be the prevailing one.

---

[17] If the undisclosed fact is palpably material—that is, if its importance would be obvious to a person of ordinary understanding—it can be inferred that the applicant was aware of its materiality, an essential element in fraud.

[18] *Penn Mutual Life Insurance Co.* v. *Mechanics Savings Bank & Trust Co.*, 72 Fed. 413 (C.C.A. 6, 1896).

[19] *New York Life Insurance Co.* v. *Bacalis*, 94 F. (2d) 200 (C.A. Fla., 1938).

Test of Fraud

The test of fraud is whether the applicant believed the fact which he did not disclose to be material to the risk. This test was approved long ago by the highest court of New York in a case involving failure of the applicant to disclose that he had once been insane.[20] The insurer must prove that an undisclosed fact is, *in the applicant's own mind,* material to the risk. As a general proposition, the insured's awareness of the materiality of the fact concealed can be proved by establishing that the fact was *palpably* material, a characteristic that would be apparent to any person of normal intelligence. However, in concealment cases, as with warranties and representations, the law takes into account the powers of understanding and state of knowledge of the particular applicant involved. Thus, the failure of an applicant who was the state agent for the company to notify the insurer of a cancerous condition of the spleen, discovered after submission of the application but before issue of the policy, was held to be fraudulent in view of the applicant's exceptional knowledge of the materiality of such a condition.[21] On the other hand, the failure of a less sophisticated applicant to disclose a toxic condition of the heart muscle, likewise discovered in the interim between submission of the application and issue of the policy, was held to be not fraudulent when evidence revealed that the applicant had refused to take additional insurance offered to him and had changed the basis of premium payments from monthly to semi-annually.[22]

Scope of the Doctrine of Concealment in Life Insurance

The requirement that a concealment be proved by the insurer to have been fraudulent has narrowed the scope of the doctrine in all forms of nonmarine insurance. Its scope has been further narrowed in life insurance through the use of a detailed written application and, in the larger cases, a medical examination. There is a presumption that the application elicits information about every matter that the insurer deems material to the risk; and if the applicant answers fully and truthfully all questions asked in the application, he is under

---

[20] *Mallory* v. *Travelers Insurance Co.,* 47 N.Y. 52 (1871). The concealment was held not to be fraudulent.

[21] *McDaniel* v. *United Benefit Life Insurance Co.,* 177 F. (2d) 339 (C.C.A. Ala., 1941).

[22] *Wilkins* v. *Travelers Insurance Co.,* 117 F. (2d) 646 (C.C.A. Fla., 1941).

no duty to volunteer additional information. This presumption can be overcome by evidence that the applicant willfully concealed other information which was material to the risk and which the applicant knew to be material. In practice, however, the doctrine is seldom invoked except for the nondisclosure of a material fact discovered by the applicant between the time he signed the application and the time the contract was consummated.

The general but not unanimous view of the courts is that the applicant must communicate promptly to the insurer his discovery of such interim facts, if they are so obviously material that the applicant could not fail to recognize their materiality. In one of the early cases on the subject, the insurance company was permitted to deny liability under a policy issued in ignorance of the fact that the applicant had undergone an operation for appendicitis during the period the application was being considered by the home office, even though the applicant was in the hospital at the time the disclosure should have been made.[23] In a later case, involving the interim discovery of a duodenal ulcer, the Supreme Court of the United States had the following to say:

> Concededly, the modern practice of requiring the applicant for life insurance to answer questions prepared by the insurer has relaxed this rule (of disclosure) to some extent since information not asked for is presumably deemed immaterial. . . .
>
> But the reason for the rule still obtains, and with added force, as to changes materially affecting the risk which come to the knowledge of the insured after the application and before delivery of the policy. For even the most unsophisticated person must know that, in answering the questionnaire and submitting it to the insurer, he is furnishing the data on the basis of which the company will decide whether, by issuing a policy, it wishes to insure him. If, while the company deliberates, he discovers facts which make portions of his application no longer true, *the most elementary spirit of fair dealing* would seem to require him to make a full disclosure.[24]

In view of the fact that not all courts impose the duty of disclosure of interim changes and, in any event, violation of the duty must be proved fraudulent, many companies rely on the delivery-in-good-health and medical treatment clauses to protect themselves against interim changes in the applicant's physical condition. These clauses

---

[23] *Equitable Life Assurance Society of United States* v. *McElroy,* 83 Fed. 631 (C.C.A. 8, 1897).

[24] *Stipcich* v. *Metropolitan Life Insurance Co.,* 277 U.S. 311 (1928). Italics supplied.

create conditions or warranties which must be fully satisfied before the company can be held liable under the contract.

The applicant is under no obligation to disclose interim developments, however material on their face, when the first premium is paid with the application and a binding receipt, conditioned on insurability at the date of application, is issued. Under such circumstances, the coverage becomes effective as of the date of application—or medical examination, if later—and changes in the insurability of the applicant after that date are supposed to be immaterial to the insurer's deliberations. Of course, interim changes in the insured's physical condition can be used as evidence to support the company's contention that the insured concealed or misrepresented facts known to him when the application was made.

CHAPTER V

Waiver, Estoppel, and Election by the Insurer

IT WAS brought out in the preceding chapter that a life insurance company may be able to avoid liability under a policy on the ground of a breach of condition, a misrepresentation, or a concealment. Not discussed there, but also a possible defense to a suit, is lack of coverage under the terms of the policy. The company, however, may not be permitted to assert any of these defenses, because of additional facts showing that it has waived the defense, has become estopped to assert it, or has conclusively elected not to take advantage of it. Various factual situations constitute the basis for a "waiver," an "estoppel," and an "election," respectively, examples of which will be dealt with in a later section of this chapter. While these are legally distinct concepts, it is customary to refer to them generically as "waiver" and to describe any factual situation which could lead to the loss of an otherwise valid legal defense as a "waiver situation." Simply and broadly stated, a waiver situation is one in which a presumably valid defense of an insurance company to a policy claim has been—or may be found to have been—waived by the company.

If the foregoing definition of a waiver situation seems vague and general, it was intended to be so. The boundaries of waiver law are very indistinct, and the concepts employed tend to be amorphous. This state of affairs is largely attributable to the underlying purpose of waiver law, which, in the case of life insurance, is to protect the policyholder and his beneficiaries against a harsh and overly legalistic interpretation of the policy and application. In perhaps no other branch of the law is there such a universal tendency to make the law fit the facts and, if that be impracticable, to create new law. It is not without justification that waiver has been described as "a kind of legal mercy, a way of tempering the wind to the shorn lamb."[1] In the process of providing mercy, the courts "have devised doctrines and asserted principles which are sometimes more creditable to the ingenuity and subtlety of the judges than easily harmonized with decisions rendered, under less violent bias, in other departments of the law."[2]

Professor Edwin W. Patterson, Cardozo Professor Emeritus of Jurisprudence, Columbia University, and an eminent authority on the law of waiver, ascribes the state of confusion existing in this field to the use of "flexible concepts to analyze the significance of foggy facts."[3] There may be hope for improvement, however, since Professor Patterson has concluded that "the doctrines of waiver, once used as judicial whitewash to cover a multitude of minor defaults, are now used more sparingly and with more discrimination."[4]

Inasmuch as the law of agency is at the foundation of most waiver situations in life insurance, it should be helpful to review the pertinent elements of that branch of the law before considering the more specific aspects of waiver.

LAW OF AGENCY

Agency may be defined as the relationship which results from the manifestation of consent by one person that another person shall act on his behalf and subject to his control, along with the consent of the other person so to act. The one for whom action is to be taken is the *principal*, while the one who is to act is the *agent*. Generally speaking, any person who has the capacity to make a contract has the capacity to act as an agent. By the same token, any person who has the capacity to perform a certain act may appoint an agent to perform the act.

In the case of a life insurance company, the agents—in the legal

---

[1] Edwin W. Patterson, *Essentials of Insurance Law* (2d ed.; New York: McGraw-Hill Book Co., Inc., 1957), p. 476.

[2] John Skirving Ewart, *Waiver Distributed* (Cambridge, Mass.: Harvard University Press, 1917), p. 192.

[3] Patterson, *op. cit.*, p. 494.

[4] *Ibid.*, p. 483.

sense—include the directors (acting as a body), the officers, home office supervisory personnel, agency supervisors, medical examiners, and soliciting agents. In the business sense, only agency field supervisors and soliciting agents are regarded as "agents." Here, the term "agent" will be used in its broader, legal meaning, with the expression "soliciting agent" being used to designate field sales personnel. Most of the waiver situations involve actions of soliciting agents.

General Rules

There are four general rules of the law of agency which are of particular relevance to life insurance.

Presumption of Agency. There is no presumption that one person acts for another. There must be some tangible evidence of an agency relationship. Thus, if a person claims to represent a certain life insurance company and collects a premium with which he later absconds, the company is not responsible for his actions if it has done nothing to create the presumption that the person is its authorized agent. If, however, the person is in possession of a rate book, application blanks, and receipt forms of the company, a presumption will be raised that the person is in fact representing the company. The presumption could, in all likelihood, be overcome by proof that the company materials were improperly acquired.

Apparent Authority of Agents. Most agency relationships are evidenced by a written instrument which expressly confers certain powers on the agent; it may also expressly withhold certain powers. The agency contract of a life insurance company usually authorizes the field representative to solicit and take applications for new business, arrange medical examinations, and collect first-year premiums. It also sets forth a number of powers specifically denied the agent, including the right to make, alter, or discharge a contract, to extend the time for payment of premiums, to accept payment of premiums in other than current funds, to waive or extend any obligation or condition, and to deliver any policy unless the applicant at that time be in good health and insurable condition.

The power of an agent to bind his principal, however, may well exceed the scope of the principal's express authorization. The latter is construed to convey authority to perform all incidental acts necessary to carry out the purposes of the agency. Such acts fall under the heading of *implied* powers. For example, if an agent is expressly authorized to deliver a life insurance policy which can be properly delivered only upon the payment of the consideration, the agent has the implied power to collect and receipt for the amount due.

The authority of an agent can also be expanded by conduct of the principal or agent which creates a justifiable belief on the part of third parties dealing with the agent that the latter possesses powers which have not been vested in him and may—unknown to the third parties—have been expressly withheld from him. If the third persons can prove that they were justified in relying on the presumption that the agent was acting within his authority, the principal will be "estopped" or precluded from denying that the agent had such powers. In proving justifiable reliance, third parties need demonstrate only that they exercised due diligence in ascertaining the agent's real authority. Authority created in this manner is referred to as *apparent authority*.

The doctrine of apparent authority can be illustrated in terms of an agent who has habitually granted his policyholders extensions of time in the remitting of premiums. If, in the past, the company has not taken action to deal with this infraction of its rules, it would be precluded from denying that the agent had such authority until such time as it notifies the policyholders involved of the limitations on the agent's powers. Such action with regard to one policyholder, however, would not create any presumption as to the agent's power to deal in a similar manner with other policyholders.

Responsibility for Acts of Agents. The principal is responsible for all acts of his agent when the latter is acting within the scope of either his express, his implied, or his apparent authority. This responsibility embraces wrongful or fraudulent acts, omissions, and misrepresentations, provided the agent is acting within his apparent authority. It is likewise responsible for any libel committed by an agent in the pursuit of his official duties. While there is no unanimity in the decisions, the weight of authority is that—in the absence of restrictions—a company is liable not only for the acts of its agents, but also for the acts of the subagents and employees to whom the agent has delegated responsibility; the liability of the company in such situations may depend on whether it has given the agent actual authority, or its actions have created an apparent authority, to delegate responsibility.

Secret limitations on the agent's authority will, under the doctrine of equitable estoppel, be inoperative as to third persons. They will, of course, be effective as between the agent and his principal; and if the agent exceeds his actual authority, he is liable to the principal for any loss or damage. The agent, as might be expected, is also liable to his principal for any loss or damage caused through his fraud, misconduct, or mere negligence.

In the course of their daily business, insurance agents are frequently asked to express an opinion as to the meaning of a particular provision, and it is of some importance to determine the legal effect of such an opinion. The general rule is that no legal effect is to be given to such opinions. This holding is based on the theory that an agent's opinion as to the meaning of any section does not create new or modify old obligations. It is followed particularly where the authority of the agent is limited and the provision involved is clear and unambiguous. In certain jurisdictions, however, a company is bound by the opinions of its agents, especially where the opinion is not inconsistent with the language of an ambiguous clause in the policy and is relied upon by the insured.[5]

Knowledge of the agent as to matters within the scope of his agency is presumed to be knowledge of the principal. This rule is applied even though matters coming to the attention of the agent are not, in fact, communicated to the principal. This rule is of critical importance, since in all their dealings with prospective and actual policyholders, soliciting agents and medical examiners are regarded to be the legal agents of the company. Hence, loyalty to the company, as well as common decency, demands that these field representatives communicate to the company all matters of underwriting or other significance that come to their attention.

Limitation on Powers of Agents. Limitations on the powers of an agent are generally effective when the limitations have been properly communicated and are not in conflict with existing law. All companies communicate to their policyholders by means of a clause in the application blank or in the policy, or in both, the customary limitations on the powers of soliciting agents and other representatives of the company with whom the policyholder may come in contact. Such provision, generally referred to as the *nonwaiver clause,* usually states that only certain specified representatives of the company (executive officers) have the power to extend the time for payment of a premium or to modify the terms of the contract in any other respect. The clause further requires that any modification of the contract must be evidenced by a written endorsement on the contract. The clause used by some companies goes on to state that no knowledge on the part of any agent or medical examiner or any other person as to any facts

[5] G. J. Couch, *Cyclopedia of Insurance Law* (Rochester, N.Y.: Lawyers Cooperative Publishing Co., 1929), Sec. 531.

pertaining to the applicant shall be considered to have been made to —or brought to the knowledge of—the company unless contained in the application, including the section completed by the medical examiner.

The nonwaiver clause will not be enforced with respect to acts or statements occurring prior to issue of the policy unless it is contained in the application and the application is attached to the policy. In other words, the applicant cannot be presumed to have knowledge of a limitation in an instrument which will come into his possession only after the transaction has been consummated. On the other hand, it would be assumed that limitations on the agent's authority contained in the application or the policy would be effective with respect to acts done subsequent to delivery of the policy. Unfortunately for the insurance companies, experience has not always borne out this assumption. In one case,[6] the court held that an agent can waive the very clause that says he cannot waive, alter, or modify any terms or conditions of the contract. Having waived the nonwaiver clause, the agent can proceed to waive any provision beneficial to the company. This, it will be recognized, is an extreme point of view.

Brokers as Agents

An insurance broker is a person (individual, partnership, or corporation) who acts as an agent of the insured in negotiating for insurance and in procuring the issuance of an insurance contract. In the eyes of the law, the broker is requested by the prospective insured to act for him, although in practice, the "request" is usually solicited by the broker. The broker usually receives all his compensation (in the form of commissions) from the insurance company, he delivers the policy for the company, and he collects the premium from the insured. As a consequence, the broker has come to be regarded as the agent of the company for the purpose of delivering the policy and collecting the premium. In fact, this status is recognized by statute in some states.

Where the broker is regarded as the agent of the company only for these limited purposes, knowledge of the broker as to facts affecting the risk is not imputed to the company for the purpose of establishing a waiver or estoppel, or for the purpose of obtaining reformation of the contract on the ground of mistake.[7] In many states, however, there is legislation which provides that any person who solicits insurance

[6] *West* v. *National Casualty Co.*, 61 Ind. App. 479, 112 N.E. 115 (1916).

[7] *Mishiloff* v. *American Central Insurance Co.*, 102 Conn. 370 (1925); *Ritson* v. *Atlas Assurance Co.*, 279 Mass. 385 (1932).

for anyone other than himself and procures a policy from the insurer shall be deemed the agent of the insurer with respect to that policy. Under some of these statutes, the solicitor's knowledge of facts constituting a breach of condition sufficient to make the contract voidable immediately has been imputed to the insurer.[8] This places the company in a position of issuing a policy it knows to be worthless—which, under the doctrine of waiver or estoppel, will preclude it from avoiding the contract on the known breach of condition. A few courts have rejected this imputation of knowledge, on the ground that the statute does not specify the *precise* powers conferred upon the solicitors.[9]

MEANING OF WAIVER, ESTOPPEL, AND ELECTION

It has been intimated that the legal concepts and rules employed in the adjudication of waiver situations have often been lacking in logic and consistency, with the result that the distinctions among waiver, estoppel, and election have become decidedly blurred, perhaps irretrievably so. Basically, however, the legal conceptions of waiver, estoppel, and election are derived from two elemental principles: (1) an individual should be bound by that to which he assents, and (2) an individual whose conduct has led another to act or not to act in reliance upon a belief as to a fact or an expectation as to future performance ought not to be allowed to act in a way contrary to the belief or expectation so created.[10] The first principle is at the foundation of waiver and election, while the second suggests the basis for several varieties of estoppel.

Waiver

The term "waiver" has been used with so many meanings that it almost defies analysis. Some courts try to distinguish it from estoppel, while other courts treat it as synonymous or interchangeable with estoppel. For example, one court might hold that the failure to demand an answer to an unanswered question in an application for life insurance constituted a *waiver* of the right to make the demand, whereas another might hold that the company was *estopped* from demanding the answer. When a court does attempt to distinguish between waiver and estoppel, it ordinarily treats waiver as a manifestation of assent

---

[8] *Welch* v. *Fire Insurance Assn. of Philadelphia,* 120 Wis. 456 (1904).

[9] *John Hancock Mutual Life Insurance Co.,* v. *Luzio,* 123 Ohio St. 616 (1931).

[10] Patterson, *op. cit.,* pp. 493 and 494.

and estoppel as nonconsensual, since the purpose of the latter is to redress a wrong and prevent inequitable treatment of one party to a contract by the other. Thus, if waiver is to be given a specific meaning, it would probably be appropriate to define it as "a manifestation of intent to relinquish a known right or advantage."[11] This is quite similar to the definition provided many years ago by the highest court of New York: "A waiver is the voluntary abandonment or relinquishment by a party of some right or advantage."[12]

While the foregoing definitions set waiver apart from estoppel, they do not distinguish it clearly from *election,* which, it will presently be noted, likewise connotes a voluntary act.

Estoppel

The doctrine of estoppel developed centuries ago in the English courts and is a limitation on the right of a person to change his mind. The law recognizes the right of an individual to change his mind, but it imposes certain restraints on that right. The law of contracts attempts to distinguish the serious promise from the casual or jesting promise by means of a *consideration.* In the law of estoppel, a detrimental reliance or change of position by the other party is the test.

There are two broad types of estoppel: *equitable estoppel* (also called *estoppel by representation* and *estoppel in pais*) and *promissory estoppel.* Historically, equitable estoppel, so called because it originated in the equity courts, was the first to develop. It was confined to a representation of past or present fact. There was no element of futurity. This original meaning has been preserved through the years and is reflected in the following comprehensive definition of an equitable estoppel: "An [equitable] estoppel is a representation of fact made by one person to another which is reasonably relied upon by that other in changing his position to such an extent that it would be inequitable to allow the first person to deny the truth of his representation."[13]

The essence of the equitable estoppel is that if a party purports to make a true statement about a past or present fact to another party who relies on the truth of the statement to his substantial detriment, the first party will not be permitted later to deny the truth of the statement. The case is tried on an assumption contrary to fact. Thus, equi-

---

[11] *Ibid.,* p. 495.

[12] *Draper* v. *Oswego County Fire Relief Assn.,* 190 N.Y. 12, 82 N.E. 755 (1907).

[13] Patterson, *op. cit.,* p. 496.

table estoppel is a rule of evidence rather than one of substantive law.

The doctrine of promissory estoppel has developed within the last century and can be distinguished by the fact that it is concerned with a statement of future conduct. It has been defined as "a statement as to his future conduct made by one person to another which is reasonably and foreseeably relied upon by that other in changing his position to such an extent that it would be inequitable to allow the first person to conduct himself differently from that which he stated."[14]

A promissory estoppel has been illustrated as follows.[15] Suppose that A promises to give B $5,000 if B will enter a particular college and receive his bachelor's degree. Suppose, further, that B matriculates at the designated college and has completed all the requirements for the degree except passing the examinations for the final term when A notifies him of an intention to revoke the promise. Since B has made a substantial sacrifice in effort and money to attend college in reliance upon A's promise, the courts would not permit A to revoke his promise. A's promise would be enforced, despite the fact that it was not supported by a consideration.[16] In other words, the law would recognize a valid contract.

The foregoing example illustrates the creation of a new obligation through a promissory estoppel. Some courts will not go that far in applying the doctrine, limiting its application to modifications of existing contracts. The latter application is the typical one in life insurance situations. It is of growing importance.

Election

In its original sense, election means a voluntary act of choosing between two alternative rights or privileges. Thus, if a married man dies testate (with a will), his widow usually has the right to take under the will or under the appropriate intestate law. These are alternative rights, and the widow's act of choosing one is a voluntary relinquishment of the other. The similarity to a waiver is readily apparent.

The concept of election has had only limited application in life insurance. Despite the fact that an election is an overt, manifested intent to be bound, the courts have occasionally found an election in the

---

[14] *Ibid.*

[15] H. M. Horne and D. B. Mansfield, *The Life Insurance Contract* (2d ed.; New York: Life Office Management Association, 1948), p. 81.

[16] Some would argue that B's action is a consideration for A's promise, making A's obligation contractual in nature, rather than one based on estoppel.

inconsistent conduct of the insurer. For example, the acceptance of a premium by the company after the discovery of a material misrepresentation has been viewed as an election by the company not to void the contract.

WAIVER SITUATIONS

In the remainder of this chapter, no attempt will be made to distinguish between waiver, estoppel, and election. The practical effect is the same, irrespective of the particular doctrine which the court uses to justify its decision. The emphasis hereafter is on the types of factual situations in which the courts are likely to invoke one of the doctrines outlined above to deprive a life insurance company of a defense which would have enabled it to avoid the payment of a claim.

Breach of Condition Precedent

The validity of most life insurance policies is contingent upon the fulfillment of three conditions precedent: payment of the first premium, good health of the applicant at the time the policy is delivered, and the absence of new elements affecting insurability (e.g., medical treatment) in the interim between the submission of the application and the delivery of the policy.

Payment of First Premium. The existence of a life insurance policy is usually conditioned upon payment of the first premium, or the first installment thereof, *in cash.* The cash-premium clause is typically coupled with the delivery-in-good-health clause.

The requirement that the first premium be paid in cash has been rather strictly enforced by the courts. Upon proof that the soliciting agent delivered the policy without payment of the premium, or any part thereof in any form, the courts in most jurisdictions hold that the policy is not in force, even though the agent orally assured the applicant that it would take effect at once. The view is that an agent having authority merely to solicit insurance and to collect premiums in cash has no actual or apparent authority to extend credit.

In reaching this conclusion, the courts seem to place great emphasis on the existence of a nonwaiver clause in the *application,* as opposed to the policy. In the leading New York case on the subject,[17] the court, in holding that the requirement had not been satisfied through the

[17] *Drilling* v. *New York Life Insurance Co.,* 234 N.Y. 234 (1922).

payment of the premium by the soliciting agent on behalf of the applicant, stressed the nonwaiver clause in the application. In another case,[18] the taking of a promissory note, payable to the soliciting agent, was not deemed a waiver of the cash-premium clause, since there was also a nonwaiver clause in the application.

The nonwaiver clause will not prevent a finding of waiver in all cases; it is merely notice to the applicant of the agent's limited authority. If it can be proved that the agent actually has authority to extend credit for all or a part of the premium, his doing so will, in most courts, constitute an effective waiver of the cash-premium requirement. Thus, an agent whose powers extended to the employment of subagents and who had received from his home office detailed instructions as to how to deal with premium notes, was held to have authority to issue a binding receipt in exchange for the applicant's note.[19] In another case, it was proved that the insurer followed a practice of requiring its soliciting agents to remit only the difference between the gross premium and the agent's commission; and—the applicant having paid more than this amount to the agent—it was held that the latter had authority to extend credit for the balance, despite the existence of cash-premium and nonwaiver clauses in the application.[20] In cases of this kind, the formal printed instructions to the agency force will not be conclusive proof of an agent's actual authority, as against proof of what was done by way of relaxation of those rules. To avoid a waiver, a company's action must be consistent with its announced policy.

It is common practice, of course, for premiums to be paid by check. If the check is honored by the bank upon which it is drawn, the premium—for all intents and purposes—has been paid in cash. A check is considered to be a cash payment, likewise, when for a reasonable period of time, the applicant had sufficient funds in his bank account to cover the check.[21] If a check tendered in payment of the first premium is not honored upon presentation within a reasonable time, however, the status of the policy depends upon the terms under which the check was accepted. If the premium receipt states that the check is accepted as payment only on condition that it be honored—a common practice—the policy will not go into force if the check is not honored. If the premium receipt does not so state, however, some courts have

---

[18] *Bradley* v. *New York Life Insurance Co.,* 275 Fed. 657 (C.C.A. 8, 1921).
[19] *Schwartz* v. *Northern Life Insurance Co.,* 25 F. (2d) 555 (C.C.A. 9, 1928).
[20] *New York Life Insurance Co.* v. *Ollich,* 42 F. (2d) 399 (C.C.A. 6, 1930).
[21] *State Life Insurance Co.* v. *Nolan,* 13 S.W. (2d) 406 (Tex. Civ. App., 1929).

construed the issuance of a premium receipt to be an *election* to treat the check as payment of the premium. In that event, of course, the condition of the policy has been fulfilled, and nonpayment of the check merely entitles the insurer to sue the drawer of the check.

A final question relates to policies which contain a clause acknowledging receipt of the first premium. Such a clause might read as follows: "This contract is made in consideration of the application therefor and the payment in advance of the sum of $......, the receipt of which is hereby acknowledged. . . ." Does such a clause prevent the company from showing that the first premium has not been paid? In the majority of cases, it is held that an acknowledgment contained in the policy itself is not *conclusive* (i.e., only prima-facie) evidence of payment, although the burden is on the company to prove nonpayment—a negative sort of undertaking which can be extremely difficult. There are some cases, however, which hold that in the absence of fraud, such a clause is conclusive evidence of payment. A number of states have statutes to that effect. Typical, perhaps, is a provision in the California Civil Code which provides that: "An acknowledgment in a policy of the receipt of premium is conclusive evidence of its payment so far as to make the policy binding, notwithstanding any stipulation therein that it shall not be binding until the premium is actually paid." Presumably, under such statutes, the company—while not being permitted to deny the existence of a binding contract—would still have the right to collect the premium from the insured or his estate, if it were proved that the first premium had not been paid.

Delivery-in-Good-Health and Medical Treatment Clauses. By their very nature, the *delivery-in-good-health* and *medical treatment* clauses are a fertile source of waiver litigation. While the clauses are explicit and unequivocal, if a policy is delivered by an agent with knowledge of a breach of either of the clauses, the presumption can always be raised that the condition was waived by the agent. The issue then turns on the authority of the agent.

The leading case on this subject is *Bible* v. *John Hancock Mutual Life Insurance Company*.[22] It involved an industrial life insurance policy containing a delivery-in-good-health clause and the following medical treatment clause:

> This policy shall be void . . . if the insured . . . has attended any hospital, or institution of any kind engaged in the care or cure of human

[22] 256 N.Y. 458, 176 N.E. 838 (1931).

health or disease, or has been attended by any physician, within two years before the date hereof, for any serious disease, complaint or operation . . . unless each such . . . medical and hospital attendance and previous disease is specifically waived by an endorsement in the space for endorsements on page 4 hereof signed by the secretary.

The policy likewise contained a clause to the effect that "agents are not authorized to waive any of the terms or conditions of this policy." There was no such clause in the application, which was not attached to the policy.

The applicant, Anna Bible, was a patient in the Hudson River State Hospital, suffering from a manic depressive psychosis. An agent for the John Hancock Company visited her in the hospital and procured her signature to an application.[23] He delivered the policy to her at the hospital in the presence of her husband and collected the first premium. That same agent collected premiums at the hospital at weekly intervals thereafter for a period of three months, the premiums thereafter being collected by another agent. The insured died about twenty months after the policy was delivered, and the beneficiary filed a claim for the benefits. The company disclaimed liability on the ground that the contract had been avoided by the breach of the good-health and medical treatment clauses.

The New York Court of Appeals, however, affirmed a judgment for the plaintiff-beneficiary on the ground that the conditions had been waived. The court pointed out that the agent was more than a soliciting agent; he had the authority to deliver policies and to collect weekly premiums. He thus had the apparent authority to effectuate a waiver or, at least, to acquire knowledge that could be imputed to his principal, the company. The applicant was not put on notice as to any limitations on the agent's authority before the policy was delivered, and the court held that the insured "was not chargeable with notice that the limitation would apply by retroaction so as to nullify a waiver or estoppel having its origin in conduct antecedent to the contract."

The case expresses the rule followed by the majority of courts—namely, that *when an agent with actual or apparent authority to deliver the policy does so with knowledge of facts constituting a breach of either the delivery-in-good-health or medical treatment clause, or both,* the breach is waived.[24]

---

[23] As a matter of fact, several policies were involved.

[24] This rule will obviously not apply when there has been collusion between the agent and the applicant.

The court indicated that there would have been no waiver if the application had contained a clause limiting the agent's authority, and if a copy of the application had been attached to the policy. Inasmuch as the application for ordinary insurance policies (as contrasted with industrial policies) generally contains a limitation on the agent's authority and is customarily attached to the policy, the waiver problem in this area would not be serious if the courts in general share the view expressed in the Bible case. It is a matter of conjecture, however, how far the courts will go in enforcing the limitation-of-authority clause, even when in the application and attached to the policy.

Misrepresentation in Application

The applicant for a life insurance policy must submit a written application in which he supplies various types of information, including that relating to his past and present health. He may also have to undergo a medical examination, including an interrogation by the medical examiner. It is standard practice for the soliciting agent to fill out the application for the applicant, and the medical examiner writes in the answers to the questions which he asks the applicant.

There is always the possibility that the information supplied by the applicant will be incorrectly recorded in the application by the agent or medical examiner. This may occur through inadvertence or through design. Unless there is collusion, the medical examiner has little or no reason to falsify the medical report; but unfortunately, the agent—being on a commission basis—does have an incentive to falsify information that might adversely affect acceptance of the application. If the agent should falsify the answers in the application, he might do so with or without the knowledge of the applicant. If he informs the applicant that he is not recording some item of information correctly, it is likely to be accompanied by an observation that the matter is immaterial and should not be permitted to complicate consideration of the application by the home office underwriting officials. If the truthful answers of the applicant are falsely recorded in the application by the agent or medical examiner, it becomes important to determine the legal effect of such misstatements.

It is a well-settled rule that one who signs and accepts a written instrument with the intention of contracting is bound by its terms. However, if the instrument contains false statements, the aggrieved party has the right to avoid the contract. Hence, in accordance with strict contract law, material misstatements in the application should give the insurance company power to avoid the contract, irrespective of the circumstances surrounding the falsification of the statements. However, the courts, recognizing that a life insurance policy is a contract of adhesion, seldom read by the insured, do not apply strict contract law in these cases. The rule supports by the weight of authority is that if the application is filled out by an agent of the company who—without fraud, collusion, or knowledge of the applicant—falsely records information truthfully provided by the applicant, the company cannot rely upon the falsity of such information in seeking to avoid liability under the contract. The desirability of the rule has been expressed by one court in the following terms: "To hold otherwise would be to place every simple or uneducated person seeking insurance at the mercy of the insurer who could, through its agent, insert in every application, unknown to the applicant, and over his signature, some false statement which would enable it to avoid all liability while retaining the price paid for supposed insurance."[25]

The key to the above rule is that the agent, in filling out the application, is acting for thc company, not the insured. In other words, the soliciting agent is, in a legal sense, the agent of the company, the principal. This finding can support either of two legal theories, both of which have been used by the courts to justify their decisions. The first theory holds that there is no deception of the insurance company, since it knew, through its agent, that the written statement or statements were not true.[26] The second theory, more widely used, recognizes that there is deception but holds that since the company, through the knowledge of its agent, knowingly issued a voidable policy, it is estopped from voiding it.

To find an estoppel, the courts must permit testimony, usually from the beneficiary, as to the answers provided by the applicant to the agent. This would seem to be in violation of both the parol evidence rule and an "entire-contract" statute. The courts of New York, Pennsylvania, and a few other states have held that the entire-contract statute does bar testimony to show a waiver or an estoppel.[27] Other states with similar statutes have permitted oral communications to the agent to be introduced into evidence, the statute not being mentioned. In Colorado, the highest court faced the issue squarely and held that

[25] *State Insurance Co. of Des Moines* v. *Taylor,* 14 Colo. 499, 24 Pac. 333, 336 (1890).

[26] *Heilig* v. *Home Security Life Insurance Co.,* 222 N.C. 231 (1942).

[27] See Patterson, *op. cit.,* p. 514, n. 80, for citations.

the statute did not exclude oral testimony to establish waiver or estoppel.[28]

The courts are likewise inclined to find a waiver or an estoppel when the applicant knows the falsity of an answer but the agent asserts that it is immaterial. The view is that the applicant is entitled to rely upon the superior knowledge of the agent or medical examiner, as the case may be. Even a stipulation in the application that oral statements made to the agent shall not be binding upon the company has been held unenforceable. However, where the applicant knows that the agent or medical examiner is not truthfully reporting obviously material facts to his company, the applicant himself is guilty of fraud and cannot invoke the doctrine of estoppel, which requires honest reliance. The applicant's behavior in this situation would be regarded as collusive.

Waiver Subsequent to Issuance of Policy

A breach of condition that occurs after a policy has gone into effect can be waived in either of two ways: (1) by an express statement, usually in writing, of a representative of the insurer having the authority to waive the condition; or (2) by the inconsistent conduct of the company and its representatives.

With respect to the first method, attention must again be directed to the clause embodied in the application for a life insurance policy, stipulating that no provision of the contract can be waived except by a *written* endorsement on the contract signed by a designated officer of the company. This restriction is likely to be enforced with respect to *express* waivers, although the courts occasionally find that the company bestowed the waiver authority on representatives not designated in the nonwaiver clause, even local agents. Moreover, oral statements may be accepted as evidence of waiver. This, it should be noted, is not inconsistent with the parol evidence rule, which applies only to oral statements made prior to or contemporaneously with the formation of the contract. Most of the litigation concerning express waivers involves the authority of the person who allegedly approved the waiver. It is clear that if an important official of the company purports to waive a breach of condition, the waiver will be recognized and enforced by the courts. The validity of other alleged waivers will depend upon the actual or apparent authority of the company representative making the utterance.

---

[28] *New York Life Insurance Co.* v. *Fukushima,* 74 Colo. 236 (1923).

A waiver after issuance of the policy is more likely to be found in the inconsistent conduct of the company. It has been said that the company cannot "run with the rabbits and bark with the hounds." When the company has knowledge of a breach or nonperformance of a condition, and wishes to avoid the contract on that ground, it must pursue a course of conduct consistent with that intention. In their zeal to protect policyholders, the courts will seize upon inconsistent conduct on the part of the insurer as evidence of an intention not to exercise its power of avoidance.

An example of inconsistent conduct may be found in the treatment of overdue premiums. If a company has followed a general practice of accepting and retaining premiums tendered after the expiration of the grace period, it will be estopped from denying the punctuality of any premiums so paid. Perhaps more important, it will be estopped from insisting on the timely payment of premiums in the future, unless it makes unmistakably clear to the policyholder or policyholders from whom overdue premiums have customarily been accepted that future payments will have to be made before expiration of the grace period. The same rule applies when a company has established a practice of sending premium notices, although not required by statute or the policy. If, without adequate notice to the policyholders, the company should discontinue its practice, it would probably be held to have waived its right to insist on payment within the grace period, provided payment is tendered within a reasonable time. In recent years, many companies that formerly sent two premium notices—the second sometimes during the grace period—have discontinued the second notice. The companies were careful to notify their policyholders of the change in practice, in order to avoid the possibility of a waiver.

Any attempt of the company to collect a premium after the expiration of the grace period may be held to be a waiver, unless accompanied by an invitation to the insured to submit an application for reinstatement.

CHAPTER VI

The Incontestable Clause

THE PRECEDING chapter discussed the impact of the doctrines of waiver, estoppel, and election on the right of a life insurance company to avoid liability under a policy because of fraud, misrepresentation, or breach of condition at the inception of the contract. This chapter will consider an even more restrictive influence—the incontestable clause. This clause, without counterpart in any other type of contract, has been the source of much misunderstanding and considerable litigation. The opinion has been expressed that no other provision of the typical life insurance contract has been the center of so much "controversy, misinterpretation, and legal abuse" as the incontestable clause.[1] The provision has a vital bearing on the protection afforded by a life insurance contract and is worthy of careful study.

NATURE AND PURPOSE OF THE CLAUSE

In General

In its simplest form, the incontestable clause states that "this policy shall be incontestable from its date of issue, except for nonpayment of premium." The purpose of such a clause is to enhance the value of a life insurance contract by providing assurances that its validity will not be questioned by the insurance company years after it was issued and has possibly given rise to a claim. It was voluntarily adopted by the companies, partly as a result of competitive pressures, to overcome

---

[1] H. M. Horne and D. B. Mansfield, *The Life Insurance Contract* (2d ed.; New York: Life Office Management Association, 1948), p. 181.

prejudices against the life insurance business created by contests based upon technicalities and to give an assurance to "persons doubtful of the utility of insurance, that neither they nor their families, after the lapse of a given time, shall be harassed with lawsuits when the evidence of the original transaction shall have become dim, or difficult of retention, or when, perhaps, the lips of him who best knew the facts are sealed by death."[2]

The incontestable clause is a manifestation of the belief that the beneficiaries of a life insurance policy should not be made to suffer for mistakes innocently made in the application. After the insured's death, it would be extremely difficult, if not impossible, for the beneficiary to disprove the allegations of the insurance company that irregularities were present in the procurement of the policy. Were there no time limit on the right of the insurance company to question the accuracy of the information provided in the application, there would be no certainty during the life of the policy that the benefits promised by it would be payable at maturity. The honest policyholder needs an assurance that, upon his death his beneficiary will be the "recipient of a check and not of a lawsuit."[3] The incontestable clause provides that assurance. It is based upon the theory that after the company has had a reasonable opportunity to investigate the circumstances surrounding the issue of a life insurance policy, it should thereafter relinquish the right to question the validity of the contract.

Originally introduced by voluntary action in 1864, the incontestable clause had become so firmly entrenched and so obviously beneficial to all parties concerned by the time of the Armstrong Investigation in 1906 that the legislation which grew out of the investigation made mandatory the inclusion of the clause in life insurance policies. Other states followed New York's example so that, today, the clause is generally required by statute. The laws of the various states differ as to the form of the clause prescribed, but none permits a clause which would make the policy in general contestable for more than two years.

Effect of Fraud

It is generally agreed that the original purpose of the incontestable clause was to protect the beneficiary of a life insurance policy against the *innocent* misrepresentations or concealments of the insured. As a matter of fact, there was considerable doubt in the early years of its

[2] *Kansas Mutual Life Insurance Co.* v. *Whitehead,* 123 Ky. 21, 26 (1906).

[3] Horne and Mansfield, *op. cit.,* p. 181.

use that the incontestable clause could operate as a bar to the denial of liability on the grounds of fraud. It is a basic tenet of contract law that fraud in the formation of a contract renders such contract voidable at the option of the innocent party. Moreover, in general, parties to a contract are not permitted to contract for immunity from the consequences of their fraud. These two rules would seem to limit the applicability of the incontestable clause to inadvertent misrepresentations or concealments. Nevertheless, over the years, judicial interpretation has firmly established the principle that the incontestable clause is effective against fraud. Even more to the point, since no reputable life insurance company is likely to contest a policy unless there is evidence of intent to deceive, it may be concluded that the primary function, if not the purpose, of the incontestable clause is to protect the insured and his beneficiaries against the consequences of his fraudulent behavior.

In holding that the expiration of the contestable period precludes a defense even on the grounds of fraud, the courts have been careful to emphasize that they are not condoning fraud. They justify their action on the ground that the company has a reasonable period of time in which to discover any fraud involved in the procurement of the policy and is under obligation to seek redress within the permissible period of time. In line with this reasoning, one court stated:

> This view does not exclude the consideration of fraud, but allows the parties to fix by stipulation the length of time which fraud of the insured can operate to deceive the insurer. It recognizes the right of the insurer, predicated upon a vast experience and profound knowledge in such matters, to agree that in a stipulated time, fixed by himself, he can unearth and drag to light any fraud committed by the insured, and protect himself from the consequences. . . . The incontestable clause is upheld in law, not for the purpose of upholding fraud, but for the purpose of shutting off harassing defenses based upon alleged fraud; and, in so doing, the law merely adopts the certificate of the insurer that within a given time he can expose and render innocuous any fraud in the preliminary statement of the insured. . . .[4]

The incontestable clause has been described as a private contractual "statute of limitation" on fraud, prescribing a period shorter than that incorporated in the statutory enactment. This analogy with conventional statutes of limitations has been questioned by some,[5] but the

[4] *Kansas Mutual Life Insurance Co.* v. *Whitehead,* 123 Ky. 21, 26 (1906).

[5] Critics of this analogy point out that (*a*) the usual statute of limitations begins to run from the time the fraud is discovered, whereas under the incontestable clause, the

basic purpose of the two instrumentalities is the same: to bar the assertion of legal rights after the evidence concerning the cause of action has grown stale and key witnesses are no longer readily available.

The courts recognize that some unscrupulous persons are permitted to profit by their fraudulent action through the operation of the incontestable clause, but they proceed on the premise that the social advantages of the clause outweigh the undesirable consequences. "The view is that even though dishonest people are given advantages under incontestability clauses which any right-minded man is loath to see them get, still the sense of security given to the great mass of honest policyholders by the presence of the clause in their policies makes it worth the cost."[6]

There is a minority view that a policy procured through fraud should be contestable at any time. The fact that the burden of proof is upon the company is deemed sufficient to protect the honest policyholder. An advocate of this view has stated:

> If the laws had exempted cases of fraud from the operation of the provision, or if the courts had interpreted the provision as not applying in cases of fraud, not a single person of the class intended to be protected by the provision could possibly have suffered. Fraud is never assumed to exist; it must be proved affirmatively, and all policies would, therefore, fall into two completely separated groups—those proved to have been secured by fraud and those not so proved. It is, therefore, wholly possible to secure the full protection desired for all policyholders not proved to have secured their policies by fraud without the incidental condonation of fraud.[7]

Despite the general adherence of the courts to the doctrine that the incontestable clause is a bar to a defense of fraud, there are some species of fraud so abhorrent that their nullification through the incontestable clause is regarded to be in contravention of public policy. For example, the incontestable clause has been held not to apply when the contract was negotiated with intent to murder the insured, even

---

period runs from the beginning of the contract; and (*b*) the typical statute of limitations applies to actions and not to defenses such as those invoked by life insurance companies during the period of contestability. See Benjamin L. Holland, "The Incontestable Clause," in Harry Krueger and Leland T. Waggoner (ed.), *The Life Insurance Policy Contract* (Boston: Little, Brown & Co., 1953), p. 58. These critics are content to identify the incontestable clause as a constituent part of the contract and peculiar to a life insurance policy.

[6] *Maslin* v. *Columbian National Life Insurance Co.,* 3 *Fed. Supp.* 368 (1932); Dist. Ct. S.D.N.Y.

[7] J. F. Little, "Discussion of the Incontestable Clause," *Transactions of the Actuarial Society of America,* Vol. XXXVI (1935), p. 429.

though the murderer was not the beneficiary.[8] In cases where the applicant lacks an insurable interest, the courts generally permit the insurer to deny liability beyond the contestable period.[9] Likewise, in those cases where someone, presumably a healthier person and usually the beneficiary, has impersonated the applicant for purposes of undergoing the medical examination and answering the questions pertaining to the health of the applicant, the courts have uniformly held the purported contract to be null and void, on the grounds that there has been no real meeting of minds.[10] Finally, in a few cases, the courts have recognized execution for crime as legitimate grounds for denial of liability,[11] although in other cases, the company has been held liable.[12]

Meaning of a Contest

A policy can be prevented from becoming incontestable only by appropriate legal action on the part of the company during the contestable period or, under one type of incontestable clause (to be described later), by the death of the insured during the contestable period. The courts hold that there must be a "contest" during the contestable period, and it becomes a matter of interpretation as to what constitutes a "contest" within the meaning of the clause.

In some jurisdictions, a notice of rescission, accompanied by a return of the premium, is deemed to constitute a contest. The majority of the courts, however, have held that the requirement can be satisfied only by a suit for rescission before a court of competent jurisdiction or by a defense to a judicial proceeding in such a court seeking to enforce the contract. In the first instance, the company would be seeking rescission by a suit in equity; in the second case, it would be defending against an action at law instituted by the beneficiary in an attempt to collect the proceeds. A suit for rescission is permitted only when there is no adequate remedy at law; and in most jurisdictions, defense against a beneficiary's action is regarded as an adequate remedy. Equity proceedings, however, are always available to the com-

---

[8] *Columbian Mutual Life Insurance Co.* v. *Martin,* 175 Tenn. 517, 136 S.W. (2d) 52 (1940).

[9] See Holland, *op. cit.,* p. 68, n. 27, for citations.

[10] *Ibid.,* p. 69 and citations in n. 31.

[11] *Scarborough* v. *American National Insurance Co.,* 171 N.C. 353, 88 S.E. 482 (1916); and *Murphy* v. *Metropolitan Life Insurance Co.,* 152 Ga. 393, 110 S.E. 178 (1921).

[12] *Afro-American Life Insurance Co.* v. *Jones,* 113 Fla. 158, 151 So. 405 (1933).

pany while the insured is alive (during the contestable period) and, as is pointed out below, are usually available after the death of the insured under certain types of incontestable clause.

Detailed rules of legal procedure have been evolved to establish the precise moment at which a contest has materialized. Once the contest has been joined, the running of the contestable period is stopped; and irrespective of the outcome of the initial contest, the incontestable clause cannot be invoked to forestall any other proceeding. Thus, if a contest is initiated with the insured during the contestable period, the beneficiary may be made a party to the proceedings after the expiration of the period specified in the incontestable clause.

The interpretation of the term "contest" is important in another respect. Broadly interpreted, the incontestable clause could prohibit the denial of any type of claim after the contestable period has expired. It could force the company to pay a type of claim that was never envisioned under the contract. Fortunately, the majority of the courts do not interpret the clause in that manner. They make a distinction between contests that question the validity or existence of a contract and those that seek to clarify the terms of the contract or to enforce the terms of the contract. In one widely cited case, the court said:

> It must be clear that every resistance by an insurer against the demands of the beneficiary is in one sense a contest, but it is not a contest of the policy; that is, not a contest against the terms of the policy but a contest for or in favor of the terms of the policy. In other words, there are two classes of contests; one to enforce the policy, the other to destroy it. Undoubtedly the term "incontestable" as used in a life insurance policy means a contest, the purpose of which is to destroy the validity of the policy, and not a contest, the purpose of which is to demand its enforcement.[13]

The significance of this distinction will be brought out in the discussion dealing with the application of the incontestable clause to other contract provisions.

Inception of the Contestable Period

Where the *operative date* of a life insurance policy coincides with the *effective date*, there can be no question as to when the contestable period begins to run. It begins the day following the date on the policy. Where, however, the effective date of protection is earlier than the date of the policy, some courts have made the beginning of the contestable period coincide with the commencement of insurance cover-

[13] *Stean* v. *Occidental Life Insurance Co.,* 24 N.M. 346, 171 Pac. 786 (1918).

age, regardless of the date of the policy. On the other hand, where the policy has been antedated so that the date of the policy is earlier than the effective date of coverage, the courts, applying the rule of construction most favorable to the insured, have usually held that the contestable period begins with the date of the policy. This is true whether the clause provides that the policy shall be incontestable after a specified period from the "date of the policy" or the "date of issue." Where the policy makes it clear that the contestable period starts to run only from the time the policy actually becomes effective, there is no reason to apply the rule of construction most favorable to the insured, and the courts will give effect to the contract as written.

TYPES OF INCONTESTABLE CLAUSES

The incontestable clause has gone through a period of evolution, various changes in wording having been made from time to time, usually to nullify the unfavorable interpretations developed out of litigation. The earliest forms were quite simple, and one that was to become involved in a precedent-making court decision read as follows: "After two years, this policy shall be noncontestable except for the nonpayment of premiums as stipulated. . . ." This clause served satisfactorily for many years until the celebrated "Monahan Decision" impaired its usefulness to the companies.[14] In that case, the insured died within the two-year period; and the company denied liability, alleging a breach of warranty. The beneficiary waited until the two-year period had expired and then brought suit against the company. The company defended on the grounds of breach of warranty, but the Supreme Court of Illinois held that the policy was incontestable and found for the beneficiary. This decision, which was accepted as a precedent in virtually all jurisdictions, established the far-reaching principle that the contestable period continued to run after the insured's death.

The practical effect of the Monahan decision was that if the policyholder should die within the contestable period, the company was forced to go into court during the contestable period to seek a rescission if it wanted to deny liability for any reason. If no action was brought before the period expired, the company was estopped from erecting any defense other than lapse from nonpayment of premiums. Much litigation was thus thrust upon the companies to avert claims

[14] *Monahan* v. *Metropolitan Life Insurance Co.*, 283 Ill. 136, 119 N.E. 68 (1918).

which they regarded to be unwarranted, to their detriment in the esteem of the public.

In an effort to avoid the undesirable consequences of the Monahan case, many companies adopted a clause which provides that the policy shall be incontestable after it has been *in force* for a specified period. It was believed that with such a clause, the death of the insured would stop the running of the period, since the policy would no longer be in force. When the clause was tested in the courts, however, the decisions, with some exceptions, held that a policy does not terminate with the death of the insured but continues "in force" for the benefit of the beneficiary. In other words, the contract still has to be performed. Thus, this clause has the same weakness as that which was litigated in the Monahan case. Despite this disadvantage, many companies have continued to use the clause, since it permits suits in equity, which are usually tried without a jury.

Those companies that were willing to give up the advantage of suits in equity modified their incontestable clause to make the policy incontestable after it has been in force *during the lifetime of the insured* for a specified period. The courts have uniformly agreed that under this clause, the death of the insured during the contestable period suspends the operation of the clause and fixes the rights of the parties as of the date of death. Under such a clause, if the insured dies during the specified period, the policy never becomes incontestable, and the claimant cannot gain any advantage by postponing notification of claim until the specified period has expired. However, since a legal remedy is available—i.e., a defense against a suit instituted by the beneficiary—the company cannot obtain rescission of the policy by a suit in equity, except during the lifetime of the insured.

A final type of clause that is used by a number of leading companies provides that (with certain exceptions, to be noted) "this policy shall be incontestable after one year from its date of issue unless the insured dies in such year, in which event it shall be incontestable after two years from its date of issue." This clause does not solve the problem created by the Monahan decision, since the death of the insured during the first year does not suspend the running of the period. However, should the insured die during the first year, the company will have a *minimum* of one year in which to investigate the circumstances of the case and, if desired, to institute a suit for rescission. Under all of the other types of clauses except the one requiring survivorship of the insured, it is possible for the company to have only a few days in which to investigate a suspicious death; in fact, it is quite likely that in many cases, the company would receive no notice of the death of the insured until the contestable period had expired. The clause described in this paragraph is more favorable to the insured than the usual clauses, since, if he survives the first year, the policy becomes incontestable at that time, and if he does not survive the first year, the company's rights are no greater than they would have been under the typical clause. It should be noted, however, that some companies limit the contestability of their policies to one year, whether or not the insured survives the period.

At one time, some companies, in the thought that they were making their policies more attractive, introduced a clause providing that the policy should be incontestable *from the date of issue,* except as to nonpayment of premiums. As it turned out, this clause provided less protection to the insured than any of the other types that have been used. The courts generally regarded this clause as an attempt to provide immunity to the insured against the consequences of his own fraud and refused to enforce it where fraud was involved. The clause protects the policyholder against an innocent misrepresentation or concealment, but does not prevent a defense based on fraud. In other words, the policy *never* becomes incontestable with respect to *fraud.* This unusual and unanticipated result is based on the fact that the clause made provision for no period during which the validity of the policy could be attacked on the ground of fraud.[15]

It is interesting to observe that the policies issued to members of the military and naval service by the federal government under its various insurance programs contained this type of incontestable clause. As a matter of fact, the clause specifically excluded fraud (and certain other conditions) from the benefits of incontestability. Yet, in its promotional material, the Veterans Administration has consistently pointed to the incontestable clause as one of the favorable (to the insured) features of its policies.

---

[15] There is a minority view that such clauses are enforceable even as against fraud, on the reasoning that if the insurer can properly limit its right to ferret out fraud in the procurement of the policy to a specified period after issuance of the policy, it can delay the issuance until it is satisfied that no fraud is present (*Duvall* v. *National Insurance Co. of Montana,* 28 Idaho 356, 154 Pac. 632 [1916]; *Pacific Mutual Life Insurance Co.* v. *Strange,* 223 Ala. 226, 135 So. 477 [1931]; *Mutual Life of New York* v. *Weinberg,* 319 Ill. App. 177, 49 N. E. [2d] 44 [1943]).

MATTERS SPECIFICALLY EXCLUDED FROM OPERATION OF THE INCONTESTABLE CLAUSE

Nonpayment of Premiums

The original incontestable clause excluded the nonpayment of premiums from its operation, and the practice has continued to the present. This exception is not only superfluous today, but has created confusion as to the applicability of the clause to matters not specifically excluded. Payment of the first premium, or the first installment of the first premium, is a consideration of the life insurance contract and is usually made a condition precedent. Unless this requirement is satisfied, there is no contract and hence no incontestable clause. If subsequent premiums are not paid, the contract does not fail as of its inception and may, in fact, continue in force under the surrender provisions.

This has not always been the case, however, and there was probably some justification for the inclusion of the exception in the original clause. Early policies contained no surrender values; and default in premium, even years after issue of the policy, resulted in avoidance of the contract from its inception. It is clear, though, that the termination or modification of a modern policy through nonpayment of premiums is not a contest of the policy. Nevertheless, the historical precedent and the requirements of state statutes have made the exception a fixture.

The express exclusion of nonpayment of premium and other conditions from the operation of the incontestable clause has caused many courts to apply the doctrine of *expressio unius est exclusio alterius*[16] to the attempts of the company to avoid liability under other provisions of the policy. Under such a doctrine, if a particular hazard were not specifically excluded from the operation of the clause, a claim arising from that hazard could not be avoided beyond the contestable period.

Disability and Accidental Death Benefits

It is also customary to exclude from the operation of the incontestable clause the provisions of the policy relating to disability and acci-

[16] "The enumeration of some is the exclusion of others," usually paraphrased as "enumeration implies exclusion."

dental death benefits. A typical clause containing these exclusions might read as follows: "This policy shall be incontestable after it shall have been in force for two years from its date of issue except for nonpayment of premiums and except as to provisions relating to benefits payable in the event of total and permanent disability and provisions which grant additional insurance specifically against death by accident."

If the courts could be relied upon to interpret the incontestable clause in accordance with its basic objective, it would be unnecessary specifically to exclude disability and accidental death benefits from its scope. Unfortunately, they have had some difficulty in distinguishing between a contest involving the validity of the policy and one relating to the coverage of an admittedly valid policy. The distinction is a critical one in connection with disability and accidental death provisions, since it is frequently difficult to determine whether a claim filed under one of these provisions is valid. In order to avoid any possible conflict with the incontestable clause in the adjudication of such claims, the companies chose to keep the provisions entirely outside the operation of the clause. Under the type of clause cited above, the *validity* of the provisions relating to disability and double indemnity can be attacked at any time, even after the expiration of the contestable period. The courts' interpretations frequently turn on the precise wording of the clause; and in some cases, it has been held that the validity of the provisions cannot be questioned beyond the period of contestability. In New York, a provision relating to total disability benefits must be incontestable after three years.

The exclusion of disability benefits from the protection of the incontestable clause is not in conflict with the intent of the clause. The purpose of the clause is to forestall a contest over the validity of the contract after the insured is dead and cannot defend the representations he made in the application for insurance. Disability claims are filed during the lifetime of the insured, and he can defend his actions, both at the time he applied for the policy and at the time of the claim.

Military or Naval Service

The laws of most states permit, as a specific exception to the incontestable clause, "violation of any provision of the policy relating to naval or military service in time of war." Except during wartime or when war was imminent, it has not been the practice to include in the policy any restrictions as to military or naval service. Even when a so-called "war clause" has been used, it has not been customary to exclude it from the operations of the incontestable clause.

RELATIONSHIP TO OTHER POLICY PROVISIONS

Excepted Hazards

At one time, it was the view of the courts and the state insurance departments that once the contestable period had expired, no denial of liability on the grounds of lack of coverage could be sustained unless the hazard involved in the litigation was specifically excluded in the incontestable clause itself. Moreover, no hazard could be excluded from the scope of the incontestable clause unless such exclusion was recognized in the statute governing the clause.[17] This doctrine was attacked when the Superintendent of Insurance of the state of New York refused to approve a proposed aviation exclusion in a policy of the Metropolitan Life Insurance Company, on the ground that the exclusion was in conflict with the New York statute prescribing the substance of the incontestable clause. The decision of the superintendent was appealed to the courts, and the issue was resolved in what is known as the "Conway Decision." The New York Court of Appeals, with Judge Cardozo sitting as chief judge, ruled that there was nothing in the law which prohibited the issuance of such a restricted policy. The decision declared that the New York statute requiring an incontestable clause "is not a mandate as to coverage, a definition of hazards to be borne by the insurer. It means only this, that within the limits of the coverage, the policy shall stand, unaffected by any defense that it was invalid by reason of a condition broken. . . .[Where] there has been no assumption of risk, there can be no liability. . . ."[18] Following the Conway decision, the various insurance commissioners reversed their rulings on the inclusion of aviation riders; and today, it is the accepted view that a company may exclude any hazard which it does not wish to cover.

In general, the right to limit coverage has been invoked only with respect to aeronautical activities, military and naval service in time of war, and suicide. With advances in aeronautics, the aviation exclusion has lost most of its significance, and war clauses are not currently

[17] This is still the case.

[18] *Metropolitan Life Insurance Co.* v. *Conway,* 252 N.Y. 449, 169 N.E. 642 (1930).

being added to policies. Limitations on the coverage of suicide, however, are contained in all policies. In New York and a few other states, there are now statutes listing permissible exclusions.

Since the Conway decision, the companies could undoubtedly exclude death from suicide throughout the duration of the contract, unless prohibited by statute. They feel, however, that it is a risk which should properly be assumed by insurance companies, and their only concern is that they not be exposed to the risk of issuing policies to persons contemplating suicide. Consequently, they exclude death from suicide, whether the insured be sane or insane, for the first year or two after issue of the policy, with the risk thereafter being assumed in its entirety by the company. If the insured should commit suicide during the period of restricted coverage, the company's liability is limited to a refund of the premiums paid.

While the suicide exclusion is normally of the same duration as the contestable period, the suicide clause is independent of the incontestable clause. Since most suicide exclusions are of two years' duration and some policies are contestable for only one year, a conflict could develop if the insured commits suicide during the second year of the contract. With few exceptions, the courts have upheld the right of the company to deny coverage of suicide beyond the contestable period.

Conditions Precedent

The incontestable clause is a part of the policy and cannot become effective until the policy has gone into force. There must be a contract before there can be an incontestable clause. Therefore, the incontestable clause does not bar a defense that the policy was never approved.[19]

On principle, it would seem that if a policy provides that it will not become effective until certain conditions have been fulfilled, there would be no contract at all until such conditions had been satisfied. Hence, the incontestable clause itself, being a part of the contract, would not be operative. This would suggest that the incontestable clause should not prevent the insurer from denying liability on the grounds that the applicant was not in good health at the time the policy was delivered or that some other condition precedent was not fulfilled. However, most of the courts have reached the conclusion that

---

[19] *McDonald* v. *Mutual Life Insurance Co. of New York,* 108 F. (2d) 32 (C.C.A. 6, 1939); *Harris* v. *Travelers Insurance Co.,* 80 F. (2d) 127 (C.C.A. 5, 1935).

the delivery-in-good-health requirement and other such conditions precedent should be accorded the same treatment as representations. Since the incontestable clause was designed to deal with misrepresentations, it follows that the clause should bar suits based on nonfulfillment of conditions precedent, if, at any time, both parties had treated the policy as having been operative.[20] This is the rule in most jurisdictions.

Misstatement of Age

Most life insurance policies contain a provision which stipulates that in the event of a misstatement of age, the amount payable under the policy will be such as would have been purchased at the correct age by the premium actually paid. In most states, a provision to this effect is required by statute. In jurisdictions where the provision is mandatory, no conflict with the incontestable clause can arise. Even where the clause is not a matter of statute, the right of the company to reduce the amount of insurance after the contestable period has expired has seldom been questioned. This is undoubtedly due to the fact that the misstatement-of-age adjustment was firmly established before any controversy developed over the right of a company to limit the coverage of a policy beyond the contestable period. If it had been held that misstatement-of-age adjustments were subject to the incontestable clause, the companies would probably have found it necessary to require proof of age before issuance of a policy.

A misstatement of age which contravenes a company's underwriting rules may, at the company's option, serve as a basis for rescission. It has been held, however, that such action would have to be taken during the contestable period.[21] If the misstatement were discovered beyond the contestable period, it could still be dealt with in the conventional manner.

Reformation

It sometimes happens that a life insurance policy in the form issued by the company does not represent the actual agreement between the company and the applicant. This may be due to simple clerical errors, such as a misspelled name or an incorrect date, or to more substantial mistakes, such as an incorrect premium, wrong face

---

[20] See Holland, *op. cit.* p. 64, n. 10, for citations.

[21] *Kelly* v. *Prudential Insurance Co.*, 334 Pa. 143, 6 A. (2d) 55 (1939).

amount, inappropriate set of surrender values, or incorrect set of settlement options. The mistake may favor either the insured or the company. The overwhelming majority of such mistakes are rectified without any controversy or litigation. From time to time, however, a policyholder will oppose the correction of a mistake in his favor. In one such case,[22] the policy actually applied for and issued was an ordinary life contract; but through a printer's error, the surrender values shown in the contract were those for a twenty-year endowment insurance policy. The company discovered the error two months after the policy was issued but had to resort to legal action to rewrite the contract.

The appropriate legal action in such circumstances is a suit for reformation of the contract. This is an equitable remedy under which the written instrument is made to conform to the intention of the parties.[23] The party seeking relief must establish the fact that there was either a mutual mistake in the drafting of the written instrument[24] or a mistake on one side and fraud on the other.

The remedy of reformation is clearly available to an insurance company during the contestable period. Moreover, it has long been the rule that reformation to correct a clerical error is not barred by the incontestable clause. A suit to rectify a mistake "is not a contest of the policy but a prayer to make a written instrument speak the real agreement of the parties."[25] In 1948, however, the Ninth Circuit Court of Appeals departed from the rule that had been regarded as well established and held that reformation was in conflict with incontestability.[26] The court reasoned that the words "this contract" appearing in the incontestable clause apply to the printed provisions of the policy of which the clause is a part, and not to the oral conversation and negotiations that preceded the execution of the contract. It was pointed out that "the clause does not say that the insurer shall not contest his liability under the actual agreement; it says *this* contract shall be incontestable." This case was later held to be contrary to the law of Cali-

---

[22] *Columbian National Life Insurance Co.* v. *Black,* 35 F. (2d) 571 (C.C.A. 10, 1929).

[23] The introduction of oral testimony is permitted in such cases, notwithstanding the fact that in so doing, the terms of the written instrument are changed. This is an exception to the parol evidence rule, discussed earlier.

[24] In this connection, it is held that knowledge by one party of the other's mistake is equivalent to a mutual mistake.

[25] *Columbian National Life Insurance Co.* v. *Black,* 35 F. (2d) 571 (C.C.A. 10, 1929).

[26] *Richardson* v. *Travelers Insurance Co.,* 171 F. (2d) 699 (C.C.A. 9, 1948).

fornia,[27] and the only other reported case since the Richardson decision followed the majority rule that reformation is not barred by the expiration of the contestable period.[28]

Reinstatement

All life insurance policies contain a provision permitting reinstatement in the event of lapse, subject to certain conditions. One of the conditions is usually "evidence of insurability satisfactory to the company." Reinstatement will almost always necessitate a statement by the insured as to the current status of his health and will frequently involve a complete medical examination. It will also involve aspects of insurability other than health, just as at the time of original issue. A question arises as to the legal effect of a misrepresentation or concealment in the reinstatement application not discovered until after the policy has been reinstated. Specifically, can a reinstated policy be rescinded after the original contestable period has expired?

There are conflicting views on this point. One view, greatly in the minority, holds that the concept of incontestability does not apply to the reinstatement process.[29] Under this view, a suit for rescission or a defense against a claim would be subject only to the conventional statute of limitations on fraud—which, it will be recalled, begins to run only *after the fraud has been discovered.*

At the other extreme, and likewise in the minority, is the view that the reinstatement clause is subject to the original incontestable clause.[30] If the original period of contestability has expired before the application for reinstatement is submitted, the reinstated policy is incontestable from the date of reinstatement. If a policy is reinstated during the original period of contestability, the reinstated policy can be contested during the remaining portion of the contestable period.

The majority opinion adopts a middle ground and holds that a reinstated policy is contestable for the same period of time as is prescribed in the original incontestable clause.[31] If the policy was originally con-

---

[27] *Mutual Life Insurance Company of New York* v. *Simon,* 151 Fed. Supp. 408 (1957).

[28] *Prudential Insurance Co.* v. *Strickland,* 187 F. (2d) 67 (1951). See also G. Frank Purvis, Jr., "Reformation of Life Policies," *Proceedings* of the Legal Section of the American Life Convention, 1957, p. 179.

[29] *Acacia Mutual Life Assn.* v. *Kaul,* 114 N.J. Eq. 491, 169 Atl. 36 (Ch. 1933); *Chuz* v. *Columbian National Life Insurance Co.,* 10 N.J. Misc. 1145, 162 Atl. 395 (Cir. Ct. Essex Co., 1932).

[30] See Holland, *op. cit.,* p. 78, n. 2, for citations.

[31] *Ibid.,* p. 78, n. 3.

testable for a period of two years, the reinstated policy would again be contestable for the same length of time. This is true even when the policy is lapsed and reinstated before the original period of contestability has expired. The reasoning is that the company needs the same period of time in which to detect any fraud in the application for reinstatement as it needed in connection with the original issue. It is hardly necessary to add that the policy becomes contestable again only with respect to the information supplied in connection with the reinstatement process. In other words, the company does not have restored to it the right to question the validity of the contract on the grounds of irregularities in the original application.

CHAPTER VIII

The Beneficiary

THE BENEFICIARY is the person named in the life insurance contract to receive all or a portion of the proceeds payable at maturity. The section of the contract dealing with the designation and rights of the beneficiary is, in many respects, the most significant one in the entire contract. It is the only one over which the insured has any control. In effect, this portion of the contract is written by the insured. It reflects the decisions of the insured concerning the disposition of his human life value. It is the means by which he can provide financial security to his family after he has passed from the scene. In a well-planned estate, the beneficiary designations will be integrated with the election of settlement option in such a manner as most effectively to carry out the insured's objectives.

There are many facets to a study of the beneficiary in life insurance, and the starting point should be a description of the various categories of beneficiaries and beneficiary designations. Emphasis is placed on customary situations and policy provisions, and the reader is cautioned that any particular case is decided on the basis of its own facts and the policy wording involved.

TYPES OF BENEFICIARIES

Beneficiaries can be classified from various points of view. For the purposes of this discussion, they will be classified as to (1) nature of the interest, (2) manner of identification, (3) priority of entitlement, and (4) revocability of the designation.

Nature of the Interest

From the standpoint of the interest involved, beneficiaries fall into two broad categories: *the insured* or his estate; and a person or persons other than the insured, normally referred to as a *third-party beneficiary*.

The insured normally designates himself as the person to receive the proceeds of an endowment insurance policy or a retirement income policy, since those policies were primarily designed to provide benefits to the policyholder himself. He may designate someone else to receive the proceeds in the event of his death, or he may specify that the proceeds be payable to his estate. Proceeds are usually made payable to the estate only for a purpose associated with the settlement of the estate, such as the payment of last-illness and funeral expenses, debts, mortgages, and taxes. If any proceeds remain after the claims against the estate have been satisfied, they are distributed in accordance with the decedent's will or the appropriate intestate law. It is considered highly undesirable, however, to have the proceeds of a policy payable to the insured's estate when it is intended that they should go to certain specific individuals. The proceeds will be subject to estate administration and may be reduced through probate costs, taxes, and the claims of creditors. Moreover, distribution to the intended beneficiaries will be delayed until settlement of the estate has been completed.

When it is intended that the proceeds be paid to the insured's estate and be subject to the control of the executor or administrator, as the case may be, the proper designation is "the executors or administrators of the insured." If the policy involved is an endowment or a retirement income policy and the proceeds are to be paid to the insured if he survives to the date of maturity and to his estate if he does not so survive, the proper designation is "insured, if living; otherwise to his executors or administrators." The simple designation "insured's estate" would undoubtedly be effective; but such terms as "heirs," "legal heirs," or "family" would not be. When the latter terms are used, the proceeds do not become part of the probate estate. The appropriate intestate law will be followed in determining the legal heirs; but the latter will receive the proceeds directly, being treated as named beneficiaries, rather than heirs. In other words, the proceeds will pass outside the probate estate.

When the insured was the applicant and designates himself or his estate as beneficiary, he is regarded as the owner of the policy and can exercise all rights under the policy without the consent of any other person. The policy is his property and can be dealt with like any other property.

The insured as beneficiary has been considered at some length, since the remainder of the chapter will be concerned with third-party beneficiaries.

Any person or organization other than the insured who is designated to receive insurance proceeds is known as a *third-party beneficiary*. Three general types of third-party beneficiary can be distinguished. The first is the owner-applicant, sometimes referred to as the "assured." This is the situation in which one person procures insurance on another person's life and becomes the owner of the policy. Ordinarily, the owner will designate himself as beneficiary, although it is not inconceivable that he would direct that the proceeds be paid to someone other than himself, particularly in the event that he should predecease the insured. This type of arrangement is identified with key-man insurance and business continuation agreements, but it is by no means confined to such situations. It may be used by a creditor to protect his interest, or by a family group to provide estate liquidity and minimize death taxes. From the standpoint of ownership rights, the third-party owner occupies the same position as the insured who designates himself as beneficiary. There is the difference—of no legal significance—that the insured owns his policy because he is the only party involved, whereas the third-party owner has his rights established by an express provision in the contract.

The third-party applicant must have an insurable interest in the insured at the inception of the contract. There need be no insurable interest at the date of the insured's death; and the third-party owner, or the beneficiary of his choice, is entitled to retain the full amount of the proceeds.

The second type of third-party beneficiary is the person who has furnished a valuable consideration in exchange for the designation. A creditor may be designated as beneficiary under a policy on his debtor's life, although it is much more common for the policy to be assigned to the creditor. In either event, the creditor is permitted to retain only that portion of the proceeds equal to his interest at the time of the debtor's death. During the insured's lifetime, he could exercise no rights in the policy without the consent or joinder of the insured. Occasionally, a wife is designated beneficiary under a policy as part of a divorce settlement. Her rights would depend upon the terms of the settlement. The designation is usually irrevocable or, if revocable, can be changed only by an appropriate court order.

The third type of beneficiary other than the insured is the person who has furnished no consideration. Technically, this type is known as the *donee* or *gratuitous* beneficiary. This is the typical situation where the insured designates a member of his family as beneficiary for no consideration other than "love and affection." It is not necessary for the donee beneficiary to have an insurable interest, although she usually does. The discussion in the succeeding pages will be directed at the donee beneficiary, unless a specific notation is made to the contrary.

Manner of Identification

Classified as to the manner of identification, beneficiaries may be termed *specific* or *class*. A specific beneficiary is an individual who is designated by name or in any other manner which clearly sets him or her apart from any other individual. A class beneficiary is a person not mentioned by name who belongs to a clearly identifiable *group* of persons designated as beneficiaries.

In making specific designations, it is customary to identify the person both by *name* and *relationship* to the insured, if there is a legal or blood relationship. For example, a wife would be designated as "Mary Smith Doe, wife of the insured." A son would be designated as "Charles William Doe, son of the insured." The full name—i.e., the first, middle, and surname—should preferably be given. The wife's maiden name should be included to prevent confusion and litigation in the event that there should be an antecedent or subsequent wife with the same given name. It invites litigation to designate the insured's spouse simply as "wife," without any name, or to use the insured's name with the word "Mrs." prefixed, such as "Mrs. John Doe." In both of these cases, if the insured should be married more than once, there is likely to be controversy as to whether the designation refers to the woman who was married to the insured at the time he made the designation or the one married to him at the time of his death.

The relationship stated in the designation is regarded as descriptive only and not as a condition of entitlement. That is, if a beneficiary is identifiable by name or otherwise, she will be entitled to the proceeds even though the stated relationship to the insured is no longer applicable—or never was. For example, if a man were to purchase a policy prior to marriage and designate his fiancée by name as beneficiary, describing her as his wife, his death prior to the marriage ceremony would not deprive her of the proceeds. Nor would an invalid marriage have any effect on the beneficiary's entitlement.

A class designation is appropriate whenever the insured desires that the proceeds be divided equally among the members of a particular group, the composition of which may not be definitely fixed as of the time of designation. Examples of such groups are children, grandchildren, brothers, sisters, or heirs. Perhaps the most common class designation is "children of the insured." This type of class designation is especially favored for the designation of secondary or contingent beneficiaries. It may also be used in combination with a specific designation, such as where the insured designates his living children by name and then adds "and any other surviving children born of the marriage of the insured and Mary Smith Doe, wife of the insured."

From the standpoint of the law, class designations are entirely proper. Courts have repeatedly sustained the validity of such designations. From a practical standpoint, however, class designations present the problem of identifying the members of the class. No class designation is entirely free of possible complications. Even the simplest designations can cause difficulties. For example, the designation "children of the insured" would seem to circumscribe the class precisely enough to permit of ready identification; but in discharging its responsibilities under such a designation, the insurance company would have to determine whether the insured was survived by any illegitimate children, children by a previous marriage or marriages, or adopted children. If the surviving children are adults, there is always the possibility that one has severed normal ties with the family, his whereabouts unknown to the other members of the family and perhaps even his existence denied or concealed by them. The designation "children born of the marriage of the insured and Mary Smith Doe, wife of the insured," while quite precise, does not of itself indicate whether adopted children of the marriage should be accorded the same status as natural children. For the sake of clarity, and to avoid possible litigation, some designations include a statement that the word "children" shall be construed as including adopted children. The use of the term "heirs" in a beneficiary designation will make it necessary for the company to refer to previous court rulings as to the meaning of the term in the jurisdiction involved or, lacking these, to seek court interpretation. Then, the company will have to identify and locate the heirs. The perils to the company in this process are such that many companies will not accept the designation of "heirs."

When either the insured or his wife has children by a previous marriage, a class designation must be carefully worded to carry out the insured's intentions. He may wish to provide for all his children and those of his wife by her former marriage, or he may want to confine his bounty to the children of his current marriage. If he specifies that the proceeds are to be paid to "my children" or "children of the insured," his children by any marriage would be included, but the children of his wife by her previous marriage would be excluded. On the other hand, by speaking of "my wife, Mary Smith Doe, and our children," he is not only excluding his wife's children by her former marriage but also any children he may have had by an earlier marriage and any he may have by a subsequent marriage.

Most companies today restrict the use of class designations. They will not accept designations of a class whose relationship to the insured is remote or whose composition will be difficult of determination. Where the class is acceptable, it must be described as precisely as possible. All companies permit the designation of children as a class. This is a useful device in protecting the interests of unborn children. Unless the companies were willing at least to supplement specific designations with a class designation of children not yet born, many children would be deprived of insurance protection through failure of the insured to revise his settlement plan after the birth of an additional child or children. At best, class designations lead to delays in the settlement of death claims. At their worst, they can involve considerable trouble and expense for the company and possibly even the double or multiple payment of some claims.

Priority of Entitlement

With respect to priority of entitlement, beneficiaries may be classified as *primary* and *contingent*. Among the various classes of beneficiary, the primary beneficiary has the first claim to the proceeds if the conditions on which they are payable to her are fulfilled. There may be two or more primary beneficiaries, in which event they will share the proceeds in the proportion specified by the insured. It is not implicit in such an arrangement that the beneficiaries share equally in the proceeds, except as to the members of a class. Class beneficiaries do share equally in the proceeds, since, without mentioning names, it is impracticable to provide disproportionate shares. With respect to her particular share, any one of a group of primary beneficiaries, whether specifically named or designated as a class, enjoys rights in the policy equal to those of any other beneficiary.

The contingent beneficiary, frequently called the *secondary* beneficiary, has a claim to the proceeds which ripens only upon the death or removal of the primary beneficiary. The basic concept of a contingent beneficiary is that of a person or an organization that takes the place of the primary beneficiary in the event that the latter should predecease the insured or lose her entitlement in some other manner before receiving any proceeds. With the increased use of installment settlement plans, however, the contingent beneficiary has assumed importance in another role—namely, to receive the benefits under an installment option payable beyond the death of the primary beneficiary. In this role, the contingent beneficiary can become entitled to benefits even though the primary beneficiary survives the insured. This function is of importance in connection with the interest option, installment time option, installment amount option, and guaranteed installments under life income options.

The two functions of the contingent beneficiary are quite distinctive, and her rights thereunder are quite different. Under the original concept, the contingent beneficiary becomes the primary beneficiary upon the death of the erstwhile primary beneficiary during the lifetime of the insured—subject, of course, to being divested of her position by the insured. In her new status, the former contingent beneficiary succeeds to all the rights of the original primary beneficiary, including those arising under the provisions for optional settlement. Upon the death of the insured, she would be regarded as a "first taker" beneficiary, with all that this status implies under company settlement option practices. She might be given the right to take the proceeds in a lump sum, to elect her own settlement option, and to designate her own contingent beneficiaries to receive any benefits unpaid at the time of her death.

Upon the death of the insured, proceeds payable in a lump sum vest immediately in the primary beneficiary (in the absence of a delay clause), and the interest of the contingent beneficiary or beneficiaries is terminated. Even though the primary beneficiary should die before receiving a check from the insurance company, the proceeds would go to her estate, rather than to the contingent beneficiary. If the proceeds are payable under an installment option, the contingent beneficiary would become entitled to the benefits upon the death of the primary beneficiary. She would be a "second taker" beneficiary, however, and under the practices of most companies, would have to take the proceeds under the distribution pattern prescribed for the primary beneficiary. In other words, a "second taker" contingent beneficiary is not usually permitted to commute the unpaid installments or to elect to have them paid out under a settlement arrangement different from that in effect for the primary beneficiary.

There may be, and usually are, two or more contingent beneficiaries of the first order of priority. The typical insured designates his wife as primary beneficiary and his children, by name or as a class, as contingent beneficiaries. For a lump-sum distribution, the designation might read as follows: "Mary Smith Doe, wife of the insured, if she survives the insured; otherwise in equal shares to the surviving children of the insured." If the proceeds are to be distributed under an installment option, a more complex designation is necessary.

There may be various degrees of contingent beneficiaries, each successive level having a lower order of entitlement to the proceeds. Thus, there may be "first contingent," "second contingent," and "third contingent" beneficiaries. Two levels of contingent beneficiaries are provided for in the following designation: "Mary Smith Doe, wife of the insured, if she survives the insured; otherwise in equal shares to the surviving children, if any, of the insured; otherwise to Harry Doe, father of the insured, if he survives the insured." If the proceeds are to be paid out under an installment option, the agreement usually specifies that any installments remaining unpaid at the death of the last surviving contingent beneficiary shall be paid in a lump sum to the estate of such beneficiary. This obviates the necessity of reopening the estate of the insured to receive the unpaid installments, which—if one or two levels of contingent beneficiaries have passed out of the picture—might precipitate a series of estate reopenings, with considerable expense and little benefit. Many persons designate an educational institution, hospital, or religious organization as the last contingent or ultimate contingent beneficiary. Among other purposes, it assures that the insured will not have a reversionary interest in the proceeds which, if of sufficient value, could cause the proceeds to be includable in his estate for federal estate tax purposes.

Right of Revocation

Under modern practice, the applicant for insurance is asked to indicate in the application whether or not he reserves the right to change the beneficiary. If he reserves such right, the designation is referred to as *revocable* and the designee as the *revocable beneficiary*. If the insured does not reserve the right to change the beneficiary, the designation is properly described as *irrevocable* and the designee as the *ir-*

revocable beneficiary. This distinction is so significant that a word on the historical development of the concept of revocability seems warranted.

Historical Development. The early contracts of life insurance in the United States made no provision for a change of beneficiary. The insured simply entered into a contract with the insurance company that upon his death, the company would pay a specified sum of money to the person designated as beneficiary—usually, the wife. Since there were no surrender values or other prematurity rights of significance to the insured, the person entitled to receive the death proceeds was regarded to be the owner of the policy. One of the early students of American insurance law had the following to say about the interest of the beneficiary:

> We apprehend the general rule to be that a policy, and the money to become due under it, belong the moment it is issued to the person or persons named in it as the beneficiary or beneficiaries, and that there is no power in the person procuring the insurance by any act of his or hers, by deed or by will, to transfer to any other person the interest of the person named.[1]

In 1888, the United States Supreme Court defined the interest of the beneficiary in substantially the same terms.[2]

In consonance with this concept of ownership of the policy by the beneficiary, the majority of the early court decisions held that the death of the beneficiary before the insured did not terminate her interest.[3] That is, the insured was not permitted to designate a substitute beneficiary; and upon his death, the proceeds were payable to the estate of the beneficiary originally named in the policy.

Around the turn of the century, some of the larger companies adopted the practice of including in their policies a provision which permitted the insured to substitute a new beneficiary even during the original beneficiary's lifetime, provided he had specifically reserved the right. Moreover, the change could be effected without the consent of the beneficiary. There was some doubt as to the validity of this practice until the standard forms which grew out of the Armstrong Investigation of 1905 and 1906, and became statutory (or compulsory) in New York on January 1, 1907, included a change of bene-

---

[1] George Bliss, *The Law of Life Insurance* (1871), quoted in James S. Burke, "Designation of the Beneficiary," in *The Beneficiary in Life Insurance* (Dan M. McGill, ed. (rev. ed.; Homewood, Ill.: Richard D. Irwin, Inc., 1956), p. 8.

[2] *Central National Bank* v. *Hume,* 128 U.S. 195, 9 Sup. Ct. 41 (1888).

[3] *Couch on Insurance,* 1006 (1930), and cases cited.

ficiary clause. This clause was supplemented shortly thereafter by another which stipulated that the beneficiary's interest, whether revocable or irrevocable, would terminate upon her death during the insured's lifetime, with such interest reverting to the insured. The designation of a contingent beneficiary to succeed to the interest of a deceased primary beneficiary was the next logical development.

Status of the Revocable Beneficiary. For some time after the validity of a reserved right to change the beneficiary had become well recognized, the revocable beneficiary was generally regarded to have a vested interest in the policy which could be defeated only by the exercise of the insured's right to revoke the designation. This view became known as the "defeasible vested interest" concept. Under that concept, it was believed that the consent of the beneficiary was necessary to the exercise of any policy rights by the insured other than the right to change the beneficiary. For example, the insured could not surrender or assign the policy, make a policy loan, or elect a settlement option without the consent of the beneficiary. Of course, there was nothing to prevent the insured from revoking the beneficiary designation and then exercising the various policy rights and privileges.

During the last quarter century, however, court after court has rejected the defeasible vested interest theory in favor of a more practicable rule which simplifies considerably the administration of policy rights. This modern rule, now prevailing in all but three states, holds that the interest of a revocable beneficiary is, at most, a mere expectancy, which is subject to every other interest created by the insured and to every policy right or privilege exercisable by the insured alone. Under this concept, consent of the beneficiary is not needed for the exercise by the insured of any policy right or privilege. Three states—Colorado, Massachusetts, and New Jersey—still maintain the view that a revocable beneficiary has a vested interest which is subject to divestment through a change of beneficiary accomplished in the manner prescribed by the policy. Even in those states, however, the insured is now permitted to make a policy loan without the consent of the revocable beneficiary.[4]

---

[4] *Anderson* v. *Broad Street Bank,* 90 N.J. Eq. 78, 105 Atl. 599 (1918); *John Hancock Mutual Life Insurance Co.* v. *Heidrich,* 135 N.J. Eq. 325, 38 A. (2d) 442 (1944); *David* v. *Metropolitan Life Insurance Co.,* 135 N.J.L. 106, 50 A. (2d) 651 (1947); *Strachan* v. *Prudential Insurance Co. of America,* 321 Mass. 507, 73 N.E. (2d) 840 (1947); *Muller* v. *Penn Mutual Life Insurance Co.,* 62 Colo. 245, 161 Pac. 148 (1916).

The interest of a revocable beneficiary, such as it is, terminates upon her death during the insured's lifetime. This is true even though there is no contingent beneficiary and the insured fails to appoint a successor beneficiary. Thus, the nature of the revocable beneficiary's interest comes into sharper focus. She has no enforceable rights in the policy prior to maturity and cannot interfere in any way with the exercise by the insured of his rights in the policy. She has an "expectancy" in the proceeds which will materialize only if *all* of the following conditions are fulfilled: (1) the policy remains in force until the death of the insured, (2) the beneficiary designation remains unchanged, (3) the policy is not assigned, and (4) the beneficiary outlives the insured. Despite the fulfillment of these conditions, the beneficiary's interest can be greatly impaired through policy loans negotiated by the insured.

On the positive side, the right of the insured to revoke a beneficiary designation is extinguished by his death, and the interest of the revocable beneficiary vests absolutely at that point. Her interest in the proceeds is, of course, subject to any deferred settlement agreement that might be operative, as well as to the rights of any contingent beneficiaries.

There are circumstances under which an insured who has reserved the right to change the beneficiary will not be permitted to exercise that right. If the policy was procured to secure a debt, or if—by agreement—the named beneficiary is to pay the premiums on the policy, the right to change the beneficiary is forfeited.[5] It has also been held that delivery of the policy to the insured's wife in consideration of marriage gives her a vested interest which cannot be defeated by the designation of another beneficiary by the insured.[6] Similarly, when a wife is designated beneficiary of a policy under an agreement made in contemplation of divorce, or when—by court order—an insured is directed to designate his divorced wife as beneficiary of a policy intended to serve as security for alimony payments or in lieu of such payments, the right to change the beneficiary is relinquished.[7] It should be understood that in all these circumstances, the insurance company would permit a change of beneficiary if it had received no notice of the limitation on the insured's right.

---

[5] *Wellhouse* v. *United Paper Co.*, 29 F. (2d) 886 (C.C.A. 5, 1929).

[6] *McDonald* v. *McDonald*, 110 So. 291 (Ala., 1926).

[7] *Mutual Life Insurance Co. of New York* v. *Franck*, 50 P. (2d) 480 (Cal. App., 1935).

Status of the Irrevocable Beneficiary. It is well settled that whenever the insured designates a particular person as beneficiary of a policy and does not reserve the right to revoke the designation, the beneficiary acquires a vested interest in the contract. The exact nature of the interest depends upon the terms of the contract. If there are no conditions under which the beneficiary could be deprived of the right to receive the full amount of proceeds payable under the terms of the policy, her interest would be vested absolutely or unconditionally, and she would be regarded as the sole owner of the policy. She could exercise all policy rights without the joinder of the insured and would even have the right to pay premiums to keep the policy in force. The insured would have no rights in the policy and, consequently, could do nothing with the contract, without the beneficiary's consent, which would in any way diminish or adversely affect the beneficiary's right to receive, at the insured's death, the full amount of insurance provided by the policy. If the beneficiary should predecease the insured, her interest in the policy would become a part of her estate, and her heirs would be entitled to the proceeds upon maturity of the policy.

Such absolute vesting is not common in modern policies. Most policies today provide that the interest of a beneficiary, even one irrevocably designated, shall terminate upon her death during the lifetime of the insured, with all rights reverting to the insured. This is sometimes called a *reversionary* irrevocable designation. Under this type of designation, the interest of the irrevocable beneficiary is only conditionally vested. There is a condition—namely, her death before maturity of the policy—which can destroy her interest. Since the insured can acquire ownership rights in the contract through the death of the beneficiary during his lifetime, he possesses a contingent interest in the policy from the beginning. His interest is considered substantial enough to necessitate his concurrence in all negotiations concerning the policy. Thus, in the usual circumstances, neither the insured nor the beneficiary can exercise any policy rights or dispose of the policy without the consent of the other. For all intents and purposes, the insured and the beneficiary are regarded as joint owners of the policy when the beneficiary designation is irrevocable.

It is possible for an insured to procure a policy under which he would not reserve the right to change the beneficiary but would retain the normal policy privileges.[8] Even though the insured can diminish the beneficiary's interest in such a policy or destroy it com-

[8] *Morse* v. *Commissioner,* 100 F. (2d) 593 (C.C.A. 7, 1938).

pletely by surrender, he cannot revoke her interest, such as it may be, and give it to another, without the beneficiary's consent. As courts have pointed out, the terms and conditions of the policy are determinative of the rights of the insured and the interest of the beneficiary. In the majority of policies issued today, however, there are no specific conditions that would permit the insured to impair or destroy the interest of an irrevocably designated beneficiary.

Irrevocable beneficiary designations are not widely used. In most situations where their use might be justified, an absolute assignment, ownership policy, or ownership clause is likely to be more appropriate. An irrevocable beneficiary designation does offer the advantage of protecting the beneficiary's interest in the proceeds during her lifetime, and automatically vesting complete ownership rights in the insured in the event that he should survive the beneficiary; but the same result may be achieved by an appropriately worded ownership clause.

SUCCESSION IN INTEREST

Whenever there is only one beneficiary in a beneficiary classification—i.e., primary, first contingent, and so forth—the interest of any beneficiary who predeceases the insured passes in the manner and according to the rules described in the preceding pages, unless the contract provides otherwise. Whenever there is more than one beneficiary in a beneficiary classification, however, a question arises as to the disposition of the interest of any beneficiary who should die before his interest materializes. The problem has frequently arisen in connection with class designations, such as "my children," but it is equally relevant to multiple specific designations.

To pin-point the problem, assume that A, the insured, names his three children, B, C, and D, as primary beneficiaries of his insurance, share and share alike, without designating any contingent beneficiaries, and without specifying what should be the disposition of the share of any child who should fail to survive him. Assume further that D predeceases A, leaving three children E, F, and G. Who is entitled to D's share?

A policy provision on this point is controlling; but in the absence of a pertinent policy provision, D's interest might conceivably be disposed of in one of three ways. It might pass to A's estate, on the theory that where there are multiple designations, the interest of each beneficiary is severable and is contingent on the beneficiary's survival of the insured. The share might pass to B and C, on the theory that the designation of multiple beneficiaries creates a form of undivided interest, analogous to a joint tenancy, with right of survivorship. Finally, the share might pass to D's children, E, F, and G, on the theory that a primary beneficiary has a vested interest in the proceeds which cannot be defeated by his failure to survive the insured.

In the litigation that has developed around this question, there has been no support for the view that the interest of a deceased beneficiary should revert to the insured's estate, despite the fact that this would have been the outcome had the deceased beneficiary been the sole primary beneficiary. The majority of the decisions have followed the rule that the surviving beneficiaries of the classification to which the deceased beneficiary belonged are entitled to take the share of the deceased beneficiary. In the example cited, B and C would be entitled to the full amount of proceeds. This doctrine is known as the "New York Rule," since it was first espoused by the New York courts. From a practical standpoint, much can be said in favor of the rule. Most of the cases involve children, which means that if the share of the deceased child were to revert to the insured's estate, it would ultimately be distributed to the surviving children, the other beneficiaries, reduced by its share of administration expenses and bequests to other persons, including the widow. A substantial minority of the courts have followed the "Connecticut Rule," which holds that the heirs of the deceased beneficiary are entitled to his share. In the above example, E, F, and G would receive the proceeds to which D would have been entitled had he survived A. Each would receive one ninth of the total proceeds, with B and C receiving one third each. This rule is in conflict with the prevailing view of a beneficiary's interest in a life insurance policy, but it reflects the desire of the jurists involved to carry out what they conceive to be the wishes of the insured.

In anticipation of this problem, many companies have incorporated a provision in their policies which—in the absence of contrary instructions from the insured—will control the disposition of the interest of any beneficiary who dies before becoming entitled to payment of his share of proceeds. This provision, commonly known as the "succession-in-interest clause," is applicable to both primary and contingent beneficiaries, and to beneficiaries designated irrevocably as well as revocably. A typical clause might appear as follows:

SUCCESSION IN INTEREST OF BENEFICIARIES

The proceeds of this policy whether payable in one sum or under a settlement option shall be payable in equal shares to such direct beneficiaries as survive to receive payment. The share of any direct beneficiary who dies before receiving payments due or to become due shall be payable in equal shares to such direct beneficiaries as survive to receive payment.

At the death of the last surviving direct beneficiary payments due or to become due shall be payable in equal shares to such contingent beneficiaries as survive to receive payment. The share of any contingent beneficiary who dies before receiving payments due or to become due shall be payable in equal shares to such contingent beneficiaries as survive to receive payment.

At the death of the last to survive of the direct and contingent beneficiaries:

(*a*) if no settlement option is in effect, any remaining proceeds shall be paid to the owner or to the executors, administrators, successors, or transferees of the owner; or

(*b*) if a settlement option is in effect, the withdrawal value of payments due or to become due shall be paid in one sum to the executors or administrators of the last to survive of the direct and contingent beneficiaries.

A direct or contingent beneficiary succeeding to an interest in a settlement option shall continue under such option, subject to its terms as stated in this policy, with the rights of transfer between options and of withdrawal under options as provided in this policy.

It will be noted that this clause applies not only to the situations where either a primary or a contingent beneficiary fails to survive the *insured,* but also to cases where a contingent beneficiary fails to survive a *primary beneficiary*. The latter is important when proceeds are being paid out on an installment basis. If the proceeds are to be paid in a lump sum, the problem can be met by specifying in the beneficiary designation that the proceeds will be paid only to those beneficiaries who survive the insured, provided this solution is in accord with the insured's wishes.

The disposition of the interest of deceased beneficiaries envisioned by the succession-in-interest clause does not represent the desires of all policyholders. In designating their children as beneficiaries, many insureds want the share of a deceased beneficiary to go to the latter's children, the insured's grandchildren. This can be accomplished by directing that the proceeds be distributed *per stirpes,* a Latin expression meaning "by the trunk." For example, in designating his wife as primary beneficiary and his children as contingent beneficiaries, an insured could use the following wording: "Mary Smith Doe, wife of the insured, if she survives the insured; otherwise in equal shares to the surviving children of the insured, and to the surviving children of any deceased children of the insured, per stirpes." The expression "per stirpes" means that the issue or lineal descendants of a deceased person take the share of an estate or of the insurance proceeds that the deceased would have taken had he survived. It is used in wills and trusts, as well as insurance policies. The children represent the parents, and grandchildren represent the children, and so on down the "trunk." As a matter of fact, the words "by representation" are sometimes used in lieu of "per stirpes." The "Connecticut Rule," referred to earlier, embodies the per stirpes concept.

An insured sometimes wants the children of a deceased beneficiary to share equally with the surviving members of the original beneficiary group. In the example used earlier, A might have wanted D's children to share equally with B and C, each taking one fifth of the proceeds. He could have achieved this objective by specifying that the proceeds should go "in equal shares to such of B, C, and D, children of the insured, as may survive the insured, and to the surviving children of such of said children as may be deceased, per capita."

In all these matters, the insurance company accedes to the wishes of the insured, requiring only that his desires be clearly expressed in the designation.

OWNERSHIP RIGHTS

Life insurance policies issued today offer many valuable rights and privileges in addition to the basic obligation of the company to pay the face of the policy upon maturity. Most of these rights—such as surrender options, dividend options, policy loans, assignments, and change of beneficiaries—can be exercised during the insured's lifetime and are referred to as *prematurity rights*. It is essential, therefore, that the ownership of the various rights be clearly established and known to all parties concerned.

When a person applies for insurance on his own life and designates himself or his estate as beneficiary, all ownership rights in the policy are vested in him. The same is true if he designates another person as beneficiary, but reserves the right to revoke the designation. In all but three states, the interest of such a third-party beneficiary is regarded as a "mere expectancy," so ephemeral as not to interfere with the exercise of the prematurity rights by the insured. In three states, the interest of a revocable beneficiary is judicially recognized as a qualified or defeasible vested interest which can be divested only by a change of beneficiary. In those states, consent of the beneficiary is necessary to the exercise of all prematurity rights except policy loans and change of beneficiary. When a person applies for insurance on his own life and designates another person as beneficiary without reserving the right to revoke the designation, the insured and the beneficiary are considered to be joint owners of the policy, and neither can exercise any prematurity rights without the consent of the other. It will be noted that in none of these situations is the beneficiary considered to be the sole owner of the policy.

In today's complex world of business and finance, there are more and more situations in which it is desirable—or even essential—that the beneficiary (in the broadest sense) be the absolute owner of the policy. For example, if the insured wants to keep the proceeds out of his gross estate for federal estate tax purposes, he must divest himself of all incidents of ownership. A creditor wants all ownership rights in a policy taken out on the debtor to secure a loan. Partners need to be absolute owners of policies on the lives of fellow partners used to finance business continuation agreements. Employers must be the owners of policies on the lives of key employees.

Sole and complete ownership of a policy can be vested in a person other than the insured in one of three ways. The first is through procurement of the policy by the prospective beneficiary in the first instance. The beneficiary applies for the insurance, with the consent of the insured, and has himself designated as owner of the policy, as well as beneficiary. Some companies have developed special forms, called *owner policies,* for this purpose, while others use regular policies with an ownership clause. This clause declares the beneficiary to be the owner of the policy, any provisions in the policy to the contrary notwithstanding, and specifically states that the beneficiary shall have the right to exercise all the rights which would otherwise be vested in the insured.

The second method consists of the *transfer* of ownership rights in a policy originally issued to the insured by means of an endorsement on the policy. The insured directs the company to vest all his rights, privileges, and options in the beneficiary, and the policy is endorsed accordingly. The endorsement is known as an *ownership clause;* and in some companies, it may be identical to the clause endorsed on a policy at the time it is issued.

The third method is identical with the second, except that it involves the use of an absolute assignment form. This is the oldest procedure and one that is still preferred by many. It will be discussed in detail in Chapter IX.

The owner of a policy, whether he procured it on his own application or by transfer from the insured, can designate a person other than himself to receive the proceeds of the policy and can reserve the right to revoke the designation. He may also transfer his ownership to another person, provided the transfer takes effect at the time it is made. It is generally agreed, likewise, that an insured—in transferring ownership of his policy to another person—may nominate a successor to take ownership in the event that the original transferee should die before the insured. There seems to be considerable disagreement, however, as to whether an owner—either as the procurer of the original policy or by transfer from the insured—may himself designate another person to succeed to his ownership in case of his death before that of the insured, other than by a provision in his will. The question is whether such a disposition, to take effect only upon the death of the owner, would be testamentary in nature and hence in conflict with the statutes of wills as they exist in the various states. Because of the uncertainty concerning the matter, some companies will not recognize any disposition of the owner's interest, in the event that he should predecease the insured, other than to the owner's estate. The disposition of the interest by the legal representatives of the owner would depend entirely on the provisions of his will or of the laws of intestacy.

CHAPTER VIII

The Beneficiary (Continued)

SIMULTANEOUS DEATH AND SHORT-TERM SURVIVORSHIP

Simultaneous Death of Insured and Beneficiary

It should now be clear that the rights of various parties can be vitally affected by the question of whether the primary beneficiary survives the insured, or vice versa. Under normal circumstances, this is a question of fact which can be easily and conclusively established. If, however, the insured and the beneficiary are killed in an automobile accident, airplane crash, explosion, or other such untoward circumstances, it may well be impossible to determine which survived the other. Inasmuch as valuable property rights are involved in this situation, including the disposition of the estates of the insured and beneficiary, the courts have had to adopt rules which will permit them to solve the dilemma.

Six states—Georgia, Louisiana, Mississippi, New Mexico, Ohio, and Oklahoma—follow the old Napoleonic Code (which, in turn, was based on the Roman Civil Code), which created a set of *conclusive presumptions* as to survival, reflecting the age and sex of the parties involved. These presumptions, now embodied in statutes in the states indicated, are as follows: A male is presumed to have survived a female if both were between the ages of fifteen and sixty; if both persons were under fifteen, the older—regardless of sex—is presumed to have survived; if both were over sixty, the younger is presumed to have survived, regardless of sex; if one was under fifteen and the other over sixty, the younger is presumed to have survived, regardless of sex; finally, if one was under fifteen or over sixty and the other was between those ages, the latter is presumed to have survived, regardless of sex.

Until recent years, all the other states followed the English common-law rule, which makes no presumption as to survival. Under this rule, the problem is resolved through the device of placing on one party or the other the legal burden of proving survivorship. If the legal representative (executor or administrator) of the party on whom the burden was placed cannot prove survivorship (and it is assumed in such cases that adequate proof cannot be adduced), it is presumed that the other party survived. With respect to each type of property involved, the burden of proof will be placed on the party who must survive in order to establish entitlement to the property. Thus, the incidence of the burden can vary with the species of property rights involved.

In the case of life insurance, the burden of proof, under the common-law rule, depends upon whether the beneficiary designation is revocable or irrevocable. If the designation is revocable, the beneficiary has only an expectancy and must survive the insured before the proceeds vest in her. Thus, her legal representatives would have the burden of proving that she survived the insured; and if there were no evidence to substantiate their claim, the insured would be presumed to have survived.[1] If the designation is irrevocable, the beneficiary has a vested right to the proceeds which can be defeated only by her failure to survive the insured. Thus, the insured's representatives should properly have the burden of proving that he outlived the beneficiary and consequently divested her of her rights. In the absence of proof, the proceeds would go to the estate of the beneficiary, or if there are contingent beneficiaries, to the latter.

In an attempt to avoid the litigation inherent in this procedure for establishing survivorship and to provide an equitable basis for disposing of the property of the parties involved, forty-three states and Hawaii have adopted the so-called "Uniform Simultaneous Death Act." The measure applies to all types of property and property rights. The underlying theory of the act is that, in the absence of evidence to

---

[1] In some of the early cases, the courts held that the revocable beneficiary had a *vested* interest which could be divested only by a change of beneficiary during the insured's lifetime or by failure of the beneficiary to survive the insured. Since the interest had already vested, the courts reasoned, the burden should be on the insured's representatives to prove that he survived the beneficiary and thereby divested her of her rights. See *Cowman* v. *Rogers,* 73 Md. 403, 21 Atl. 64 (1891).

the contrary, each person is presumed to be the survivor as to his own property. In the case of jointly held property, each party is presumed to be the survivor as to his share of the property. The act makes specific references to life insurance, stating that where the insured and the beneficiary have died and there is no sufficient evidence that they died otherwise than simultaneously, the proceeds shall be distributed as if the insured had survived the beneficiary. This is a conclusive presumption, and it applies whether the beneficiary is designated revocably or irrevocably. This presumption is not in complete harmony with the underlying theory of the act when the designation is irrevocable; but it seems justified, in view of the fact that the overwhelming majority of beneficiary designations are revocable, the insured being the owner of the policy.

In those states which have not yet enacted the Uniform Simultaneous Death Act, the same results can be achieved through the inclusion of a so-called *common disaster clause* in the policy. With language similar or even identical to that of the act, the clause states that when the insured and beneficiary perish in a common accident, the insured shall be presumed to have survived.

Short-Term Survivorship

The Uniform Simultaneous Death Act settles the question of survivorship when there is not sufficient evidence as to whether the insured or the beneficiary survived, but it does not eliminate the possibility of harassing legal action by the personal representative of the beneficiary bent on proving that the beneficiary survived the insured. Moreover, it is not effective when the beneficiary, in fact, did survive the insured, even by a moment. In the absence of contrary instructions in the policy, the proceeds would, under such circumstances, go to the estate of the beneficiary.

When there are contingent beneficiaries and the proceeds are held under the interest option or are payable in installments (other than a life income), the short-term survivorship of the primary beneficiary creates no particular problems. The estate of the primary beneficiary would be entitled to one monthly payment at most, and the remainder of the proceeds would go to the contingent beneficiaries. Under all other circumstances, however, the survival of the beneficiary for only a short period is generally considered to be an unfavorable event.

If the proceeds are payable to the primary beneficiary under a life income option, there is likely to be a substantial forfeiture of proceeds, even though there are surviving contingent beneficiaries. If there are no refund features in the option, the company's obligation would be discharged completely by the payment of one monthly installment to the beneficiary's estate.[2] If the payments are guaranteed for a specified number of years, some forfeiture would be inevitable—the extent, of course, varying inversely with the length of the period. There would be no forfeiture, other than loss of interest, under the cash refund or installment refund form of life income option.

If the proceeds are payable in a lump sum and the wife was the primary beneficiary, the proceeds, after probate, may go to relatives of the wife—a generally unintended and, perhaps, undesired result. This would be the case where the insured and beneficiary were not survived by children or grandchildren. Even though there were surviving children, the proceeds would get to them only after having gone through estate administration and suffering some shrinkage. This, however, is the fault of the lump-sum settlement and not the short-term survivorship of the beneficiary. The consequences would have been the same had the insured survived the beneficiary and died shortly thereafter, unless contingent beneficiaries were named to take the proceeds in that event.

In an effort to avoid the undesirable consequences of short-term survivorship of the beneficiary (which is a far more common occurrence than simultaneous death), some companies stipulate that the proceeds will be payable to the beneficiary only if she be alive at the time of payment. Other companies use a provision which states that the proceeds will be payable to the beneficiary only if she survives the insured by a specified period of time, such as ten, thirty, or sixty days. The companies are understandably reluctant to delay payment for a protracted period, but some are willing to defer payment up to 180 days. Such clauses solve the problem very effectively, although no reasonable period would be long enough to cover every case that might arise.

The delayed payment clause has one disadvantage for the policyholder who anticipates a federal estate tax liability. Such policyholder would normally want the proceeds of his life insurance policies to qualify for the so-called "marital deduction," which is a deduction allowed for property passing outright to the decedent's spouse, up to one half of the adjusted gross estate. The vesting of insurance pro-

---

[2] The first payment is due immediately after the death of the insured.

ceeds, or any property includable in the decedent's gross estate, can be delayed up to six months without jeopardizing their qualification for the marital deduction, provided the spouse survives the period and obtains complete dominion over the proceeds. If the spouse does not survive the period, the proceeds do not qualify. This disadvantage of the delayed payment clause has caused some companies to advocate the use of the interest option with contingent beneficiaries, to meet the problem of short-term survivorship of the beneficiary. If the beneficiary is given the unlimited right of withdrawal, the proceeds will qualify for the marital deduction even though she never had an opportunity to exercise the right. If she is injured in a common disaster and dies from her injuries, or dies from any cause shortly after the insured, the beneficiary is not likely to withdraw the proceeds, and they will pass to the contingent beneficiaries. In the event that the beneficiary survives the insured by an extended period, she would be permitted, under the practices of most companies, to elect a liquidation option at contract rates within a specified period, such as one or two years, after the insured's death. The proceeds passing to others on her death would be includable in her gross estate for federal estate tax purposes; but if she dies within a specified period after the insured, the law allows a credit for any taxes paid on the same property in the insured's estate.

Another method of assuring the availability of the marital deduction when there is no evidence of survivorship is through the use of a *reverse* common disaster clause in the insurance policy. This clause makes the presumption that the *beneficiary* survives. Obviously, it should be used only when it is compatible with the over-all estate plan of the insured.

It should be emphasized that a perfectly satisfactory method of dealing with the short-term survivorship hazard is through the use of installment options (except life income options) with contingent beneficiaries. Again, this method would be used only if it meets the distribution objectives of the insured. Perhaps a better way to state the proposition is that neither the simultaneous death of the insured and the beneficiary nor the short-term survivorship of the beneficiary presents any problems when the proceeds are to be distributed under the installment time or installment amount options, or are held under the interest option, with contingent beneficiaries to succeed to the interest of the primary beneficiary.

EFFECTING CHANGE OF BENEFICIARY

As was indicated earlier, the applicant for insurance is always given the opportunity to reserve the right to change the beneficiary. If he does so, he can remove not only the original beneficiary, but also any successor beneficiaries that he might appoint, provided he does not, in the meantime, relinquish the right. This is a matter of contract, and the company cannot refuse to assent to a change of beneficiary on the ground that the prospective beneficiary has no insurable interest, or on any other ground. On the other hand, the company can—and does—prescribe the procedure which must be followed in effecting a change of beneficiary. Such procedure is also a condition of the contract.

All companies require written notice of a change of beneficiary, and most specify that the change must be endorsed on the policy. This is not a burdensome requirement from the insured's standpoint[3] and, in the usual case, would pose no difficulties. There are occasionally situations, however, in which the insured is not able to produce the policy for endorsement. It may have been lost, or it may be in the possession of a person who refuses to release it. A common example of the latter difficulty is possession of the policy by an estranged or a divorced wife. In such cases, the company may recognize the change of beneficiary despite the lack of formal compliance with the procedural requirements, but would probably do so only if it were satisfied that there is no danger of the prior beneficiary's establishing a claim. The courts have consistently held that the policy provisions concerning change of beneficiary are for the protection of the company and can be waived under proper circumstances.

Divorce between the insured and the beneficiary deserves special mention. The general rule is that divorce in itself does not terminate the interest of the beneficiary. This is based on the doctrine, mentioned earlier, that the interest of a named beneficiary is a personal one, not dependent on the relationship to the insured which may have been stated in the designation. This general rule prevails in cases where the insured has reserved the right to change the beneficiary but

---

[3] Endorsement is burdensome on the company, and some companies which now require endorsement are searching for a way of avoiding it in the future—for both new and old policies.

has not done so, as well as in those where the right to revoke the wife's interest has not been reserved; but in the latter situation, a settlement agreement between the divorced husband and wife, or the divorce decree, may affect the wife's rights.

In a few states, this rule has not been followed by the courts, or is modified by statute. In Kentucky, the interest of a wife is *automatically* terminated by divorce, whether she was revocably or irrevocably designated; but where insurance on the life of the husband has been procured by the wife during the marriage and paid for by her with her own funds, the rights of the wife therein are not abrogated or impaired by a subsequent divorce.[4] In Michigan, the wife's interest is automatically terminated by the divorce, whether she was revocably or irrevocably designated, unless the court decree specifies otherwise. In Missouri and Minnesota, divorce does not automatically terminate the wife's interest; but the husband is given the power to change the beneficiary, even though he had named his wife as irrevocable beneficiary. In New York, the aggrieved party in a divorce action may apply to the court granting the final decree or bring an action in supplementary proceedings for an order directing the insurance company to change the beneficiary, even one irrevocably designated.

THE MINOR AS BENEFICIARY

The designation of a minor as beneficiary creates problems that are not ordinarily encountered with an adult beneficiary. Perhaps the most obvious complication is that which may arise if an insured designates a minor as beneficiary without reserving the right to revoke the designation. If, thereafter, the insured should wish to change the beneficiary, assign the policy as collateral for a loan, make a policy loan, or surrender the policy for its cash value, he could do so only with the minor's consent, which he does not have legal capacity to give. The insured might seek to have a guardian appointed for the minor, but it is highly unlikely that a court would permit the guardian to waive the rights of the minor.

Problems will almost certainly arise if the policy matures while the beneficiary is still a minor. The insurance company cannot safely make payment directly to the minor, since the latter is not legally competent to receive payment. Upon the attainment of his majority, he might

[4] *Ficke* v. *Prudential Insurance Co. of America,* 305 Ky. 181, 202 S.W. (2d) 429 (1947).

repudiate the release contained in his receipt and demand payment of the proceeds once again. To protect itself, the company would have to insist on the appointment of a guardian, which involves expense to the minor's estate. In a number of states, insurance companies are authorized by special statutes to waive the guardianship requirement and make payment on behalf of the minor to an adult person, usually a parent or someone standing in place of a parent. However, the amounts which can be distributed under these statutes tend to be nominal, the usual limit being less than $500. A few states permit amounts up to $1,000 to be paid in this manner.

In Arizona, Kentucky, Louisiana, Utah, and Washington, it is provided by statute that a minor who has attained the age of eighteen years shall be competent to receive and give full acquittance and discharge for an amount not exceeding $2,000 in any one year in the form of benefits payable upon the death of the insured, as long as the insurance policy or the policy settlement agreement specifically provides for direct payments to such minor. In Louisiana, Utah, and Washington, the statute applies only to *periodical* payments, not exceeding in the aggregate $2,000 in any one year. In Arizona and Kentucky, the statute applies to either a lump-sum payment in an amount not exceeding $2,000 or periodical payments not exceeding $2,000 in any one year. New York has a statute which permits the payment of $3,000 to a minor, either in a lump sum or in periodic payments not exceeding that sum per year. The New York statute also pertains to benefits payable upon the maturity of a policy as an endowment; while in Arizona and Kentucky, the statute also embraces benefits payable under annuity contracts.

Pennsylvania, alone among all the states, has a statute which permits the insured, in designating a beneficiary, to appoint a guardian of the estate or interest of any beneficiary who shall be a minor or otherwise incompetent. The law further provides that payments of the proceeds by the insurance company to such guardian shall discharge the insurance company for the payment to the same extent as if payment had been made to an otherwise duly appointed and qualified guardian.

Difficulties also exist with respect to the election of settlement options by a minor or a guardian acting on his behalf. The statutes referred to above authorize installment payments direct to minors only when the settlement option was elected by the insured or other owner of the policy. They do not authorize the minor to elect a settlement option. It is quite clear that a minor lacks legal capacity to elect a settlement option; and most companies are not willing to run the risk of repudiation of the contract by the minor, unless the amounts involved are small. However, if the beneficiary is within a year or two of attaining his majority, a company may agree to a settlement involving the payment of interest only, with a provision for payment of principal to the minor upon attaining his majority, or to his estate in the event of his death.

The law is unsettled with respect to the right of a guardian to elect a settlement option on behalf of his minor ward. There are no statutes expressly authorizing such an election, and the few court decisions on the point are conflicting. The basic question involved is whether the election of a settlement option by the guardian is an investment of the ward's funds and, if so, whether it is a legal investment. In a case involving the election of the interest option, the majority opinion held that the right of election was an interest "in the nature of a property right" given by the policy to the beneficiaries which could properly be exercised by the guardian on behalf of the minor beneficiaries.[5] Judge Lehman, dissenting from the majority of the court, took the view that the exercise of the right of election was an investment of the proceeds, and that since the investment was not one permitted by statute, the guardian had no right to elect.

A more serious question is involved when the guardian wishes to elect a liquidating option. This runs contrary to the basic rule of guardianship law that the principal cannot be used for the ward's support without court approval. Thus, it seems agreed that a liquidating option can be elected only with court approval, which would be granted only upon demonstration that the action was in the best interests of the ward. Moreover, the election could not operate to deprive the ward of the free and unrestricted use of his funds after attaining his majority. Hence, if the settlement were to extend beyond the ward's age twenty-one, he would have to be given the right to withdraw the unpaid balance at that time. Since the guardian has no authority to dispose of the ward's property after the latter's death, any installments unpaid at the time of the ward's death should be payable to his estate.

Many insureds stipulate that any proceeds becoming payable to a minor will be paid to a trustee, to be administered for the benefit of

---

[5] *Latterman* v. *Guardian Life Insurance Co.,* 280 N.Y. 102, 19 N.E. (2d) 978, 127 A.L.R. 450 (1939).

the minor. This procedure is described in the following section and will not be dealt with further at this point.

If the proceeds are not needed for the maintenance and support of the minor, some companies are willing to accept a provision that the funds will remain with the company, at interest, until the beneficiary has legal capacity to accept them. This is possible under the laws of New York and other states which permit the accumulation of interest during the minority of a beneficiary.

THE TRUSTEE AS BENEFICIARY

There are circumstances under which it is advisable to have life insurance proceeds administered by a trustee. A trust can serve many useful purposes, but it is especially desirable when there is need for great flexibility in the administration of the proceeds, or when some of the beneficiaries are minors. There appears to be a growing tendency to designate a trustee as contingent beneficiary to administer proceeds for the benefit of minor children, the mother being primary beneficiary. Such an arrangement is called a *contingent trust,* since it goes into effect only if the proceeds become payable to the children while they are still minors. It takes the place of guardianship.

Irrespective of the nature of the trust, the trustee may be a natural person or a corporation, and the designation may be revocable or irrevocable, whichever is consistent with the terms of the trust. If the trust is irrevocable, however, the proceeds are usually made payable to the trustee under the instrumentality of an absolute assignment.

It is highly desirable, if not essential, that there be a trust agreement at the time the trustee is designated beneficiary. If the insured should die before instructions have been provided the trustee, the trust would undoubtedly be dissolved as unenforceable. In such cases, the courts have held that, there being nothing to guide the trustee as to the purpose or manner of distribution of the trust estate, the funds must be paid over to the person or persons presumably entitled to them. If the distributees were children, the proceeds would be paid to duly appointed guardians. The trust agreement need not be a separate instrument, although it normally is. The terms of the trust may be incorporated in the settlement agreement, particularly if it is a contingent trust. The following provision illustrates the latter procedure and also brings out certain other aspects of an insurance trust that should be noted:

Regardless of any provision herein to the contrary, any sum payable as herein provided to any of said children during such child's minority shall be paid to *John Doe,* brother of insured, as trustee for such child. In the event said brother shall fail to serve or shall cease to serve as trustee for such child, because of death or otherwise, any sum payable as herein provided to such child during minority shall be paid to *Richard Doe,* nephew of the insured, as successor trustee. Any permissible right of withdrawal or election of options by such child during minority shall be exercisable by said trustee. All sums payable to said trustee shall be held and expended for the maintenance, support, and education of such minor child in the discretion of the trustee, except as may be otherwise provided in a separate trust instrument; and when such child shall attain the age of twenty-one, trustee shall pay over any unexpended funds. As respects any payment made to said trustee, the company shall be under no liability to see to or be responsible for the proper discharge of the trust or any part thereof, and any such payment to said trustee shall fully discharge the company for the amount so paid. The company shall not be charged with notice of a separate trust instrument, a change of trustee, the death of such child, the termination of the trust, or rights under the trust, until written evidence thereof is received at the home office.

When a trustee is designated as beneficiary, it is usually intended that the trustee shall collect the proceeds in one sum and administer them in accordance with the terms of the trust agreement. There are occasions, however, when the trustee deems it advantageous—either to himself or to the trust beneficiary—to make use of the deferred settlement facilities of the insurance company. It becomes important, under such circumstances, to determine whether a trustee can avail himself of such facilities.

Trustees, as a class, first developed a real interest in insurance policy settlement options in the 1930's, when the going interest rate on new investments dropped below the rate of return guaranteed in insurance company settlement options. Many companies, feeling that trustees were attempting to shift their investment responsibilities (for which they were compensated) to the life insurance industry, and having other reservations about the practice, refused to honor settlement option elections by trustees. Litigation[6] established the right of a trustee to elect a settlement option, unless that right is denied in the insurance policy. Thereafter, many companies inserted a prohibition against the use of settlement options by trustees and have continued the practice to the present.

---

[6] *First Trust Co. of St. Paul* v. *Northwestern Mutual Life Insurance Co.,* 204 Minn. 244, 283 N.W. 236 (1939).

In the absence of express permission in the trust instrument, there is a serious question whether a trustee has the legal right to use settlement options, even though made available by the insurance company. The issue, as in the case of guardianship, hinges on whether or not a life insurance settlement option is a legal investment for a trustee. Where the investment statute is of the "prudent man" type, a strong argument can be made in favor of the legality of the practice. Many legal experts have concluded, however, that a trustee has an unquestioned right to elect a settlement option only when (1) the trust instrument expressly confers the right and (2) the insurance policy does not deny the right.

REMARRIAGE CLAUSE

When the settlement agreement calls for the proceeds to be paid to the surviving widow under an installment option not involving life contingencies, or to be held at her disposal under the interest option, the insured frequently requests that provision be made for termination of the widow's interest if she should remarry, with the undistributed proceeds going to the children as contingent beneficiaries. Such a provision is called a *remarriage clause.*

All companies discourage the use of a remarriage clause, and many refuse outright to include it in the settlement agreement. When the clause is included, the companies attempt by the wording of the clause to avoid the responsibility of determining whether the widow has entered into a valid marriage. The hazards associated with such a determination are serious enough in ordinary circumstances; but in jurisdictions which recognize common-law marriages, the difficulties are compounded.

The remarriage clause places on the contingent beneficiaries or their guardian the responsibility of providing proof of remarriage of the widow and relieves the company of any liability for payments made to the widow after her remarriage but before proof has been furnished by the contingent beneficiaries. Since the widow will normally be the guardian of the children, there is some doubt that proof of her remarriage will be provided. If the guardian is an outsider, the existence of the clause may not be known to him. If the widow becomes the guardian, it is doubtful that the interests of the secondary beneficiaries would be served any more effectively than if the proceeds had been paid to her as primary beneficiary.

CHAPTER IX

Assignment of Life Insurance Contracts

THE LIFE insurance contract, with its valuable prematurity rights and promise to pay a specified sum of money upon maturity, is an ideal form of collateral for credit transactions. Hence, it is not surprising that the assignment of life insurance policies as collateral security has reached large proportions. They are, in addition, frequently assigned as a means of transferring ownership rights to another person or organization. It is important to note the circumstances under which a life insurance contract can be assigned and the manner in which the rights of the various parties involved are affected by the assignment.

RIGHT OF ASSIGNMENT

Assignment by the Insured or Owner of the Policy

It is a settled rule of law that anyone having an interest in a life insurance contract can transfer that interest, with or without a consideration, to another person. Hence, the contract does not contain a provision expressly authorizing the insured or owner to transfer his interest; it is an inherent right which can be restricted only by contract. Industrial life insurance policies contain limitations on the right of assignment, but ordinary insurance policies are free of restrictions.

In the usual situation, all ownership rights in a policy are vested in the insured. Among the incidents of ownership is the right to assign the policy. This right carries with it the power to transfer all rights and interests in the policy to another person. When someone other than the insured is owner of the policy, it is customary for the policy to restrict the right of assignment to the owner. This is not a restriction on the assignability of the policy as such; it merely identifies the person who shall have the right to assign it.

The person assigning the policy cannot transfer any greater interest than he possesses or enlarge the obligation of the insurer. This means that he cannot, by his action, impair or defeat the vested interest of another person in the contract. In the typical case, only one other party could be adversely affected by the assignment, and that is the beneficiary. But is the interest of the beneficiary such that it is entitled to protection against infringement? The answer obviously depends upon whether the beneficiary designation is revocable or irrevocable.

If the designation is revocable, the majority rule is that the insured, or other owner of the policy, can assign the policy without the consent of the beneficiary and without complying with the formalities for changing the beneficiary designation. More important, the assignment is held to extinguish the interest of the beneficiary to the extent of the assignee's interest. As might be expected, the majority rule reflects the decision of those courts that view the interest of the revocable beneficiary as a mere expectancy. Those courts that adhere to the defeasible vested interest theory hold that the insured cannot assign the policy without either obtaining the consent of the beneficiary or revoking the designation. The latter step is perhaps the safer course of action, since in some jurisdictions, it may be held that a joinder by a wife-beneficiary is an invalid act if the purpose is to provide collateral for her husband's debts.[1]

It is the rule in all states that when the beneficiary designation is irrevocable, the policy cannot be assigned without the joinder of the beneficiary. The foregoing caveat concerning the wife's approval of an assignment designed to serve as collateral for her husband's debts is appropriate here.

Assignment by the Beneficiary

In the absence of a provision to the contrary, the beneficiary can assign her interest, both before and after maturity of the policy. Prior

[1] *Douglass* v. *Equitable Life Assurance Society*, 150 La. 405. 90 So. 834 (1922).

to maturity, her interest is virtually worthless if the insured reserved the right to change the beneficiary. If such right was not reserved, there is something of substance to be transferred; but the interest is contingent upon the original beneficiary's survival of the insured, unless the beneficiary's estate is designated to receive the proceeds if she predeceases the insured.

Upon maturity of the policy, proceeds payable in a lump sum vest in the beneficiary and can be assigned by her, probably without regard to any restrictive provisions in the policy. When the proceeds are held by the company under a deferred settlement agreement, the beneficiary's right of assignment is subject to the rights of the contingent beneficiaries, if any, and restrictive provisions in the policy or settlement agreement. Apropos the latter, it is common practice for the policy or settlement agreement to contain a so-called *spendthrift clause*, which denies to the beneficiary the right to commute, alienate, or assign her interest in the proceeds.[2] Furthermore, the laws of a few states which protect insurance proceeds from the claims of the beneficiary's creditors prohibit an assignment of the beneficiary's interest.

EFFECT OF ASSIGNMENT ON RIGHTS OF BENEFICIARY

The effect of an assignment on the rights of the beneficiary depends not only on the type of beneficiary designation but also on the type of assignment involved. The latter may take one of two general forms: an *absolute* assignment or a *collateral* assignment.

In form, the absolute assignment purports to divest the insured or owner of all incidents of ownership, and to transfer absolutely and permanently all rights and interests in the policy to the assignee. It is designed for those situations, involving a gift or a sale, where the clear intent is to make the assignee the new owner of the policy. The collateral assignment, on the other hand, is the form designed to transfer to the assignee those rights—and only those rights—needed to protect a loan from the assignee to the assignor. It resembles a mortgage of land or a pledge of marketable securities. The arrangement is intended to be temporary; and upon repayment of the loan, the assignment is terminated, with all rights reverting to the insured or previous owner. The assignee's interest in the policy is limited to the amount of the indebtedness and unpaid interest, plus any pre-

---

[2] See pp. 181–83.

miums paid by the assignee to keep the policy in force. For reasons to be explained later, absolute assignment forms have frequently been used when only a security arrangement was intended. In such cases, the assignment is treated as collateral in character and is released upon satisfaction of the assignor's obligation to the assignee. In fact, the courts will enforce such a result if the assignor can prove that, as between the assignor and assignee, a collateral assignment was intended.

If a policy is assigned in absolute *form,* and the parties intended the assignment to be absolute in *substance* as well, the interest of the beneficiary is completely extinguished, provided the designation was revocable or, if irrevocable, the beneficiary joined in the assignment. If an assignment is collateral in *substance,* irrespective of its *form*, the interest of the beneficiary will be extinguished to the extent of the assignee's interest, which is limited in the manner described above. If the insured attempts to assign the policy without the consent of the beneficiary when such consent is necessary, a valid transfer of his interest takes place, but the interest of the beneficiary is not affected. If she is a revocable beneficiary in a jurisdiction which sees a defeasible vested interest, she remains the beneficiary until a change has been accomplished in the prescribed manner. If she is an irrevocable beneficiary, she remains such, and no rights and privileges in the contract can be exercised by the assignee without her consent.

By what legal process is the interest of a third-party beneficiary subordinated to that of the assignee, without a change of beneficiary? The policy instructs the insurance company to pay the proceeds to a designated individual, subject to the right of the insured to substitute a different person. Assignment of the policy does not change those instructions; the beneficiary remains the payee of record. Theoretically, the assignment merely puts the assignee in the shoes of the assignor, who, prior to the assignment, was not slated to receive the proceeds. By what rationale does the new owner *automatically* become the payee of the policy, extinguishing the interest of the original payee?

This poses something of a legal riddle; and for many years, the courts held that an assignment did not, per se, subordinate the interest of the beneficiary. In one of the early cases, the court stated: "After a careful examination of the authorities, I am of the opinion that whether the interest be regarded as vested and defeasible, contingent, a mere expectancy, or whatever the characterization may be, if the policy stipulates the course by which the beneficiary's interest is to be nullified, he cannot be deprived of his right unless the prescribed mode for its destruction is followed. . . ."[3] Today, however, this view is entertained in only three states—Colorado, Massachusetts, and New Jersey—and the dominant philosophy is that the interest of an assignee will prevail over that of a revocable beneficiary.

In general, the courts have based their rulings purely on the intent of the parties. Most of the litigation has involved collateral assignments; and in such cases, there is usually a clear intent to subordinate the beneficiary's interest to that of the creditor-assignee. Since it is generally recognized that the assignee can perfect his claim by observing the formalities of a change of beneficiary, the courts are willing to spare him the trouble of doing so. Consent of the beneficiary to the assignment is regarded in all jurisdictions as conclusive evidence of intent to give a preferred status to the rights and claims of the assignee. In cases involving absolute assignments, not incidental to a credit transaction, some courts have concluded that a formal assignment, with notice to the insurance company, substantially conforms to the requirements for a change of beneficiary and operates as such. This rationale is patently inappropriate for collateral assignments, since the beneficiary of record receives the proceeds in excess of the claims of the assignment.

In all states, it is held that whenever the beneficiary of a policy is the insured or his estate, the claims of the assignee will prevail over those of the executor or administrator of the insured's estate.[4] This is true whether the assignment is absolute or collateral in form. Accordingly, it has been the practice of most companies, whenever the beneficiary does not join in the assignment, to advise the insured to change the beneficiary to his estate before executing an assignment. This is a precautionary measure, designed to avoid litigation by a disgruntled beneficiary. In the execution of assignments incidental to policy loans, the companies *require* this procedure, unless the wording of the policy makes it unnecessary.

This procedure is not without its disadvantages when used in connection with an assignment intended only as security for a loan. Unless the original beneficiary designation is restored after execution of the assignment, any proceeds remaining after satisfaction of the assignee's claims will be payable in a lump sum to the insured's estate.

---

[3] *Anderson* v. *Broad Street National Bank,* 90 N.J. Eq. 78, 105 Atl. 599 (1918).

[4] See citations in Harry Krueger and Leland T. Waggoner (eds.), *The Life Insurance Policy Contract* (Boston: Little, Brown & Co., 1953), p. 89, n. 17.

It would be even more unfortunate were the insured to neglect to restore the original beneficiary designation and settlement plan after release of the assignment. Among other disadvantages, it would mean the loss of protection of the cash value and proceeds against the claims of creditors of the insured.

To avoid such undesirable contingencies, many companies have developed administrative procedures that call for reinstatement of the original beneficiary designation immediately following assignment of the policy. In some companies, this involves three separate documents, executed in proper sequence. The first document changes the beneficiary to the insured's estate; the second assigns the policy on a collateral basis; the third restores the beneficiary designation existing before the first document was executed. In other companies, all three actions are accomplished in one document. This document contains a provision similar to the following:

> If this assignment is executed by the insured alone or by the insured and not all the beneficiaries of record, and if the right to change the beneficiary is reserved to the insured, then I, the insured, for the purpose of subjecting to this assignment the designation of beneficiary in force immediately preceding this assignment, (*a*) hereby revoke that designation and designate as beneficiary of the policy at the time of this assignment my executors or administrators; and (*b*) reinstate, effective immediately after this assignment, the designation of beneficiary in force immediately preceding the change of beneficiary made in (*a*) above.

This may appear to be legal legerdemain, but it does take the third-party beneficiary out of the assignment picture. At the moment the assignment is being executed, the estate is the beneficiary; one moment later, the original beneficiary is back in the picture. Any settlement options previously elected by the insured would remain in full force and effect, except that the amount payable thereunder might be reduced.[5]

The foregoing practices are used in connection with the bulk of outstanding policies. However, the recently issued policies of the major companies contain a provision intended to make it unnecessary to follow such a confusing procedure. One such provision reads as follows: "The interest of any revocable beneficiary in this policy and any

---

[5] A shorter provision, designed to accomplish the same objectives as the above-cited clause, reads as follows: "To the extent that he has the right to do so, the undersigned changes the designation of beneficiary in force immediately preceding this assignment and reinstates it to the same effect as if such designation had been executed subsequent to the assignment."

settlement option elected shall be subordinate to any assignment made either before or after the beneficiary designation or settlement option election."

The effectiveness of this type of provision has been upheld[6] even under the laws of New Jersey which, historically, has been one of the states requiring the consent of a revocable beneficiary to an assignment of the policy. Nevertheless, it would seem that an assignee who wants to avoid any possible legal complications upon the death of the insured would be well advised to designate himself as beneficiary. Then, there could be no doubt as to his right to receive the proceeds. This step is neither necessary nor permitted if the A.B.A. assignment form, to be discussed later, is used.

EFFECT OF ASSIGNMENT ON OWNERSHIP RIGHTS

Concept of Ownership

There are two sets of rights in a life insurance policy: those that exist during the lifetime of the insured and those that arise after his death. The first set is known, quite logically, as prematurity rights, and the second set as maturity rights. The most important of the prematurity rights are the right to surrender the policy for cash or paid-up insurance, the right to borrow against the policy, the right to designate and change the beneficiary, and the right to assign the policy. Among the lesser—but still significant—prematurity rights are the right to elect settlement options, elect dividend options, reinstate the policy, convert or exchange the policy for another, and take advantage of the automatic premium loan feature. The maturity rights include the right to receive the proceeds, to elect settlement options (unless usurped by the insured or owner), and to designate direct and contingent beneficiaries (only under certain circumstances).

The concept of ownership of these rights has undergone dramatic development during the last fifty to sixty years. The original concept was that all prematurity and maturity rights were vested in the beneficiary and her estate. In other words, the beneficiary was regarded as the absolute owner of the policy. Once the right of the insured to change the beneficiary was recognized, the insured and the beneficiary were considered to be joint owners of the prematurity rights and the beneficiary the sole owner of the maturity rights—subject, however,

---

[6] *Phoenix Mutual Life Insurance Co.* v. *Connelly*, 188 F. (2d) 462 (C.C.A. 3, 1951), reversing 92 Fed. Supp. 994 (D. N.J., 1950).

to the right of the insured, if reserved, to divest the beneficiary of all her interest in the policy and the proceeds. Over the years, this concept has been modified until today, in the absence of a contrary ownership arrangement, the insured is regarded to be the absolute owner of the prematurity rights and the possessor of the power to dispose of the maturity rights. If the insured has designated a third person as beneficiary, without reserving the right to revoke the designation, such beneficiary is considered to be the sole owner of the proceeds (when due at maturity), subject to the reversionary interest of the insured; and the insured and the beneficiary are looked upon as the joint owners of all prematurity rights.

Ever since the concept of a beneficiary change was recognized, around the turn of the century, the insured has been identified with ownership rights, either as sole or as joint owner. The most recent development is the complete dissociation or disattachment of the insured from ownership rights in the policy. This development received its impetus from the growth of business insurance, juvenile insurance, and insurance for estate transfer purposes, where there is a distinct need to have ownership of the policy in a person other than the insured; but it was also motivated by the desire of the companies to clarify the ownership status of the various rights in the contract. The dissociation is accomplished by specifying on the face of the policy that a particular person or firm shall be the owner of the policy and restricting the exercise of the various policy rights and privileges to the owner. In most cases, the insured is designated as owner; but the insured, as such, has no rights in the policy. All prematurity rights are vested in the owner, including the right to control the disposition of the maturity rights. The owner is given express authority to designate and change primary and contingent beneficiaries. Furthermore, during the lifetime of the insured, the owner can exercise all the rights and privileges in the policy without the consent of the beneficiary. Thus, it is apparent that the concept of the irrevocable beneficiary is negated with the ownership form of policy. The application makes no reference to the question of whether the applicant does or does not reserve the right to change the beneficiary. If the applicant wishes to create a joint ownership of the policy by the insured and the beneficiary, reminiscent of the irrevocable beneficiary designation, he can designate them as joint owners, with whatever survivorship provisions might be appropriate or desired.

The owner is given the sole right to assign the policy, and the interest of any beneficiary is made subject to the assignment. The assignee does not necessarily become owner of the policy. The policy may stipulate the manner in which a transfer of ownership is to be accomplished, and some policies state that ownership of the policy can be transferred only by a written instrument, satisfactory to the company, endorsed on the policy.

It can be seen that a minimum of *five* parties, other than the insurance company, may be associated with a modern life insurance policy. These are the applicant, the insured, the owner, the beneficiary, and the assignee. In the great majority of cases, the applicant, insured, and owner are one and the same person. Nevertheless, the ownership of all rights and privileges is made crystal clear, irrespective of the number of parties or interests involved. The next problem is to determine what happens to these rights and privileges when the policy is assigned.

Throughout the following discussion, it should be borne in mind that few of the policies involved in assignments to date have contained such a clear delineation of ownership rights as that found in the owner form of policy currently being issued.

Collateral Assignments

A collateral assignment is nothing more than a pledge and is subject to the general rules of law governing such a transaction. The pledgor is entitled to get his property back upon paying the debt when due and, after tendering the correct amount at the proper time, may recover the property in a legal proceeding. On the other hand, if the debt is not paid when due, the pledgee may, under authority of a court obtained in a suit for that purpose—or, more commonly, under the authority of the pledge agreement itself—have the property sold to satisfy his claim, including expenses of sale. The sale can be private, if the agreement gives the pledgee such alternative. The surplus remaining after the pledgee has been satisfied belongs to the pledgor. Since the pledgee is not the absolute owner of the policy, it is doubtful whether he can surrender the policy in the absence of a specific agreement to that effect. If the pledgor of an insurance policy dies before paying the debt for which it is security, the pledgee has a claim against the proceeds of the policy and may enforce it to the extent of his debt and other charges. However, since the collection of the proceeds is not a sale, the pledgee would not have the power, in the absence of an express stipulation, to collect the full amount of the proceeds, holding the excess for the pledgor's representatives.

It was not customary, before the development of the A.B.A. assignment form, for collateral assignment forms to confer on the assignee specific rights and powers in the policy. Hence, when the assignee attempted to surrender a pledged policy or take other action concerning it, most companies insisted that the owner of the policy join in the action. Furthermore, upon maturity of the policy, the assignee was permitted to collect only the amount of the oustanding indebtedness, unpaid interest, premiums paid on the policy, and other expenses incurred in connection with the loan. The remaining portion of the proceeds, if any, was paid to the beneficiary of record.

Many creditors resented having to prove the extent of their interest to the insurance company, preferring to receive the entire amount of proceeds and accounting to the beneficiary for the excess over their claims, as computed by them. To make matters worse, the collateral notes (not the collateral assignment form) used by some banks proved to be defective, in that they failed to give the bank the unquestioned right to pay premiums on the policy in the event of default by the insured and to add the sums thus paid to the principal of the indebtedness. The only recourse of the bank in some circumstances was to obtain title to the policy through foreclosure proceedings, thus establishing its right to pay premiums and to bring these outlays under protection of the collateral assignment. To obviate such difficulties, the A.B.A. assignment form contains a provision which specifically authorizes the assignee to pay premiums and add them to the amount of the indebtedness.

Whatever the impact of a collateral assignment on ownership rights, it is intended to be temporary in nature. Once the loan is repaid by the assignor, the assignment is released, and all ownership rights revert to their status before the assignment. An irrevocable beneficiary, for example, in joining in a collateral assignment, does not relinquish her vested rights in a policy; she merely agrees to subordinate her interest to that of the assignee during the time the assignment is in force. Once the assignment is terminated, the former status of all rights is restored. Repayment of the loan cancels the assignment, even though there may not be a formal release of the encumbrance.

Absolute Assignments

As was pointed out earlier, an absolute assignment in form conveys to the assignee all the title, rights, and interests possessed by the assignor. If the assignor owned all the rights in the policy, or if all persons having an interest in the policy joined in the assignment, the assignee becomes the new owner of the policy and can exercise all the rights therein, without the consent of any other person. The transfer is intended to be permanent. Until recent years, this was the conventional way of transferring ownership of a policy to another person. It was used, for example, when the insured wanted to make a gift of the policy or, on rare occasions, to sell the policy. It was the approved method of divesting the insured of all incidents of ownership in a policy, to the end that the proceeds would not be includable in his gross estate for federal estate tax purposes. In recent years, however, the practice of transferring ownership rights by means of an ownership endorsement has gained favor; and in some of the newest policy forms, it is specifically stated that ownership in the full legal sense can be transferred only by means of a written instrument, acceptable to the company, endorsed on the policy. The forms declare expressly that ownership *of the policy* cannot be effected through an assignment.

Be that as it may, in the days when an absolute assignment was universally regarded as a full and complete transfer of ownership rights, many creditors—particularly banks—turned to it as a more effective method of safeguarding their interests. They began to insist upon an absolute assignment when a policy was being pledged as security for a loan. In this way, they hoped to avoid the restrictions that were frequently imposed upon them in connection with collateral assignments. They wanted the right, without the consent of the insured, to surrender the policy for cash, to borrow the loan value, to elect paid-up insurance, and to exercise any of the other rights and privileges that might protect their interests. They also wanted the right to receive the full proceeds upon maturity of the policy, from which they would deduct amounts due them and pay over the excess to the insured or the beneficiary, as the case might be. In so doing, of course, they would deprive the beneficiary of the privilege of utilizing the policy's settlement options. In most cases, because of the smallness of the sums involved, this was not a serious disadvantage to the beneficiaries; but when the sums involved were substantial and the options were on a favorable basis, this practice of the banks was a potential source of great loss to the beneficiaries.

In many cases, perhaps, the absolute assignment form worked out exactly as the banks and other creditors had hoped it would. In other cases, however, the insurance company, realizing that the policy had been assigned only as collateral, refused to recognize the assignee as sole owner of the policy and insisted upon the joinder of the insured in the exercise of the various policy rights. The companies based their refusal on the failure of the assignment form to mention the specific rights conferred upon the assignee.

Dissatisfaction with the absolute assignment form on the part of both creditor and debtor interests eventually led to the development of a form especially designed for the assignment of life insurance policies. It was developed by the Bank Management Commission of the American Bankers Association, with the collaboration of the Association of Life Insurance Counsel. The official name of the form is "Assignment of Life Insurance Policy as Collateral," but it is popularly known as the A.B.A. assignment form.

A.B.A. Assignment Form

The essence of the A.B.A. assignment form is that it sets forth clearly and specifically the rights which are transferred to the assignee, and those that are not transferred and are presumably retained by the assignor.[7] The assignment is absolute and unqualified, in the sense that the rights vested in the assignee can be exercised without the consent of any other party. It is collateral, in that the assignee's rights are limited to his interest, with all rights reverting to the assignor upon termination of the assignee's interest.

The form states that the following rights shall pass to the assignee, to be exercised by him alone:

1. The right to collect from the insurance company the net proceeds of the policy when it matures by death or as an endowment.
2. The right to surrender the policy for its cash value.
3. The right to assign or pledge the policy as security for loans or advances from the insurance company or other persons.
4. The right to collect and receive all distributions of surplus to which the policy may become entitled during the time the assignment is in force, as well as all dividend deposits and paid-up additions credited to the policy as of the date of the assignment, provided appropriate notice is given to the insurance company by the assignee.
5. The right to exercise all surrender options and to receive the benefits and advantages therefrom.

It seems likely that the form will eventually be amended to add prepaid premiums and premium deposits to the list of benefits to which the assignee is entitled.

---

[7] The full text of the form is printed as Appendix D.

The form stipulates that the following rights shall not pass to the assignee, unless the policy has been surrendered:

1. The right to collect from the insurance company any disability benefit payable in cash which does not reduce the amount of insurance (the so-called *maturity type* of permanent and total disability income provision found in some of the older policies provides for the deduction of each monthly payment from the face of the policy).
2. The right to designate and change the beneficiary, subject to the assignment.
3. The right to elect settlement options, likewise subject to the assignment.

In consideration of the rights vested in him, the assignee agrees:

1. To pay over "to the person entitled thereto under the terms of the Policy had this assignment not been executed" any sums remaining after the liabilities, matured or unmatured, to the assignee are satisfied.
2. Not to surrender the policy or borrow upon it except for the purpose of premium payment, unless there has been a default in the obligations to the assignee or a failure to pay premiums when due, and in any event, not until twenty days after the assignee shall have mailed to the assignor notice of his intention to exercise such right.
3. Upon request, and without unreasonable delay, to forward the policy to the insurance company for endorsement of any designation or change of beneficiary, or any election of a settlement option.

The insurance company is authorized to make payment to the assignee without investigating the reason for any action taken by the assignee, the validity or amount of the assignee's claims, or the existence of any default on the part of the assignor. Upon surrender or maturity of the policy, the assignee is entitled to all the monies due but may, at his option, request a smaller sum. From the standpoint of the assignee, the right to receive the full proceeds eliminates one of the objections to the collateral assignment; but if he wants to permit the proceeds in excess of his claims to be paid under the settlement plan selected by the insured, he may do so. If he requests the payment of a greater sum than the amount of his interest, he becomes what in law is known as a *resulting trustee* for the excess and must account under the principles of trusteeship to the insured or beneficiary, as the case may be, for such sum.

The assignee is relieved of the obligations to pay premiums and policy loan principal or interest; but if he pays any such items out of his own funds, the amounts so paid become part of the liabilities secured by the assignment, are due immediately, and draw interest at a rate not exceeding 6 per cent annually until paid.

Other provisions of the form establish the superiority of the assignment instrument in case of conflict with any provisions of the note for which it is security, grant administrative discretion to the assignee in the handling of its claim, and certify that the assignor has no bankruptcy proceedings pending against him and has not made an assignment for creditors.

This form can appropriately be used with any type of policy form, including the recently issued owner type. It is estimated that at least three fourths of all collateral assignments currently being filed with the companies are on the A.B.A. assignment form, either in its exact form or with slight modifications.

NOTICE TO THE COMPANY OF ASSIGNMENT

If the interest of an assignee is to be protected, the insurance company must be notified of the assignment, preferably as soon as the assignment has been executed. A life insurance policy is not a negotiable instrument; and a transfer of rights in the policy, to be effective, must be recorded with the party who is under obligation to perform. If, without notice of an assignment, a life insurance company, upon maturity of a policy, pays the proceeds to the beneficiary of record, it will be absolved under the general rules of law from any further liability or obligation under the policy, even though a valid assignment of the policy was in effect at the date of the insured's death. To implement the law, and to put all parties on notice, the companies incorporate in their policies a statement that no assignment will be binding on the company unless it is in writing and filed in the home office. This provision has no effect on the *validity* of an assignment, but it has a material bearing on the enforcement of the rights transferred to the assignee.

The issue is broader than the relative rights of the beneficiary and the assignee. At the maturity of the policy, there may be more than one valid assignment of the policy in effect, and the relative rights of the assignees must be resolved. This can happen where one of the assignees failed to demand delivery of the policy with the assignment, or where the insured obtained a duplicate copy or copies of the policy by alleging that he had lost the original. It is conceivable that an insured could innocently or inadvertently assign a policy while a valid assignment of the policy was still outstanding; but in most such cases, the insured is guilty of fraudulent behavior.

Definite rules of law have been evolved to settle the disputes arising over multiple assignments of the same interest. The English rule, adopted in a minority of American jurisdictions, holds that the assignee who first gives notice to the insurance company has prior claim to the proceeds, provided that such assignee, at the time the policy was assigned to him, had no notice of a prior assignment.[8] If he had known of an earlier unrecorded assignment still in effect, he would, of course, have been guilty of fraud in accepting a second assignment of the same interest. The American—or prevailing—rule is that the assignee who is first in point of time will be preferred, regardless of notice to the company.[9] This rule is subject to the important exception that if the prior assignee fails to require delivery of the policy and thus permits a subsequent assignee to obtain delivery of the policy with no notation of the prior assignment, the claim of the subsequent assignee will be superior to that of the original assignee. A third or general rule, applicable under either the English or American rule, is that an assignee not guilty of fraud shall be permitted to retain any proceeds that may have been paid to him. Thus, an assignee with a preferred claim will lose his priority in any jurisdiction if he fails to notify the company of his claim before it has paid another assignee of record. In jurisdictions applying the American rule, the assignee first in point of time will have his interest protected, even under the general rule, as long as he records the assignment with the insurance company at any time prior to payment by the company.

Policy loans or advances made by the company are subject to the foregoing rules. Since assignments involving policy loans or advances are automatically recorded with the company, no difficulties are likely to develop around them. The only time that a company would find its lien against the cash value and proceeds subordinate to that of another assignee would be if—with notice of another valid assignment, and without the consent of the assignee—it went ahead and made a policy loan. Presumably, this would happen only through inadvertence. If a valid assignment of the policy had been executed

---

[8] See Krueger and Waggoner, *op. cit.*, p. 69, n. 2, for a list of jurisdictions following the English rule. Such important insurance states as California, Connecticut, Ohio, and Pennsylvania follow that rule.

[9] See *ibid.*, p. 70, n. 3, for a list of states following the American rule. New York is on the list.

prior to the policy loan but with no notice to the company, the latter would be protected under the exception to the American rule.[10]

Whenever there are conflicting claims for insurance proceeds or other benefits, whether the claimants be assignees or beneficiaries, the insurance company generally seeks the assistance of the courts. To do otherwise would be to invite the possibility of having to pay the benefits more than once. In such circumstances, it files a *bill of interpleader*, an equitable device, and pays the proceeds into court. In taking such action, it admits its obligation to pay, and petitions the court to adjudicate the conflicting claims and determine who is entitled to receive the money. The company discharges its responsibility by paying the disputed sum over to the court. This is an extremely important legal remedy for insurance companies.[11]

OTHER MATTERS RELATING TO ASSIGNMENT

Company Not Responsible for Validity of Assignment

The policy provision pertaining to assignment almost invariably contains a statement that the company shall not be responsible for the validity of any assignment of the policy. Some of the more recent policies broaden the statement to include the word "effect" as well as "validity." This provision is intended to protect the company against suits by a beneficiary or some other person alleging that the assignment was invalid because of the insured's incompetence or because the assignment was tainted with fraud or executed under duress. In the only litigated case on record,[12] an insured and his wife, who was the beneficiary of the policy, executed an assignment at a time when both were of advanced age and lacking in mental capacity. Upon the

[10] *Patten* v. *Mutual Benefit Life Insurance Co.,* 192 S.C. 189, 6 S.E. (2d) 26 (1939).

[11] Strictly speaking, a "bill of interpleader" requires that the insurance company be entirely disinterested in the outcome of the litigation. Under various state statutes and the Federal Interpleader Statute, the company can file a "bill in the nature of a bill of interpleader" when it does have an interest in the outcome. An example of the latter situation is when the representatives of an insured and the beneficiary killed in a common accident are claiming the proceeds, and the settlement agreement calls for the payment of the proceeds to the beneficiary under a life income option. If the beneficiary is held to have survived, the company may be able to discharge its obligations with one monthly payment. See pp. 144, 145. A more common example of the use of a "bill in the nature of a bill of interpleader" is when a company admits a death claim but denies liability for accidental death benefits.

[12] *New York Life Insurance Co.* v. *Federal National Bank,* 151 F. (2d) 537 (C.C.A. 10, 1945), reversing 53 Fed. Supp. 924 (W.D. Okla., 1944); certiorari denied, 327 U.S. 778 (1946); rehearing denied, 327 U.S. 816 (1946).

death of the insured, the company, having no knowledge of the incompetence of the insured and beneficiary, paid the proceeds to the assignee. Subsequently, the wife's guardian sued the company to recover the proceeds, on the ground that the assignment was void. The court refused to hold the company liable for a second payment of the proceeds, giving as one of its reasons the exculpatory statement in the assignment provision. The decision was upheld by the United States Supreme Court.

This clause protects the company only when it has no knowledge of a defect in the assignment instrument or of any irregularity in the circumstances surrounding the assignment. There would seem to be some risk to the company if a defect in the assignment form provided by the company caused loss to an interested party. To date, however, there are no reported cases on this point.

Insurable Interest

The right of an insured or other owner to assign his policy to anyone of his choice, whether or not such person has an insurable interest in the life of the insured, is recognized in all jurisdictions, when no financial consideration is involved. Such donee-assignees have been regarded to be in the same class as donee-beneficiaries as far as insurable interest is concerned. The position of the courts is that it is immaterial whether the insured designates the payee of the policy within the contract itself, as by a conventional beneficiary designation, or by means of a separate instrument, i.e., an assignment. If the applicant for insurance has an insurable interest in the life of the insured at the inception of the contract, an insurable interest on the part of the assignee is not required, either at the inception of the contract or at the time of the insured's death. Of course, if the insured were induced by the assignee to take out the policy, the latter would have to have an insurable interest since, in effect, he would be the applicant.

The situation is different when an assignment is made for a consideration. If the policy is assigned to a creditor as security for a debt, the assignee is permitted to retain only the amount of his interest, even though the assignment was absolute in form. Thus, it may be said that a creditor-assignee must have an insurable interest in the life of the insured at the maturity of the contract. If his interest is extinguished prior to maturity of the policy, the assignment terminates. On the other hand, an assignment to a purchaser for value is valid in all but five states, irrespective of the question of insurable interest. In other words, in most jurisdictions, a policy can be sold to a person who has no insurable interest in the life of the insured. The rationale of this doctrine was expressed in the leading case of *Grisby* v. *Russell,* in which Mr. Justice Holmes stated:[13] "Life insurance has become in our days one of the best recognized forms of investment and self-compelled saving. So far as reasonable safety permits, it is desirable to give to life policies the ordinary characteristics of property. . . . To deny the right to sell . . . is to diminish appreciably the value of the contract in the owner's hands."

Briefly, the argument is that there should be a free market for life insurance policies where a person in poor health can obtain the true value of his policy. The minimum price at which a policy should sell is the cash value, but the real value of a policy on the life of a person in poor health is somewhere between the cash value and the face of the policy, depending upon his chances of survival. If a person is ill and needs money for medical treatment, it is argued, he should be permitted to sell his policy to the highest bidder, without regard to insurable interest. The chances of murder are thought to be remote; and in any case, the danger should not be greater than when the insured designates a beneficiary who has no insurable interest.

Five states—Alabama, Kansas, Kentucky, Missouri, and Texas—do not follow the majority rule and require the assignee to have an insurable interest when the policy is assigned for value.

---

[13] 222 U.S. 149 (1911).

CHAPTER X

Protection Against Creditors

THE PROTECTION enjoyed by life insurance against claims of creditors is a vast and complex subject, and can be dealt with here in only the most cursory fashion. Emphasis will be on guiding principles, with a minimum of substantiating detail. There are so many facets to the subject that a rather detailed outline is necessary. The most basic dichotomy distinguishes between protection available in the absence of special legislation and that available under statutes specifically designed to give life insurance a preferred status.

NON-STATUTORY PROTECTION

The topic of non-statutory protection can itself be broken down into various subtopics, but the most important distinction to be noted is that between creditors of the insured and creditors of the beneficiary.

Creditors of the Insured

Creditors of the insured may seek to satisfy their claims out of the cash value of a policy still in force or out of the proceeds of a matured policy. The legal principles involved in these two types of action are so different that they must be dealt with separately.

Before Maturity of the Contract. If the policy is payable to the insured or to a *revocable* third-party beneficiary, the insured is the owner of the policy and is entitled to the cash value upon surrender of the policy. The cash value is an asset of the insured and is reflected as such in his financial statements. It would seem, therefore, that in the absence of special statutory rules, the cash value of such an insurance policy would be available to the creditors of the insured on the same basis as any other personal property. Such is not the case, however.

In theory, the insured's creditor is entitled to the cash value of a policy owned by the insured; but in practice, he is generally unable to enforce his rights because of procedural difficulties. The normal collection processes are not effective against the cash value, since the insurance company is under no obligation to pay the money to anyone until the insured exercises his privilege of surrendering the policy. Moreover, the courts are loath to force the insured to exercise his right to surrender. Direct action against the company, in the form of a garnishment or distraint proceeding, has uniformly been unsuccessful, while attempts by judgment creditors to force the insured to surrender his policy have been successful in only a few jurisdictions—among which, however, is New York.

The situation is different when the insured is bankrupt and a trustee in bankruptcy has been appointed. The Federal Bankruptcy Act provides that the trustee of the estate of the bankrupt shall be vested with the title of the bankrupt, as of the date of the filing of the petition in bankruptcy, to all property which prior to the filing of the petition he could by any means have transferred or which might have been levied upon and sold under any judicial process. Since a life insurance policy payable to the insured or a revocable third-party beneficiary could have been transferred, title to it passes to the trustee in bankruptcy. The latter, as owner of the policy, can then surrender it for its cash value. The problem of compelling the insured to perform an act which he does not wish to perform is not involved here. It should be noted, however, that the interest of the trustee in bankruptcy is limited to the cash value of the insurance on the date the petition in bankruptcy was filed. Thus, if the insured should die prior to adjudication of the bankruptcy and before the policy is surrendered, the excess of the proceeds over the cash value must be paid to the designated beneficiary—if any—otherwise to the insured's estate. Moreover, if the insured, within thirty days after the amount of the cash value has been certified to the trustee by the insurance company, pays over to the trustee the sum of money so certified, he is entitled to recover his policy free from the claims of the creditors participating in the bankruptcy proceeding. This provision was incorporated in the act to prevent the hardship which might befall the bankrupt's family if all his life insurance policies were to pass absolutely to the trustee in bankruptcy. Funds borrowed for this purpose can be repaid almost in full from the proceeds of a policy loan. Policies without a cash value do not pass to the trustee in bankruptcy.

Entirely apart from bankruptcy, the federal government has recently been able, in actions brought against the insured, to seize the cash values of life insurance policies in satisfaction of tax liens. Even the tax authorities have not been successful in suits brought directly against insurance companies. Divorced wives also have occasionally been able to satisfy alimony and support claims by actions to seize the cash value of life insurance policies owned by their former husbands.

When a policy is payable to a third-party beneficiary and the right to revoke the designation is not reserved, creditors of the insured have no enforceable claims against the cash value of the policy. This is based on the theory that policy rights are owned by the beneficiary, and the creditors of the insured should not be permitted to destroy or impair the rights of a third-party owner. In any event, the cash value could not be obtained without the consent of the beneficiary; and unless the beneficiary were a co-debtor, she could not be made a party to a suit to compel surrender of the policy. Furthermore, since the insured cannot transfer the policy without consent of the beneficiary, title does not pass to the trustee in bankruptcy. The latter can acquire no greater rights than the bankrupt possesses. Of course, if the insured relinquished the right to change the beneficiary or took out the policy in the first instance in fraud of his creditors, his action may be successfully attacked by the creditors.

After Maturity of the Contract. When proceeds are payable to the insured or his estate, they become available to the estate creditors on the same basis as any other unrestricted assets in the estate. When they are payable to a third-party beneficiary, however, they vest in the beneficiary immediately upon the insured's death, whether the designation was revocable or irrevocable. In theory, therefore, creditors of the insured should have no claim against the proceeds. Nevertheless, in a series of recent cases, the federal government has been permitted to collect unpaid income tax liens out of proceeds payable to third-party beneficiaries, on the theory that the latter are *transferees*. Recovery is allowed only where a valid tax lien had been placed against the cash value during the insured's lifetime and is limited to the amount of the cash value at the date of the insured's death.

Creditors of the Beneficiary

The cash value of a life insurance policy cannot be levied upon by a creditor of a third-party beneficiary, whether the designation is revocable or irrevocable. When the designation is revocable, the insured is the sole and absolute owner of the policy; and when the designation is irrevocable, the insured has rights which cannot be defeated by a creditor of another person. If the insured did not reserve a reversionary interest and the beneficiary was construed to be the sole owner of the policy, it seems likely that the creditors of the beneficiary would have a valid claim to the cash value. Unless the beneficiary was bankrupt, the creditors would experience the same difficulties in enforcing their rights as those encountered by creditors of the insured.

Once the policy has matured, the proceeds are the property of the beneficiary and can be freely levied upon by her creditors, in the absence of the protective provisions to be discussed in the next section.

STATUTORY PROTECTION[1]

All states have seen fit to enact legislation providing special protection to life insurance against the claims of creditors. Such legislation has a long history, the oldest law going back to 1840. The laws are a manifestation of a public policy that sets a higher priority on a man's obligation to his widow and children than on his obligations to his creditors. They reflect a philosophy which has led to laws exempting from attachment by creditors workmen's compensation awards, veterans' benefits, and other similar payments. To a great extent, they duplicate the protection available under case law. In some cases, the protection afforded by statute falls short of that which can be invoked under decision law.

Known generically as *state exemption statutes,* these laws are very diverse in nature. The broadest among them exempt all types of life

[1] For a comprehensive and scholarly treatment of the statutory basis for protection of insurance proceeds against creditors, see Howard C. Spencer, "Rights of Creditors," in *The Beneficiary in Life Insurance* (Dan M. McGill, ed.) (rev. ed.; Homewood, Ill.: Richard D. Irwin, Inc., 1956), pp. 41–108. The classification of statutes presented in the succeeding pages is based upon—but not identical with—the classification developed by Spencer.

insurance benefits from attachment by all types of creditors. At the other extreme are laws exempting from claims of creditors of the insured modest amounts of *proceeds* payable to the widow and children of the insured. Some of the laws apply to all types of life insurance, while others protect only some particular form, such as group insurance, pensions, disability income, annuity income, or fraternal insurance. Some protect only insurance taken out by a married woman on the life of her husband. There are statutes which protect the insurance against the creditors of the insured only, creditors of the beneficiary only, or any unsecured creditors, other than the federal government. Finally, some laws protect only proceeds, while others protect all types of benefits, including especially cash values. To make matters more confusing, some states have more than one type of statute.

Types of Statutes

At first blush, it seems impossible to classify such a hodgepodge of legislation. Closer inspection, however, reveals patterns that can serve as the basis for classification. The most apparent breakdown is that between statutes of general applicability and those that apply to specialized forms of life insurance, such as group insurance, annuities, and so forth. The general statutes may, in turn, be classified into six groups.

The first group embraces those statutes that pertain only to policies taken out by or for the benefit of married women on the lives of their husbands. Appropriately known as *married women's* statutes, these were the earliest laws of this type enacted.[2] The early laws protected only a small amount of insurance per married woman, but the amount of insurance exempted under the modern statute is unlimited. As a rule, the protection is effective only against creditors of the insured.

In sequence of time, the married women's type of statute was followed by the so-called *distribution* type of statute. These laws provide, in essence, that proceeds payable to the estate of the insured will pass to his widow and children free of the claims against the estate. It would be assumed that the very language of these statutes would rule out any protection during the lifetime of the insured; but in Tennessee, by a court decision,[3] and in Florida, by statute, cash values are pro-

---

[2] At the time these early laws were enacted, married women did not have legal capacity to own separate property.

[3] *Dawson* v. *National Life Insurance Co.,* 300 S.W. 567 (1927).

tected. These laws seldom protect against claims of the creditors of the beneficiary.

A somewhat later type of statute may be called the *procedural* type. The common characteristic of these laws is that they are enacted not as a part of the insurance law, but as one of the general exemptions from execution which are frequently found in civil practice or procedure codes. Since they are general exemption statutes, they usually provide immunity from all types of creditors, including those of the beneficiary. The amount of insurance exempted is usually quite limited, and the cash values are typically not protected. This is perhaps the most heterogeneous group of statutes dealing with the protection of insurance from claims of creditors.

The type of statute which has wielded the greatest influence is that which was first enacted in the state of New York in 1927. It has served as a model for the statutes of fifteen other states and has affected the course of legislation in many other jurisdictions. Thirty states now have statutes either identical with or broadly equivalent to the New York statute. Hence, it may be described as the typical state exemption statute. The use hereafter of the expression *New York* statute will refer to that statute as a generic type, rather than to the specific law of the state of New York, unless the context suggests otherwise.

The New York type of statute applies to all policies of life insurance payable to a person or organization other than the insured or, if different, the person applying for insurance. It protects both the cash value and the proceeds against the creditors of the insured and the person procuring the insurance. The protection is available whether the designation is revocable or irrevocable, and a reversionary interest in the insured is expressly declared to be immaterial. It does not protect anyone against the claims of creditors of the beneficiary.

The broadest protection is available under the so-called *comprehensive* statutes. Found in the states of Arkansas, Kansas, Louisiana, Nebraska, New Mexico, and possibly Georgia (the law in this state is not clear), this type of statute exempts, without limitation, all types of benefits associated with life insurance from the claims of the insured, beneficiary, third-party owner, or any other person or organization.

Finally, there are the laws, called *spendthrift statutes* and found in about half of the states, which are concerned solely with the protection of proceeds held under a settlement agreement against the claims of creditors of the *beneficiary*. The statutes are designed to protect the proceeds only while they are in the hands of the company and not after they have been received by the beneficiary. Unlike the other exemption statutes, these laws do not provide automatic protection; they are, instead, permissive in nature. They permit the insurance company and the insured to agree that the proceeds will not be subject to encumbrance, assignment, or alienation by the beneficiary, or to attachment by the creditors of the beneficiary. Such an agreement must be embodied in either the policy or the settlement agreement, and the beneficiary must not be a party to it.

Functional Analysis of the Statutes

Types of Benefits Protected. The minimum objective of state exemption statutes is to provide protection against the claims of creditors of the insured for all or a portion of the proceeds payable to the widow and children of the insured upon the maturity of the policy. The maximum objective, typified by the comprehensive statutes, is to provide unlimited protection to all types of insurance benefits payable to anyone against creditors of every description. An intermediate goal, representing the public policy of most jurisdictions, is to protect—both during the lifetime of the insured and upon his death—the benefits of an insurance policy payable to anyone other than the insured's estate, against the creditors of the insured. The latter objective involves protection of the cash value of the policy; otherwise, the policy may be destroyed by seizure of creditors before it has had an opportunity of serving its basic function—namely, the support of the widow and children after the death of the insured.

Many of the early statutes spoke only of "proceeds." Some courts adopted a narrow construction of the term, but most gave it a broad enough interpretation to include cash values. To indicate that prematurity values are to be protected, many statutes use the language, "proceeds and avails." A few actually use the words "cash value." The result is that practically all statutes, other than the distributive and procedural types, exempt—by specific language or court interpretation—both the cash value and the maturity value.

The word "proceeds" has had to undergo interpretation in another direction. Does it include paid-up additions, accumulated dividends, and prepaid or discounted premiums; or is it limited to the original face amount? The usual interpretation is that it includes all amounts payable upon maturity of the policy.

The exemption of the cash value is of singular importance in connection with the Federal Bankruptcy Act. That act recognizes all exemptions from claims of creditors granted under the law of the state in which the bankrupt resides. Thus, to the extent that a state law exempts cash values, the trustee in bankruptcy cannot take title to the life insurance policies of a bankrupt policyholder. Since the revocability of the beneficiary designation does not affect the exemption, it is apparent that the bankrupt enjoys more protection under the typical state exemption statute than under case law.

As a matter of fact, the treatment of bankrupts under these laws has been the subject of severe criticism by creditor interests. These critics argue that, all too often, a business man in financial difficulty places a substantial amount of assets in life insurance payable to his wife and children, and then—after going through bankruptcy—uses the insurance to re-establish himself in business. Since most states permit a man who has become insolvent to maintain existing insurance, or even acquire new insurance, *for the protection of his family,* without being in fraud of his creditors, there is little that the latter can do to prevent abuse of an otherwise desirable relief provision. Admittedly, the law usually restricts the insurance which an insolvent debtor can acquire or maintain to a "reasonable" amount, but the courts tend to construe the limitation liberally.

Curiously enough, the federal tax authorities have not let state exemption statutes stand in the way of their collection of tax liens. This is true even under the broadest statutes. The government can obtain the cash value of a policy through either forced surrender during the insured's lifetime or collection from the proceeds after his death, provided a lien had been placed against the cash value before his death.

Among the general state exemption statutes, only those of the married women's and comprehensive types protect benefits payable to the insured or the third-party procurer of the insurance. Thus, disability income and annuity payments are usually not exempt from attachment by creditors. In some states, however, these benefits are protected by special statutes. The most liberal of these special statutes is found in New York, where both disability and annuity payments are exempt up to $400 per month, except that 10 per cent of the annuity payments are subject to garnishment, the same percentage applicable to wages. Lump-sum dismemberment benefits are completely exempt. Pennsylvania exempts disability benefits without limit, but protects only the first $100 of monthly annuity income.

Dividends payable in cash are normally subject to seizure. In a few cases, the insured was permitted to accumulate dividends or use them to pay premiums.

Parties Entitled to Protection. Broadly speaking, state exemption statutes protect all third-party beneficiaries against the claims of the insured's creditors. The New York statute and those patterned after it also protect assignees and third-party owners. The comprehensive statutes protect all the foregoing plus the insured. On the restrictive side, the married women's and distributive statutes protect only the insured's widow and children.

As a class, state exemption statutes do not protect the person procuring the insurance from his own creditors. Thus, with the exception of the comprehensive statutes, the insured enjoys no protection against his own creditors. While he cannot be compelled by his creditors to surrender a policy for cash—and thus impair the rights of third parties—if he should voluntarily do so, the funds could be attached by his creditors. It is interesting to note that the cash value and death proceeds of an endowment policy are exempt in many jurisdictions, despite the fact that the insured is beneficiary of the endowment proceeds. Of course, in New York, Pennsylvania, and a few other states, proceeds of an endowment payable to the insured in the form of income are exempt up to the limits of monthly income stated in the law.

Nature of Limitations, if Any. As a rule, the statutes of broad application contain no limitations on the amount of insurance which will be protected thereunder. Several of the statutes, however, predominantly of the procedural type, contain definite limitations, expressed in terms of either the face amount or the amount of annual premiums. For example, the law in South Dakota limits the exemption to $5,000 and to proceeds payable only to a widow, husband, or minor child. The protection is available, however, against all creditors—the beneficiary's as well as the insured's. Arizona and Minnesota restrict the application of their procedural-type law to proceeds payable to the widow or children of the insured, up to a maximum of $10,000.[4] These laws, likewise, are effective against creditors of the beneficiary. Several western states exempt only such amounts of insurance as can be purchased with a maximum annual premium of $500, without specifying the plan of insurance. Idaho restricts its

---

[4] Both of these states, however, have a statute of the New York type protecting third-party beneficiaries without limit.

exemption to insurance purchasable with a maximum annual premium of $250.

As was stated above, when protection is afforded disability and annuity payments, a limit may be placed on the amount of monthly income so exempt.

Type of Creditors against Whom Protection Is Afforded. As has been pointed out earlier, state exemption statutes, as a class, are concerned only with creditors of the insured. A sizable number of statutes, however, provide protection against the claims of *creditors of the beneficiary*. This is true of the comprehensive statutes, which tend to exempt all types of insurance benefits from all types of creditors. The procedural statutes, likewise, usually make no distinction between creditors of the insured and those of the beneficiary, but the exemption is typically available only for such amount of insurance as can be obtained with an annual premium of $500. The law in New York exempts the proceeds and avails of a policy purchased by a wife on the life of her husband against the claims of *her* creditors. Several other states provide a limited amount of protection against the claims of the wife's creditors in connection with policies purchased by the wife with her own funds.

The most prevalent and significant form of statutory protection of insurance proceeds against the creditors of the beneficiary, however, is represented by those statutes that authorize the inclusion of spendthrift clauses in life insurance policies. This type of provision originated with personal trusts and had the dual purpose of protecting the trust income from the creditors of the trust beneficiary and preventing the beneficiary from alienating or disposing of his interest in the trust.[5] The validity of such a restrictive provision was widely debated in this country during the latter half of the nineteenth century; but it was ultimately held to be valid in most jurisdictions, either by statute or by judicial decision. A few states still do not recognize the provision.

Once the validity of a spendthrift clause in a trust agreement was well established, it was a logical development to introduce it into life insurance settlement agreements. Its validity in this setting was very much in doubt, however, since life insurance companies do not segregate assets, accept discretionary powers, or otherwise conform to the trust pattern in the administration of proceeds under a deferred

[5] Some courts now allow restraints on alienation of principal, but most continue to restrict the practice to life or income estates.

settlement agreement. To remove any doubts, about half of the states have enacted statutes stating that a spendthrift clause will be enforced if, at the direction of the insured, it is contained in either the policy or the settlement agreement.

The use of spendthrift clauses has become widespread. A typical clause might read as follows: "Unless otherwise provided in this settlement agreement, no beneficiary may commute, anticipate, encumber, alienate, withdraw, or assign any portion of his share of the proceeds. To the extent permitted by law, no payments to a beneficiary will be subject to his debts, contracts, or engagements, nor may they be levied upon or attached." If enforceable, this clause will protect the proceeds while they are being held by the insurance company, but not after they have been received by the beneficiary. The clause applies to debts created after the insured's death as well as those existing at the time of his death.

If the clause is to be enforced, it must be included in the policy or settlement agreement at the request of the insured.[6] This requirement is deemed satisfied, however, by the inclusion of the clause in the printed portion of the policy or settlement agreement, a practice followed by a growing number of companies. The highest state court in New York has held that if the clause is in the policy or settlement agreement, the beneficiary can be given the unlimited right of withdrawal without affecting the validity of the clause.[7] This is an anomaly and inconsistent with the original philosophy of the clause. It means that the beneficiary can have complete control over the proceeds and yet prevent her creditors from getting at the proceeds with any type of legal process. If the clause is in the policy, whether by specific request of the insured or by company practice, the beneficiary can elect to have the proceeds held by the company under a deferred settlement agreement and still enjoy the protection of the clause. It is not believed, however, that under those circumstances, she could reserve a right of withdrawal and retain protection against her creditors.

Properly inserted in the policy or settlement agreement, the spendthrift clause may be enforced despite the absence of a statute spe-

---

[6] *Matulka* v. *Van Roosbroech,* 25 N.Y.S. (2d) 240 (City Ct., 1940), affirmed, 25 N.Y.S. (2d) 247 (App. T. 1st Dept., 1940); *Rath* v. *Kaptowsky,* 393 Ill. 484, 66 N.E. (2d) 664 (1946). For a contrary holding, see *Provident Trust* v. *Rothman,* 321 Pa. 177, 183 Atl. 793 (1936). Three states have statutes which permit inclusion of the clause at the request of the beneficiary.

[7] *Genessee Valley Trust Co.* v. *Glazer,* 295 N.Y. 219, 66 N.E. (2d) 169 (1946).

cifically authorizing it—provided, of course, that there are no decisions specifically rejecting the spendthrift trust as a matter of policy.

SCOPE OF EXEMPTION STATUTES

There is considerable uncertainty as to the length of time proceeds payable under a life insurance policy are exempt from the claims of creditors and the amount of physical change which they can undergo without losing their exempt status. With respect to claims of creditors of the insured, the proceeds are generally regarded to be exempt as long as they can be identified as such. For example, the courts have almost universally extended the exemption to cover the bank account into which the exempt proceeds have been deposited.[8] Furthermore, it has been held that real estate purchased with insurance proceeds is not subject to creditors' actions.[9]

The law is not as well settled with respect to claims of creditors of the beneficiary. Some statutes which extend their cloak of protection to such claims state specifically that the proceeds shall be exempt from claims of creditors, whether of the insured or the beneficiary, both before and after receipt by the beneficiary. These statutes are presumably enforced in accordance with their intent. Other statutes of this type do not state that the proceeds are to be exempt while in the hands of the beneficiary; and serious question may be raised as to whether, under such statutes, proceeds are protected against the beneficiary's creditors after reaching the hands of the beneficiary, particularly as to debts created after receipt of the proceeds.[10] It seems clear that the protection afforded under a spendthrift clause, even though sanctioned by statute, does not extend beyond the instant of receipt of the proceeds.

---

[8] Cohen, "Exemption of Property Purchased with Exempt Funds," *Virginia Law Review,* Vol. XXVII (1941), pp. 573 and 584.

[9] *Booth* v. *Martin,* 158 Iowa 434, 139 N.W. 888 (1913).

[10] However, in *Reiff* v. *Armour & Co.,* 79 Wash. 48, 139 Pac. 633 (1914), real estate purchased by the beneficiary with exempt life insurance proceeds was held to be not subject to debts created after receipt of the proceeds.

APPENDIXES

A. Application for Life Insurance Policy

APPLICATION FOR INSURANCE—PART I

POLICY No.

TO THE ______ MUTUAL LIFE INSURANCE COMPANY, Philadelphia, Pa.

1. Proposed Insured. (*Please print full name.*) ☐ Male ☐ Female

2. Addresses of Proposed Insured. (*Cover at least two years. Use Remarks if necessary.*)
(a) Residence: Street City County State

(b) Business: Street City County State

(c) Send premium notices to ☐ Residence ☐ Business — *If neither indicated, send to residence.*

3. (a) Place of birth. (b) Date of birth. Month Day Year (c) Age nearest birthday.

(d) Marital status. ☐ Married ☐ Single ☐ Widowed ☐ Divorced

4. (a) Principal occupation. Exact duties.

(b) Name of Employer. (c) Any other occupation?

(d) Any change of occupation contemplated? (*Give details.*) (e) Occupation during the past five years. (*Give details.*)

5. Do you intend to change your residence within, or travel outside the U.S.A.? (*Give details.*)

6. Are you now a member of, or do you intend to join the armed forces or the armed forces reserve of any nation? (*Give details.*)

7. (a) State approximately your past and contemplated passenger flying hours other than as a passenger on regularly scheduled airline flights.
Past 12 months.................... Next 12 months....................
(*If more than 25 hours in either case, give details under Remarks.*)
(b) Have you ever taken or do you intend to take instruction in the operation of an aircraft either as a pilot or as a crew member?
☐ Yes ☐ No (*If "Yes", complete Aviation Supplement.*)

8. Have you ever applied to or been examined for any insurance company, association, society or agent without a policy of the exact kind and amount applied for being issued or has any company, association or society cancelled or refused renewal or reinstatement of any policy under which you were insured? (*Give details.*)

9. (a) Sum to be insured $
(b) Plan.
(c) Premiums payable ☐ Annually ☐ Semi-Annually ☐ Quarterly ☐ Monthly
(d) If the policy contains an Automatic Premium Loan provision shall the policy be subject to such provision? ☐ Yes ☐ No
(e) Additional benefits desired.
☐ Disability Waiver of Premium ☐ Disability Waiver of Premium and Annuity ☐ Double Indemnity
(f) Dividends of surplus to be applied.
☐ To reduce premiums. ☐ To accumulate at interest.
☐ To increase sum insured. ☐ To advance maturity.
☐ To be paid in cash. *If not indicated, to be paid in cash.*

10. Policy to be issued with beneficiary and ownership as follows:
(a) *Death benefit*—Payable to the beneficiary or equally to the beneficiaries surviving the Proposed Insured in the first class in which a beneficiary survives as follows:

Class	Full Name	Relationship to Proposed Insured	Date of Birth
Class 1			
Class 2			

If no beneficiary survives Proposed Insured—the *death benefit* to be payable to the executors or administrators
☐ of Proposed Insured; ☐ of....................
(b) *Endowment* or *monthly income* if on endowment plan—Payable to the Proposed Insured unless otherwise requested as follows: (*Indicate below if another beneficiary is desired.*)
To....................if living,
otherwise to....................
(c) *Privileges of ownership* to be vested in
☐ the Proposed Insured.
☐ ....while living,
thereafter in....................

11. What is the total amount of insurance on your life, including Health and Accident Insurance?

Company	Amount of Life Insurance	Disability Benefits Per Month	Accidental Death Benefit	Date of Issue

State what amount, if any, is business insurance.

12. Are any applications for insurance now pending or contemplated? (*State companies and amounts of insurance applied for in each.*)

13. Has full payment for the first premium on the insurance applied for been made? (*State amount. Partial payment may not be made.*)
☐ Yes $.................... ☐ No

REMARKS (*Enter Here Any Special Instructions.*)

AMENDMENTS AND CORRECTIONS (*For Home Office use only. No notation will be made by the Company in this space if such use is not permitted by statute or Insurance Department regulation.*)

I represent that the statements and answers in this Part I are written as made by me or by the Proposed Insured (to whom the statements and answers relate if the applicant is other than the Proposed Insured) and are full, complete and true and agree that they and the statements of the Proposed Insured in Part II (which shall consist of the statements made to the medical examiner or, if the policy is issued without a medical examination, to the agent) shall be a part of the contract of insurance if issued and that the Company, believing them to be true, shall rely and act upon them. I also understand and agree that:

1. No insurance shall be in force until the first premium is paid in full and the policy is delivered while the health, habits, occupation and other facts relating to the Proposed Insured are the same as described in Part I and Part II of this application and any amendments or supplements thereto, except that insurance shall be in force from the date of Part I or Part II of this application, whichever is the later, as provided in and subject to the conditions of the receipt attached to Part I of this application if (when Part I of this application is signed and in exchange for such receipt signed by the Company's agent) payment of the first premium is made in full.
2. Notice to or knowledge of an agent or a medical examiner is not notice to or knowledge of the Company, and that no agent or medical examiner is authorized to accept risks, to pass upon acceptability for insurance, or to modify, alter or enlarge any contract of insurance.
3. Acceptance of any policy issued on this application shall be a ratification of any amendments or corrections noted by the Company in the space in Part I marked "Amendments and Corrections."

A 209636

Signed at....................State of....................the..........day of....................19..........
Witness Present:

Signature of Proposed Insured

Signature of Applicant if other than Proposed Insured

PREMIUM RECEIPT

This receipt is to be given by the agent to the applicant only if payment of the first premium in full is received when Part I of the application is signed. ***Otherwise this receipt must not be detached.*** The receipt is void if altered or modified.

Received from....................$.........., the first....................premium on proposed insurance in the amount of $..........on the life of.................... for which an application bearing the number of this receipt has been made to The ______ Mutual Life Insurance Company. Insurance (subject to the terms of the policy applied for) shall be in force from the date of Part I or Part II of the application, whichever is the later, if (1) the amount paid in exchange for this receipt is the amount of the full first premium for the policy applied for and this receipt is signed by the Company's agent and delivered at the time Part I of the application is signed and (2) on the date of Part I or Part II, whichever is the later, the Proposed Insured is acceptable, as later determined by the Company, under the Company's rules for insurance on the plan, at the premium rate and for the amount applied for. Such determination shall be made without regard to any change occurring after such date in health or other facts relating to the Proposed Insured. If the Company shall determine that the Proposed Insured was not so acceptable or if the above conditions are not otherwise met, the payment received shall be returned upon surrender of this receipt.

Signed this..........day of....................., 19..........
54 ✓
AGENT

A 209636

Application for Life Insurance Policy (Continued)

AGENT'S [hole]TIFICATE

AGENT NOTE: If Disability Annuity is requested a medical examinatio[hole]uired.

1. (a) How long and how intimately have you known the Proposed Insured? (b) State Proposed Insured's race.	1. (a) (b)	5. If this application was taken on a non-medical basis, did you personally obtain the answers on Part I and Part II from the Proposed Insured?	5.
2. What knowledge or information have you as to Proposed Insured's habits, particularly the use of intoxicants?	2.	6. Is this policy applied for to replace insurance now in force in this or any other company or National Service Life Insurance? *State company and reason for replacement.*	6.
3. (a) What is Proposed Insured's approximate worth? (b) What is Proposed Insured's income?	3. (a) $.......... (b) Earned—$.......... Unearned—$..........	7. Does the premium notice address, as given, apply to all existing Penn Mutual insurance?	7.
4. Do you *unqualifiedly* recommend him for acceptance?	4.	8. Was this Proposed Insured referred to you by a broker or agent of this or any other Life Insurance Company? *If so, give details including the name of such agent or broker, why referred and what commission interest, if any, he has in this business.*	8.

Give below names and addresses of three references

....

....

....

....

....

....

Date

..........19....... ....
Signature of Soliciting Agent

The General Agent is to complete and sign the following form:

(a) The Soliciting Agent in this case is..........
(Please Print)

(b) I hereby endorse the above certificate

....
General Agent

IF PROPOSED INSURED IS A WOMAN—MARRIED, WIDOWED OR DIVORCED—COMPLETE THE FOLLOWING:

FULL MAIDEN NAME..........

1. (a) Will the premium be paid with her own personal funds? (b) If not, by whom will premiums be paid?	(c) If she has an income other than that derived from her given occupation, state source and amount annually.
2. If MARRIED, state: (a) Husband's name.......... (b) How much Husband is insured for in wife's favor. (If not insured, explain reason.)	3. If a DIVORCEE, state: (a) By whom divorce was obtained..........Date.......... (b) On what grounds?

Application for Life Insurance Policy (Continued)

APPLICATION FOR INSURANCE—PART II
STATEMENTS TO MEDICAL EXAMINER
(OR AGENT IF NON-MEDICAL)

POLICY No.

THE ______ MUTUAL LIFE INSURANCE COMPANY, Philadelphia, Pa.

Full Name of Proposed Insured .... (Please Print) .... Date of Birth .... Month Day Year

1. Are you in good health?

2. (a) Family History		Age if Living	State of Health	Age at Death	Cause of Death
Father					
Mother					
Full Brothers	No. Living				
	No. Dead				
Full Sisters	No. Living				
	No. Dead				
Wife or Husband					

(b) Has either parent or any brother or sister had mental trouble, diabetes, tuberculosis or heart disease?

(c) To the best of your knowledge, have you had any association during the past year with a person having tuberculosis?

3. (a) When did you last consult or receive treatment for your health from any physician, surgeon or practitioner?

(b) For what reason? (*Give details.*)

(c) Give name and address.

(d) State name of every other physician, surgeon or practitioner who has attended or treated you or whom you have consulted for any reason or ailment, serious or not serious, within the past five years. (*Give all dates and details.*)

4. Have you ever had a health or physical examination? (*If "Yes," under Details give dates, reasons and names and addresses of persons who made examinations.*)

5. Have you ever had a special heart study or an electrocardiogram? (*If "Yes", under Details give dates, symptoms or other reason for same and names of physicians, surgeons or practitioners consulted.*)

6. *Answer "Yes" or "No". Under Details give dates, symptoms or other reason for same and names of physicians, surgeons or practitioners consulted.*

(a) Have you lost any time from your work during the past 5 years due to illness or injury? (a)..........

(b) Have you ever been X-rayed for diagnostic purposes or for treatment of disease? (b)..........

(c) Have you ever been in a clinic, hospital, sanatorium or asylum for observation, treatment or diagnosis? (c)..........

(d) Are you contemplating any operation or has any future surgery been recommended? (d)..........

(e) Have you ever applied for or received sickness, accident or disability benefits of any kind from the Veteran's Administration, any insurance company, government, employer or other source? (e)..........

7. (a) How often and to what extent during the past 5 years have you used alcoholic beverages?..........

(b) Have you ever used alcohol to excess or taken treatment or a cure for alcoholism or drug addiction? (*If "Yes", under Details give dates and full particulars.*) (b)..........

8. Have you been aware of any suspicion of, or have you ever had or been treated for any of the following diseases or ailments? (*Answer each separately—give details below.*)

(a) Convulsions, dizzy spells, fainting spells, epilepsy, nervous breakdown or any nervous trouble? (a)..........

(b) Asthma, pleurisy, spitting of blood or tuberculosis? (b)..........

(c) Rectal bleeding, fistula, any stomach, intestinal, liver, gall bladder or kidney disorder? (c)..........

(d) Palpitation of heart, shortness of breath, pain in chest, abnormal pulse, any disease of the heart or blood vessels or a high blood pressure? (d)..........

(e) Arthritis, growing pains or rheumatic fever? (e)..........

(f) Dysentery, any tropical disease, or syphilis? (f)..........

(g) Any defect in hearing or vision, ear discharge, any varicose veins or tumor? (g)..........

9. Have you ever been told that you had albumin or sugar in your urine, or have you ever been on a diet?

10. Have you ever had any illness, disease, operation or injury other than as stated by you above? (*If so, give full particulars, date, duration, severity, etc., of each. Use reverse side if necessary.*)

DETAILS

(*Give additional information when required to complete answers to previous questions. Identify by question number.*)

11. (*Omit if Part II is being completed by a medical examiner.*)

(a) Exact height..........ft..........in. (b) Present wt..........lbs.

(c) Any change past 2 yrs.?.......... Gain..........lbs. Loss..........lbs.

(d) Reasons

I represent that the statements and answers in this Part II are written as made by me, are full, complete and true and agree that they shall be a part of the contract of insurance if issued.
To the extent permitted by law I, on behalf of myself and of any person who shall have or claim any interest in any policy issued hereunder, waive all provisions of law forbidding any physician or other person who has attended or examined me, or who may hereafter attend or examine me, from disclosing any knowledge or information thereby acquired, and hereby authorize such physicians or other persons to make such disclosure to the Company or its authorized representative.

Dated at.. ...., 19.......
Witness:

....
Medical Examiner (Agent if Non-Medical)

....
Signature of Proposed Insured

5802-3 120M 11-58

....19..........

Dr..

....

In connection with an application to the ______ Mutual Life Insurance Company, detailed information is desired concerning the conditions for which I have consulted you. I will appreciate your courtesy in supplying that company with all data it may request.

Very truly yours,

....

....19..........

Dr..

....

In connection with an application to the ______ Mutual Life Insurance Company, detailed information is desired concerning the conditions for which I have consulted you. I will appreciate your courtesy in supplying that company with all data it may request.

Very truly yours,

....

Application for Life Insurance Policy (Concluded)

MEDICAL FEE VOUCHER—DETACH THIS VOUCHER AND MAIL IMMEDIATELY TO MEDICAL DIRECTOR

The ____Mutual Life Insurance Company, ____ Philadelphia, Pennsylvania.

Forward completed examination report to General Agent. Under no circumstances deliver to any one else.

Examination fees are paid the 15th of the following month. Fee for this examination must not be accepted from agents, applicants or examinees.

Name of person examined.................... Date Examined....................

Name of agent....................

Please detail confidential information of any nature....................

....

....

....

Signature of Examiner.................... M.D. Address....................

PRINT OR WRITE PLAINLY

PART III

REPORT OF EXAMINING PHYSICIAN

12. (a) Are you alone with the examinee?.......... (b) Race..........
(c) Do you believe examinee older than stated?..........
(d) How long and intimately have you known examinee?..........
(e) Does examinee appear frail, anemic, unhealthy? (*Details.*)..........

13. Is there any deformity, loss of member, impaired sight or hearing? (*Describe fully under Remarks. If any defect in vision or hearing, give degree. Is other eye or ear normal?*)

14. (a) Height (in shoes).......... ft.......... in. Did you measure?..........
(b) Weight (without coat and vest).......... lbs. Did you weigh?..........
(*If 20% over or under standard weight—Scale weight required.*)
(c) How long has present weight been maintained?..........
(d) What is the most examinee ever weighed?.......... When?..........
(*Give full details under Remarks regarding gain or loss in past two years.*)
(e) Measurement of chest, nipple level: Inspiration.......... Expiration..........
(f) Measurement of abdomen at level of umbilicus..........

15. Is there a history of, or on examination do you find any abnormality of the (*Give full details under Remarks.*)
(a) Brain or nervous system?..........
(b) Reflexes: Pupillary?.......... Knee?..........
(c) Respiratory System?..........
(d) Gastro-intestinal System?..........
(e) Genito-urinary System?..........
(f) Endocrine System?..........

16. Blood Pressure:
(a) Systolic.......... Diastolic (cessation of sound)..........
(b) Time of day.......... A.M.......... P.M..........

17. Heart rate and rhythm:

	Pulse Rate	Regular?	If Irregular No. per Min.
(a) Examinee seated at rest	....	....	....
(b) Immediately after exercise (*25 hops each foot*)	....	....	....
(c) Two minutes after exercise	....	....	....

(d) Is hypertrophy present?..........
(e) Murmur present?.......... Systolic.......... Diastolic..........
(f) Is the murmur transmitted?..........
....
(g) What is the location of the murmur?..........
....
(h) Diagnosis of the heart condition..........
....
(i) Is there a history of precordial or thoracic pain, shortness of breath or acute indigestion? (*Full details under Remarks.*)
(j) Any history of rheumatic fever or other infectious disease? (*Full details under Remarks.*)

18. Urine: (a) Specific gravity.......... (b) Albumin.......... (c) Sugar..........
(d) Do you know specimen examined was voided by examinee?..........
(*If albumin or sugar present or a genito-urinary history in past five years, send a portion of specimen examined to Home Office.*)
(e) Have you sent specimen to Home Office?..........
(f) Have you reported all specimens examined?..........

19. Are there any other factors to your knowledge or observation which might influence health or longevity?

20. FEMALES
(a) Is she pregnant?.......... (b) How far advanced?..........
(c) Has she had any gynecological disorder?..........

REMARKS

Name of Agent.......... Where was this examination made? Your office.......... Examinee's office.......... Examinee's residence..........

Signature of Examiner.......... M.D. P.O. Address.......... Date..........

B. Specimen Ordinary Life Insurance Contract

The _____ Mutual Life Insurance Company

Policy No. 0 000 000 *Age:* 35

Insured: WILLIAM PENN

Sum Insured: TWENTY FIVE THOUSAND *Dollars*

First Premium: $ 590.50 due on or before delivery of this policy.

Subsequent Premiums: $ 590.50 due on February 10, 1960 and on the 10th day of each 12th month thereafter during the lifetime of the Insured subject to any reduction provided by any supplemental agreement attached to this policy.

Policy Year Date: February 10, 1959 *Date of Issue:* February 10, 1959

Beneficiary: Death Benefit payable as provided in the Beneficiary Section

Owner: The Insured.

The _____ Mutual Life Insurance Company

Agrees to pay the Sum Insured as a Death Benefit

upon receipt of due proof of death of the Insured and upon due surrender of this policy. The provisions stated above and on the following pages are a part of this policy.

In Witness Whereof, The _____ Mutual Life Insurance Company has caused this policy to be executed at its Home Office, _____________, on the Date of Issue.

ATTEST: SPECIMEN SECRETARY

SPECIMEN PRESIDENT

DEPUTY REGISTRAR

WHOLE LIFE POLICY

Sum Insured Payable at Death

Premiums Payable During Life—Annual Dividends

NOTE: The Beneficiary Section of this specimen contract is omitted to save space since it is identical with the Beneficiary Section of the Specimen Settlement Agreement reproduced in Appendix D.

Section 1—PREMIUM PAYMENT

Payment of Premiums This contract is made in consideration of payment to the Company of premiums as provided herein.

Each premium is payable at the Home Office or to an Agent of the Company in exchange for the Company's receipt signed by the President, Vice President or Secretary and duly countersigned or for a receipt given as provided in the application for this policy.

Upon written request by the owner the method of premium payment may be changed to annual, semi-annual or quarter-annual payable in advance at the Company's premium rate applicable to this policy for the method of payment requested, subject to consent of the Company if the change would result in a premium of less than $10.

Default in Premium Payment Failure to pay any premium when due, other than the first, shall constitute a default in premium payment. The due date of such premium shall be the date of default.

Grace Period A grace period of 31 days will be granted for the payment of every premium in default during which period this policy will remain in force. Upon failure to pay a premium in default within the grace period this policy shall lapse and cease to be in force except as provided in section 4. If the Insured dies on the due date of a premium or during the grace period the amount of any premium due and unpaid shall be deducted from the Sum Insured.

Reinstatement This policy, unless it has been surrendered, may be reinstated within five years after lapse for nonpayment of premium upon receipt by the Company of evidence of insurability satisfactory to the Company, payment of all overdue premiums with compound interest at the rate of 5% per year, and payment of any excess of (1) any indebtedness which existed at the date of lapse, increased by compound interest at the rate of 5% per year to the date of reinstatement, plus any indebtedness incurred after lapse, over (2) the Loan Value at the date of reinstatement. The amount of indebtedness and interest which remains after payment of the amount required above shall constitute policy indebtedness as of the date of reinstatement.

Section 2—DIVIDENDS

This policy shall participate in divisible surplus while it is in force except as provided in sections 4 and 7. Dividends of such surplus shall be determined and apportioned by the Board of Trustees annually.

Each such dividend apportioned to this policy, unless it is in force under section 7, shall be available at the end of the policy year (except that if at the end of the first policy year the premium for the second policy year has not been paid, the dividend shall be available when such premium has been duly paid) and shall be applied under one of the following dividend options.

Such dividends may be:

(1) Applied in reduction of premium if the balance of premium is paid before the end of the grace period. If at any time payment of further premiums is not required to maintain this policy in force, dividends available thereafter shall be paid in cash unless another dividend option is elected.

(2) Applied to provide paid-up participating life insurance (herein called paid-up additions) payable upon receipt of due proof of death of the Insured.

(3) Left with the Company to accumulate at 2¼% per year compound interest, this interest rate to be increased by such addition as may be awarded annually by the Board of Trustees. Such accumulations, subject to any assignment as security for a loan under section 3, may be withdrawn in cash at any time with interest to the date of withdrawal.

(4) Paid in cash.

The dividend option elected in the application shall be applicable until a subsequent written election is filed by the owner at the Home Office. If no option is elected, Option 4 shall apply.

If this policy matures by the death of the Insured after the first policy year, the Company will pay such post-mortem dividend of surplus as may be awarded by the Board of Trustees.

When used in this policy, "dividend credits" means (a) accumulations under dividend Option 3 and accrued interest thereon, (b) any dividend as to which dividend Option 1 is applicable but which may not be applied in reduction of premium because of lapse or surrender of this policy and (c) any post-mortem dividend.

SECTION 3—LOAN PROVISION

Policy Loans Upon proper assignment the owner may obtain a loan for an amount not exceeding the Loan Value solely upon the security of this policy at any time before maturity or surrender except while this policy is in force as extended term insurance. There shall be deducted from the loan the amount of any existing indebtedness and any premium due and unpaid.

Loans shall bear interest at the rate of 5% per year payable at the end of each policy year. Interest not paid when due shall be added to the loan and bear interest at the same rate.

The Loan Value, when determined as of a premium due date or the end of a policy year, shall be the policy value (as provided in section 4) increased by the value of any paid-up additions and by any dividend credits. When determined as of any other date the loan value shall be the amount which, with interest at the rate of 5% per year to the next premium due date or, if this policy is in force as a paid-up or fully paid policy, to the end of the current policy year, will equal the sum of (i) the policy value at the next premium due date or, if this policy is in force as a paid-up or fully paid policy, at the end of the current policy year, and (ii) the value of any paid-up additions and the amount of any dividend credits at the date the determination is made.

When used in this policy the term "indebtedness" means outstanding policy loans made under this section, including automatic premium loans, together with interest due and interest accrued.

Indebtedness may be repaid in whole or in part at any time while this policy is in force before maturity and before the end of the grace period for payment of any premium in default at the time of such repayment.

If at the end of a policy year indebtedness exceeds the Loan Value, this policy shall lapse and cease to be in force upon failure to pay interest when due and within 31 days after notice shall have been mailed to the owner to his last known address.

Except in the case of a loan for the payment of a premium due the Company, the Company may defer the making of any policy loan for not more than six months from the date of receipt of application for the loan.

Automatic Premium Loan Provision If an automatic premium loan provision shall have been requested in the application or by subsequent written request filed at the Home Office and such request remains unrevoked by written notice filed at the Home Office, any premium remaining unpaid at the end of the grace period shall be paid by charging such premium as a policy loan on the last day of such period, provided (1) the amount of indebtedness after addition of such automatic premium loan will not exceed the loan value at the end of the grace period or, if earlier, on the due date of the next premium and (2) not more than two consecutive premiums shall be paid by automatic premium loans. Automatic premium loans so made shall be subject to the same terms and conditions as other policy loans.

SECTION 4—NON-FORFEITURE AND SURRENDER PROVISIONS

Non-forfeiture Benefit In event of default in premium payment at any time when there is a net policy value the Company, during continuance of default and before the death of the Insured, will grant Benefit (1) below or in place of Benefit (1) will grant Benefit (2) or (3) upon election as provided therein:

Benefit (1) Extended Term Insurance At the end of the grace period if Benefit (2) or (3) has not been elected or upon written election by the owner before the end of the grace period, the net policy value shall be applied to continue this policy as paid-up extended term insurance (without participation in divisible surplus) payable as a death benefit upon receipt of due proof of death of the Insured during the term of such insurance and upon due surrender of this policy. The amount of such insurance shall be the Sum Insured increased by the amount of any paid-up additions and dividend credits and decreased by any indebtedness. The term of such insurance shall commence as of the date of default and shall be for such period as the net policy value will provide when applied as a net single premium at the Insured's age stated on page 1 increased by the number of completed years and months from the policy year date to the date of default.

Benefit (2) Paid-up Life Insurance Upon receipt by the Company within 60 days after the date of default of a written election by the owner, the net policy value at the date of such receipt shall be applied to continue this policy as paid-up life insurance (with participation in divisible surplus) payable as a death benefit upon receipt of due proof of death of the Insured and due surrender of this policy. The amount of such insurance shall be such as the net policy value will provide when applied as a net single premium at the Insured's age determined as provided in Benefit (1).

Benefit (3) Cash Surrender The net policy value shall be paid as a cash surrender value, in accordance with the surrender provision of this section.

Surrender Provision At any time when there is a net policy value the owner may surrender this policy for its cash surrender value which shall be the net policy value at the date of receipt by the Company of a document whereby the owner fully surrenders this policy to the Company.

Deferment of Payment Payment of any cash surrender value may be deferred for a period not exceeding six months from the effective date of surrender but if deferred 30 days or more shall bear interest at the rate of 2½% per year for the period of deferment.

Net Policy Value Defined The Net Policy Value is the policy value determined as provided below increased by the value of any paid-up additions and any dividend credits and decreased by any indebtedness.

Policy Value The Policy Value, when determined as of the end of a policy year for which a full premium has been paid, is the excess, if any, of the then present value of the future guaranteed life insurance benefit provided by the policy over the then present value of the annual non-forfeiture factors shown in the table in this section payable at the beginning of each subsequent policy year. On and after the seventh policy anniversary the policy value is equal to the full net level premium reserve. When determined as of a date during a policy year, except while the policy is in force under Benefit (1) or (2), the Policy Value shall be computed as provided above with due allowance for the time elapsed in that year and the portion of such year for which premiums have been paid. The Policy Value shall be computed on the basis of $1,000 Sum Insured and adjusted in the proportion of the Sum Insured to $1,000. During the 60 day period after default, the policy value shall be the policy value as of the date of default.

If the policy is in force under Benefit (1) or (2) the policy value shall be equal to the reserve on the insurance, provided that during the 30 day period after a policy anniversary it shall be equal to the reserve as of such anniversary.

The value of paid-up additions shall be equal to the reserve on such additions but not less than the reserve as of the immediately preceding policy anniversary nor less than the amount of dividends used to provide such additions.

Basis of Computation Present values, net single premiums and reserves are based on the Commissioners 1941 Standard Ordinary Mortality Table with compound interest at 2½% per year on the assumption that death benefits are payable immediately upon death of the Insured.

Benefits provided by any supplemental agreement made a part of this policy shall be excluded from the computation of any policy value unless otherwise provided in such agreement.

All policy values and benefits are equal to or greater than those required by statute.

Table of Cash, Loan and Non-forfeiture Values The following table shows the cash surrender, loan and non-forfeiture values available at the end of policy years completed by payment of premiums, computed in accordance with the provisions of this section and section 3, without allowance for any dividend credits or paid-up additions or deduction of indebtedness; and the amounts of annual non-forfeiture factors. The amount of extended term insurance is the Sum Insured and the amounts shown in the table for paid-up life insurance, cash surrender or loan values and annual non-forfeiture factors are for $1,000 of Sum Insured.

Values for policy years not shown in the table and any cash surrender or loan values available while this policy is in force under Benefit (1) or (2) of this section will be furnished upon request.

At End of Policy Year	Term of Extended Term Insurance		Paid-up Life Insurance	Cash Surrender or Loan Value	At End of Policy Year	Term of Extended Term Insurance		Paid-up Life Insurance	Cash Surrender or Loan Value
	Years	Days				Years	Days		
1	0	0	$0	$0.00	12	16	148	$370	$214.00
2	3	197	39	18.73	13	16	233	396	232.89
3	6	198	79	38.70	14	16	293	421	251.89
4	8	347	119	58.97	15	16	330	445	270.96
5	10	325	157	79.54	16	16	348	468	290.11
6	12	169	194	100.41	17	16	349	491	309.30
7	13	273	231	121.55	18	16	334	513	328.52
8	14	196	260	139.73	19	16	307	534	347.75
9	15	65	289	158.07	20	16	267	555	366.96
10	15	252	317	176.57	25	15	293	648	462.10
11	16	35	344	195.22	30	14	162	726	553.61

Annual non-forfeiture factor $23.915 for 1st 7 years; $20.750 thereafter.

SECTION 5—OWNER AND BENEFICIARY

Ownership All privileges of ownership under this policy are vested in the owner named in this policy. Where used in this policy "owner" means such owner, his successor or transferee. "Privileges of ownership" means the right, before the death of the Insured and without the consent of any beneficiary, to change the beneficiary one or more times; to receive every benefit and exercise every option, right and privilege provided in this policy or allowed by the Company to the owner; and to assign, transfer or agree to any modification of this policy or any interest therein.

Beneficiary The beneficiary may be changed by filing at the Home Office a written beneficiary designation in form satisfactory to the Company. No beneficiary designation shall be effective until so filed, but when so filed shall take effect as of the date it was made, provided that any interest created thereby shall be subject to any action taken or payment made by the Company before its receipt at the Home Office. The interest of any beneficiary who dies before the Insured shall vest in the owner unless otherwise provided. The rights of any beneficiary shall be subject to the rights of an assignee under any assignment by the owner.

Assignment or Transfer No assignment or transfer of this policy or any interest under it shall bind the Company until the original thereof has been filed at the Home Office, and the Company assumes no obligation as to the effect, sufficiency or validity of any assignment or transfer. No assignment or transfer of this policy or any interest under it made after death of the Insured shall be valid unless consented to by the Company. Any assignment or transfer shall be subject to any indebtedness to the Company on this policy.

SECTION 6—GENERAL PROVISIONS

The Contract This policy and the application therefor, a copy of which is attached to and made a part of this policy, constitute the entire contract. All statements made in the application will be deemed representations and not warranties. No statement shall void this policy or be used as a defense against any claim hereunder unless contained in the written and printed application and a copy of such application is attached to the policy when issued.

No modification or alteration of this policy, or waiver of any of its conditions, shall be valid unless endorsed hereon and signed by the President, a Vice President, the Actuary, the Secretary, an Associate or Assistant Actuary or an Assistant Secretary. No agent is authorized to modify, alter or enlarge this contract, or to bind the Company by any promise or undertaking as to distribution of surplus or future award of interest.

Incontestability This policy shall be incontestable after it has been in force during the lifetime of the Insured for a period of two years from the date of issue except for default in premium payment.

Policy Year Date The commencement date for computing policy years and policy anniversaries shall be the policy year date stated on page 1.

Suicide If the Insured commits suicide, while sane or insane, within two years from the date of issue, the death benefit shall be limited to the amount of the premiums paid on this policy.

Age Adjustment Any error or inaccuracy in stating the age of the Insured shall be adjusted by payment under any of the provisions of this policy of such amount as the premium actually paid would have purchased if the age had been correctly stated.

Maturity and Proceeds Defined When used in this policy the term "maturity" means maturity of insurance under this policy as a death benefit and the date of death of the Insured is the date of maturity of a death benefit. The term "proceeds" means the amount payable upon maturity after adjustment as provided below.

Payment upon Maturity Upon maturity the amount payable as a death benefit shall as of the date of maturity be increased by any dividend credits and the amount of any paid-up additions, and be decreased by any indebtedness and the amount of any unpaid premium deductible as provided in section 1.

Specimen Ordinary Life Insurance Contract (Continued)

SECTION 7—INCOME OPTIONS

The owner may elect to have the whole or part of the proceeds upon maturity of this policy or the cash surrender value upon surrender paid under one of the following options. If at maturity no election by the owner is effective, the beneficiary, if entitled to payment of the proceeds in one sum, may make such election. The right to elect and payment under an option are subject to the limitations stated in this section. As used in an option "proceeds" means the amount of proceeds or cash surrender value elected to be paid under such option.

Option A An income for a fixed period of years not exceeding 30.

Option B An income for 20 years certain and thereafter during the life of the payee, terminating, after the certain period, with the last payment preceding death.

Option C An income for 10 years certain and thereafter during the life of the payee, terminating, after the certain period, with the last payment preceding death.

Option D An interest income on the proceeds at the guaranteed rate of 2% per year, increased by any additions as provided below.

Option E An income of a fixed amount composed of payments of principal and interest on the balance of principal retained by the Company at the guaranteed rate of 2% per year, increased by any additions as provided below, until the proceeds are exhausted, the final payment not to exceed the unpaid balance of principal plus accrued interest. Interest accrued at the time for any payment shall be paid in place of the fixed amount, if greater.

Option FR A refund life income payable during the life of the payee, terminating with the last payment preceding death; provided that after the death of the payee the income payments shall be continued (unless commuted as provided below) during any refund period necessary to make the total income paid equal the proceeds, the last payment to be the difference between the total preceding payments and the proceeds.

Option G A life income payable during the joint lifetime of two payees and the life of the survivor, terminating with the last payment preceding the death of the survivor.

Option H A monthly life income without refund payable during the life of the Insured commencing at maturity or surrender and terminating with the last payment preceding death of the Insured. The amount of the income payment shall be 103% of the monthly life income which the proceeds would purchase on the basis of the Company's published rate in use at maturity or surrender for a monthly life annuity without refund, adjusted to make the first payment immediate, and may be obtained upon application to the Company at any time after it is determinable.

The amount of the income under these options, except Option H, shall be determined from the tables stated below. The income period under an option shall commence as of the date of maturity unless the election is made after such date, in which event the period shall commence as of the date such election is received at the Home Office. In case of payment of the cash surrender value under an option the income period shall commence as of the date of surrender.

The income under Option A, B, C, FR or G shall be payable monthly in advance. The income under Option D or E shall be payable monthly, quarterly, semi-annually or annually at the end of the interval elected.

Election of Option—Limitations on Use Election of an option shall be in writing filed at the Home Office before payment of proceeds or cash surrender value as otherwise provided by this policy. Election by the owner shall be before maturity. Provision in this policy, a beneficiary designation, an assignment or other instrument filed with the Company directing payment under an option shall constitute an election. Consent of the Company is required to (i) an election by an owner other than the Insured or the owner designated in this policy at the date of issue, by an assignee, association, partnership or corporation or by an executor, administrator or other fiduciary, and (ii) a direction for payment under an option otherwise than to a natural person in his own right, except that consent is not required to an election by or for an authorized fiduciary if option payments will terminate within 21 years. Acceptance by the Company of an election without condition shall constitute consent.

Payment of proceeds or cash surrender value or the share of a payee therein may not be made under an option if at maturity or surrender the amount to be paid under the option (i) is less than $1,000 (ii) would produce an income of less than $10 (iii) would be payable under Option G and either payee is then under age 50 or (iv) would be payable under Option H and the Company shall have discontinued the issuance of life annuities. If, because of this limitation, payment may not be made under an option elected before maturity or surrender the amount directed to be paid under the option shall be paid in one sum to the payee to whom the first income payment under the option would otherwise be payable if the first income payment were due at maturity or surrender.

The Company may require proof of date of birth and of continued life of any person on whose life an option is based.

Commutation, Withdrawal, or Alienation The payee, except as provided below, may commute income payments still to become due under Option A, B, C, or FR during the fixed, certain or refund period, or may withdraw the principal held under Option D or E, but in no event shall there be any right to commute income payments beyond the certain or refund periods under Option B, C, or FR, or income payments under Option G or H. The Company may defer payment upon such commutation or withdrawal for a period not exceeding six months from the date of request for payment.

If an election of an option is made by the owner, no payee other than the owner (unless written consent of the owner given before maturity has been filed at the Home Office) shall have the right to commute, withdraw, anticipate, alienate or assign any payment of income or principal or interest thereunder and, to the extent permitted by law, no such payment shall be in any way subject to such payee's debts, contracts or engagements, nor to any judicial processes to levy upon or attach the same for payment thereof. The joinder by the owner with the payee, prior to maturity in an assignment of any rights under this policy shall be consent of the owner to such assignment.

The commuted value of income payments shall be calculated on the basis of compound interest at the rate of 2% per year for Option A and at the rate of 2½% per year for Options B, C and FR.

Death of Payee Upon the death of a payee entitled to payments in his own right, the commuted value of any remaining payments under the option or, in the case of Option D or E, the balance of proceeds payable thereunder, with accrued interest, shall be paid in one sum to the executors or administrators of the payee unless otherwise provided in the election and consented to by the Company.

Participation The income under Option A, the income during the certain or refund periods under Options B, C and FR and the interest under Options D and E shall be increased by such additions as may be awarded from divisible surplus by the Board of Trustees. The income under Options B and C after the certain periods, the income under Option FR after the refund period and all income under Options G and H shall not participate in divisible surplus.

NOTE: Income Option Tables are not reproduced in this specimen contract since they appear in the Specimen Settlement Agreement in Appendix D.

C. Specimen Inspection Report Form

RETAIL CREDIT COMPANY
LIFE REPORT

District, Agcy., or Branch

RETAIL CREDIT COMPANY SERVICE REPORTS ®

CONFIDENTIAL

Acct. No.

..........OFFICE

INSURANCE HISTORY

Date	Acct. No.	Amt.

Date:
NAME:
Address:
Occupation on Inq., & Employer:

Date of Birth A A&H App'd for $ Per

SPECIMEN REPORT

	1. On what date was this inspection made?	
IDENTITY	2—A. How many years have you personally known applicant? B. How many years has each of your informants known him? *(If a new resident, give previous address.)* C. How many days since you or your informants have seen him? *(If not within two weeks, explain fully.)*	A. B. C.
RACE—AGE	3—A. What is racial descent? (Answer whether Greek, Anglo-Saxon, Negro, Italian, etc.) B. Is there any reason to doubt accuracy of birth date given?	A. B.
FINANCES	4—A. What would you estimate his net worth? B. What is his annual earned income from his work or business? C. Has he any income from investments, rentals, pension, etc.? *(If so, state source, amount.)*	A. $ B. $ C.
DUTIES	5—A. Does the occupation or job differ in name from that given in heading of this report? B. Has he any part-time or off-season occupation? Does he plan work or travel in foreign countries? C. Is he a reckless driver, or does he engage in hazardous sports? D. Does he or his employer sell or manufacture beer, wine or liquor?	A. B. C. D.
AVIATION	6—A. Has he taken flying lessons, either as member of armed forces or as civilian, owned or piloted a plane, or flown in planes not operated by licensed airlines? B. Does he plan to buy a plane or to become a student pilot?	A. B.
HEALTH	7—A. Is there anything unhealthy about his appearance, such as being very thin or pale? B. Has he any deformity, excess weight, amputation, blindness, deafness, or other defects?	A. B.
	8. Do you learn of any illness, operation, or injury, past or present?	☐ **YES** **IF YES, See Questions on Back.**

		Question	Answer
		B. Has he occupied the same home with a tuberculous person?	B.
HABITS	11—A.	Is he a steady, frequent drinker?	A.
	IF SO,	B. To what extent (daily, weekly, or how often)?	B.
		C. How many drinks does he take on these occasions?	C.
		D. What does he usually drink (beer, wine or whiskey)?	D.
	12.	Does he now, or has he in past, used beer, wine, or whiskey, to noticeable excess or intoxication?	☐ YES IF YES, See Questions on Back.
REPUTATION	13.	Do any of following apply to this applicant: Heavy debts? Domestic trouble? Drug habit? Connection with illegal liquor? Irregular beneficiary?	
	14.	Is there any criticism of character or morals?	
	15.	Is there any reason why you would not recommend for life insurance?	

REMARKS: 16. COMMENT BELOW ON TOPICS LISTED AT LEFT; GIVE DETAILS OF "YES" OR INCOMPLETE ANSWERS.

A. BUSINESS: *Employer's name; line of business; number of employees; how long applicant so employed; previous occupation, if recently changed.*

B. DUTIES: *Tell exactly what he does. What articles or materials sold or handled? Any outside duties such as travel, selling, or driving delivery vehicle? How much of time so spent?*

C. PERSONAL: *Whether married, single or divorced? Children? Comment on home surroundings, standing in community.*

Signature of person making report...

RETAIL CREDIT COMPANY

OVER—SEE ADDITIONAL QUESTIONS ON BACK

LIFE REPORT

Form 1—6-55 Printed in U. S. A.

16 Continued.

DETAILS OF HEALTH HISTORY:

X TO INSPECTOR: If your answer to Question 8 is "Yes," please answer the following questions:

17. What is (was) nature of illness, operation, or injury?	
18. On approximately what date did this occur?	
19—A. How long was he confined or "laid up"?	A.
B. Has he completely recovered?	B.
20—A. What physicians attended him? (Give full names and addresses.)	A. Name .... Address .... Name .... Address ....
B. Did he go to a hospital? *(If so, give name and address.)*	B. Name .... Address ....

21. Give any additional details showing extent and any effect on present health.

DETAILS OF DRINKING HABITS:

X TO INSPECTOR: If your answer to Question 12 is "Yes," please give these additional details to show drinking

23. If not now, did he formerly indulge to this extent?

THE FOLLOWING QUESTIONS APPLY TO EITHER PAST OR PRESENT EXCESSIVE DRINKING
(as indicated in answers to Questions Nos. 22 and 23).

		How often? (Once a week, once a month, etc.)
24. Classify drinking on these occasions and state how often:		
A. Getting "drunk," stupefied, entirely out of control of usual faculties?	A.	A.
B. Loud, boisterous, or obviously under influence, although still in possession of most of faculties?	B.	B.
C. Mild excess, just getting "feeling good"; exhilaration or stimulation?	C.	C.

25. Do (did) these occasions last for an evening, a day, two days, a week, or for how long?

26. How long has (had) he been drinking to this extent?

27. WHEN WAS THE LAST OCCASION OF THIS SORT, OR IF HE HAS REFORMED, HOW LONG AGO DID THIS TAKE PLACE?

28. If applicant is an excessive drinker at present, does he drive a car during periods of intoxication?

29. Has applicant ever taken any "cure" for liquor habit? (If so, when? Any subsequent lapse?)

30. Tell how applicant drinks, if social or solitary, or if because of domestic or other trouble, whether ever arrested, and details to give clear picture of drinking habits; if reformed, what led to reformation (ill health, domestic trouble, or what)?

INSPECTOR: Do not write in this space.
(Use Memorandum Form #106 for additional remarks)

1 R—3-59

D. A.B.A. ASSIGNMENT FORM

FORM No. 10—LIFE INSURANCE ASSIGNMENT

FORM DESIGNED, PRINTED, AND DISTRIBUTED BY AMERICAN BANKERS ASSOCIATION BANK MANAGEMENT COMMISSION (REVIEWED AND APPROVED 1950)

ASSIGNMENT OF LIFE INSURANCE POLICY AS COLLATERAL

A. **For Value Received** the undersigned hereby assign, transfer and set over to ____________________

____________________ of ____________________

its successors and assigns, (herein called the "Assignee") Policy No. ____________________ issued by the

____

(herein called the "Insurer") and any supplementary contracts issued in connection therewith (said policy and contracts being herein called the "Policy"), upon the life of ____________________

of ____________________ and all claims, options, privileges, rights, title and interest therein and thereunder (except as provided in Paragraph C hereof), subject to all the terms and conditions of the Policy and to all superior liens, if any, which the Insurer may have against the Policy. The undersigned by this instrument jointly and severally agree and the Assignee by the acceptance of this assignment agrees to the conditions and provisions herein set forth.

B. It is expressly agreed that, without detracting from the generality of the foregoing, the following specific rights are included in this assignment and pass by virtue hereof:

1. The sole right to collect from the Insurer the net proceeds of the Policy when it becomes a claim by death or maturity;
2. The sole right to surrender the Policy and receive the surrender value thereof at any time provided by the terms of the Policy and at such other times as the Insurer may allow;
3. The sole right to obtain one or more loans or advances on the Policy, either from the Insurer or, at any time, from other persons, and to pledge or assign the Policy as security for such loans or advances;
4. The sole right to collect and receive all distributions or shares of surplus, dividend deposits or additions to the Policy now or hereafter made or apportioned thereto, and to exercise any and all options contained in the Policy with respect thereto; provided, that unless and until the Assignee shall notify the Insurer in writing to the contrary, the distributions or shares of surplus, dividend deposits and additions shall continue on the plan in force at the time of this assignment; and
5. The sole right to exercise all nonforfeiture rights permitted by the terms of the Policy or allowed by the Insurer and to receive all benefits and advantages derived therefrom.

C. It is expressly agreed that the following specific rights, so long as the Policy has not been surrendered, are reserved and excluded from this assignment and do not pass by virtue hereof:

1. The right to collect from the Insurer any disability benefit payable in cash that does not reduce the amount of insurance;
2. The right to designate and change the beneficiary;
3. The right to elect any optional mode of settlement permitted by the Policy or allowed by the Insurer;

but the reservation of these rights shall in no way impair the right of the Assignee to surrender the Policy completely with all its incidents or impair any other right of the Assignee hereunder, and any designation or change of beneficiary or election of a mode of settlement shall be made subject to this assignment and to the rights of the Assignee hereunder.

D. This assignment is made and the Policy is to be held as collateral security for any and all liabilities of the undersigned, or any of them, to the Assignee, either now existing or that may hereafter arise in the ordinary course of business between any of the undersigned and the Assignee (all of which liabilities secured or to become secured are herein called "Liabilities").

E. The Assignee covenants and agrees with the undersigned as follows:

1. That any balance of sums received hereunder from the Insurer remaining after payment of the then existing Liabilities, matured or unmatured, shall be paid by the Assignee to the persons entitled thereto under the terms of the Policy had this assignment not been executed;
2. That the Assignee will not exercise either the right to surrender the Policy or (except for the purpose of paying premiums) the right to obtain policy loans from the Insurer, until there has been default in any of the Liabilities or a failure to pay any premium when due, nor until twenty days after the Assignee shall have mailed, by first-class mail, to the undersigned at the addresses last supplied in writing to the Assignee specifically referring to this assignment, notice of intention to exercise such right; and
3. That the Assignee will upon request forward without unreasonable delay to the Insurer the Policy for endorsement of any designation or change of beneficiary or any election of an optional mode of settlement.

F. The Insurer is hereby authorized to recognize the Assignee's claims to rights hereunder without investigating the reason for any action taken by the Assignee, or the validity or the amount of the Liabilities or the existence of any default therein, or the giving of any notice under Paragraph E (2) above or otherwise, or the application to be made by the Assignee of any amounts to be paid to the Assignee. The sole signature of the Assignee shall be sufficient for the exercise of any rights under the Policy assigned hereby and the sole receipt of the Assignee for any sums received shall be a full discharge and release therefor to the Insurer. Checks for all or any part of the sums payable under the Policy and assigned herein, shall be drawn to the exclusive order of the Assignee if, when, and in such amounts as may be, requested by the Assignee.

G. The Assignee shall be under no obligation to pay any premium, or the principal of or interest on any loans or advances on the Policy whether or not obtained by the Assignee, or any other charges on the Policy, but any such amounts so paid by the Assignee from its own funds, shall become a part of the Liabilities hereby secured, shall be due immediately, and shall draw interest at a rate fixed by the Assignee from time to time not exceeding 6% per annum.

H. The exercise of any right, option, privilege or power given herein to the Assignee shall be at the option of the Assignee, but (except as restricted by Paragraph E (2) above) the Assignee may exercise any such right, option, privilege or power without notice to, or assent by, or affecting the liability of, or releasing any interest hereby assigned by the undersigned, or any of them.

I. The Assignee may take or release other security, may release any party primarily or secondarily liable for any of the Liabilities, may grant extensions, renewals or indulgences with respect to the Liabilities, or may apply to the Liabilities in such order as the Assignee shall determine, the proceeds of the Policy hereby assigned or any amount received on account of the Policy by the exercise of any right permitted under this assignment, without resorting or regard to other security.

J. In the event of any conflict between the provisions of this assignment and provisions of the note or other evidence of any Liability, with respect to the Policy or rights of collateral security therein, the provisions of this assignment shall prevail.

K. Each of the undersigned declares that no proceedings in bankruptcy are pending against him and that his property is not subject to any assignment for the benefit of creditors.

Signed and sealed this ________ day of ____________, 19____

____________________ *Witness*	____________________(L.S.) *Insured or Owner*
____________________	____________________ *Address*
____________________ *Witness*	____________________(L.S.) *Beneficiary*
____________________	____________________ *Address*

Index

This book has been set on the Linotype in 11 point Times Roman, leaded 2 points and 10 point Times Roman, leaded 1 point. Chapter numbers are in 14 point Times Roman caps followed by 36 point Caslon Open numerals. Chapter titles are in 24 point Times Roman italics. The size of the type page is 27 by 45 picas.